Photoshop Illuminated

FOR ANIMATORS

The ultimate guide to creating content for games, film, and effects with Adobe Photoshop

Jaimy McCann

MESMER

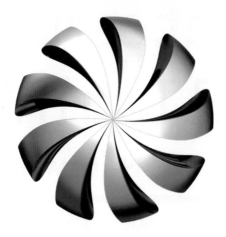

Photoshop Illuminated: For Animators

Copyright © 2003 by Mesmer Inc.

ISBN: 0-9707530-3-9

Library of Congress CCN: 2003107346

Printed in Hong Kong

First Printing: July, 2003

Author:

Jaimy McCann

with contributions by:

Brian Demong

Ryan Greene

and

Anthony Rossano

Managing Editor:

Brian Demong

User Edit:

Randy Davis

CONTACT INFORMATION

Mesmer Inc. provides the content of the book as is, and makes no warranties regarding the accuracy or completeness of the material within it. That having been said, we welcome your feedback. Please tell us how we can make this book better and better!

Questions of a technical nature, for instance those regarding software installation or hardware configuration, will not be answered.

You may email us at: info@mesmer.com

You may write to us at:

> Mesmer Animation Labs
> 1116 NW 54th Street
> Seattle WA 98107

You may call us at: 206.782.8004

Please check out our other wonderful course offerings, onsite classes, and distance learning at http://www.mesmer.com.

DIGITAL CONTENT FOR THIS BOOK

All the scene files, models, and other digital information used in this book may be downloaded free of charge from http://www.mesmer.com/

The file package is called PS4Animators.zip, and is located in the File Bank on the Mesmer web site. Either scroll through the list of files to locate PS4Animators.zip, or do a search for Courseware for Photoshop.

HELP FOR TEACHERS

We have thoughfully provided free courseware building materials to make life easier for instructors who choose to use our book in class. If you are an educator, you may download the file PS4A_TeacherResource.PDF which contains lesson plans, chapter outlines, sample tests and more useful material. You may obtain this material from the web at www.mesmer.com, in the File Bank under Courseware for Photoshop.

AUTHOR BIOS

Jaimy McCann earned a Bachelor of Fine Arts degree at Cornish College of the Arts in Seattle, WA, where she has lived all her life. She is currently the Lead Artist at Escape Factory Games.

When not working on one of several ongoing projects, she likes to explore: Seattle, the mountains, Vancouver, other cities, and other countries (other planets, too, if that were possible.) This limitless curiosity also serves as the inspiration for her work, which focuses on realistic environments and their textures.

For the future, Jaimy looks forward to continuing her career as a 3D artist, plenty of trips to interesting places, and a wonderful life with her husband Rick, 2 cats, 5 hermit crabs, and the 17 Bonsai trees that make up her family.

Anthony Rossano is the Chief Executive Officer of Mesmer, Inc. After receiving his Bachelor of Arts in Psychology from the University of Washington, Rossano went to work for the Microsoft Corporation. In 1988, Anthony Rossano deserted his post at Microsoft to found Mesmer, Inc.

Technically proficient in a wide range of authoring and animation programs, Rossano's expertise lies in Softimage 3D|Extreme, Softimage|XSI, and Alias|Wavefront Maya Composer. Anthony has taught all over the world, and counts among his training clients PDI, LucasArts, Industrial Light and Magic, Tippett Studios, Electronic Arts, Microsoft, Monolith, Psygnosis, Boeing, Lockheed, and Lear.

Ryan M. Greene graduated from the University of California at Davis, and after working various odd jobs, decided to pursue his love of art by attending the School of Communication Arts, where he studied Computer Art and Animation. Following that, Ryan got his first animation job as a medical/technical animator. He later went on to work as an artist for video/TV production, and then made the transition into games. Currently, he is working on Flight Simulator and Combat Flight Simulator for Microsoft in the Seattle area, and teaches 3d studio max at Mesmer.

Brian Demong is a fine artist schooled at Cornish College of the Arts: his primary traditional art interests are figure drawing and painting, particularly fantasy art. Brian is a certified user of Softimage|3D, Softimage|XSI, and Alias|Wavefront Composer, and certified instructor of Discreet combustion, which he teaches at Mesmer. His primary digital art interests are effects that viewers don't notice are "special", and the art and history of video games.

ACKNOWLEDGEMENTS

JAIMY SAYS:

"This book is *mostly* dedicated to my husband, Rick McCann, cause he was such a great help and support. It's also dedicated to Anthony Rossano and Brian Demong – fellow partners in publishing crime."

INTRODUCTION FROM THE EDITOR

Thank you for purchasing Photoshop Illuminated: For Animators!

There are a million and one books on Photoshop out there, but all from the perspective of using it for graphic design, web design, or for photography enhancement. Nearly every animator and aspiring animator in the world uses Photoshop to create the many 2d elements of films and video games, yet there is still a dearth of resources for them. Something had to be done, and here it is!

Since this may be the first Mesmer Press title in your library, a few words about our mission and style: many computer animation books are expensive, include a semi-functional CD, and are printed on a large scale, only once. Unfortunately, computer graphics software is not only written once; it changes very rapidly, resulting in a lot of out-of-date and inaccurate printed material. Our idea is to self-publish smaller books, in small print runs, and have our supplementary material, such as scene files and additional tutorials, available online (at www.mesmer.com) instead of on a set-in-stone CD. That way, the books themselves are inexpensive and easily updated, the supplements can be updated and refined, and new content can be added any time. This also means that your feedback is welcome, and can actually be (and has been) applied!

We also have many titles available for learning 3D animation software. Visit www.mesmer.com's Books and Courseware section to learn more about the Illuminated series, including XSI Foundation, XSI Character, 3ds max Foundation, Maya Games, and Softimage|3D Fundamentals. We are constantly working on new titles, so even if you're familiar with our offerings, be sure to check back for updates.

This book has been our most collaborative project to date, and I'd like to thank all the people that made it such a pleasure to produce: Thanks and a hearty round of applause to Jaimy for her hard work and dedication; and to Ryan Greene and Anthony Rossano for generously contributing their time and effort to this book. Thanks also to all the interviewees – John Gronquist, Jerusha Hardman, Kevin Kilstrom, Eric Kohler, Mike Nichols, and Kamal Siegel – for taking the time out to talk to us, and for contributing their awesome art. And last but not least, thanks to the fine folks at Adobe, Discreet, Softimage, and Alias|Wavefront for producing the world-class software that artists from around the globe use to make their dreams a reality.

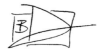

Brian Demong, Managing Editor and Mesmer Publisher

HOTKEY CHEAT SHEET

(Macintosh users substitute ⌘ for Ctrl)

Ctrl + N	New document		Ctrl + (plus)	Zoom in
Ctrl + O	Open document		Ctrl + (minus)	Zoom out
Alt + Ctrl + O	Open document as		Ctrl + 0	Fit to screen
Ctrl + W	Close		Alt + Ctrl + 0	Actual pixels
Shift + Ctrl + W	Close all		Ctrl + H	Show/hide extras
Ctrl + S	Save		Ctrl + R	Show/hide rulers
Ctrl + Shift + S	Save as		Ctrl + ;	Snap
Ctrl + Alt + S	Save a copy		Alt + Ctrl + ;	Lock guides
Alt + Shift + Ctrl + S	Save for web			
Ctrl + P	Print		A	path component selection tool
Ctrl + Q	Exit Photoshop		B	brushes
			C	crop tool
Ctrl + Z	Undo one step		E	eraser
Ctrl + Alt + Z	Undo unlimited		F	flip between screen modes
			G	paint bucket, gradient tool
Ctrl + C	Copy		H	hand tool
Ctrl + P	Paste		I	eyedropper tool
Ctrl + Shift + V	Paste into		J	healing tool, patch tool
Ctrl + X	Cut		K	slice tool
Ctrl + T	Transform		L	lasso tool
			M	marquee tool
Ctrl + L	Levels		N	notes
Ctrl + Shift + L	Auto levels		O	burn/dodge tool
Alt + Shift + Ctrl + L	Auto contrast		P	path tool
Ctrl + M	Curves		Q	quick mask mode
Ctrl + B	Color channels		R	blur/sharpen/smudge
Ctrl + U	Hue/Saturation		S	clone/pattern stamp tool
			T	text tool
Alt + Ctrl + X	Extract		U	line/vector shapes tool
Shift + Ctrl + X	Liquefy		V	move tool
			W	wand tool
Shift + Ctrl + N	New layer		X	switch fore and background colors
Ctrl + J	New layer via copy		Y	history brush
Shift + Ctrl +]	Bring to front		Z	magnifying glass
Ctrl +]	Bring forward			
Ctrl + E	Merge linked		Tab	Turn off palettes and Tools bar
Shift + Ctrl + E	Merge visible		Tab + Shift	Turn off all the showing palettes
Ctrl + Click Layer	Select layer contents			
Ctrl + Shift + Click Layer	Add to selection		[	Make brush size smaller
Ctrl + Alt + Click Layer	Subtract from selection		]	Make brush size larger
			Shift + [	Make brush softer
Ctrl + A	Select all		Shift +]	Make brush harder
Ctrl + D	Deselect		>	Cycle forward through brushes
Ctrl + Shift + D	Reselect		<	Cycle backward through brushes
Shift + Ctrl + I	Select inverse			
Alt + Ctrl + D	Feather		Up Arrow	Move selection one pixel up
			Down Arrow	Move selection one pixel down
Ctrl + Alt + F	Reset filter		Left Arrow	Move selection one pixel left
Ctrl + Shift + R	Fade filter		Right Arrow	Move selection one pixel right

1   TOOLIN AROUND IN PHOTOSHOP

IN THIS CHAPTER YOU WILL LEARN ABOUT:

- The painting tools of Photoshop
- How to choose a color palette
- What Selections are and why they are used
- Which tools are best for image editing and corrections
- Navigating around the Photoshop Interface and documents
- Vector graphics and Photoshop 7.0
- Tips and tricks for making measurements of your work

INTRODUCTION

Looking at the Photoshop interface, you will notice a vertical bar along the left side, called the tool bar. The tool bar is the main collection of implements used to begin the basics of image creation, such as paint brushes and erasers. Some of the buttons on the tool bar house more than one tool. This is indicated by a tiny black arrow in the bottom corner of the button. To access an alternative tool that lives in the same button space, hold your mouse button down and a menu with all of the tools for that button will be presented. Simply click on the one you want to select.

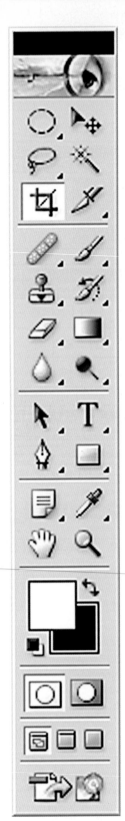

The tool Bar of Photoshop

The easiest way to choose a tool from the tool bar is to use the single-letter hotkey assigned to the tool. In this book, when a tool is mentioned, its hotkey will be in parentheses after the name of the tool. When one tool has multiple modes, you can select the alternate modes by holding Shift while pressing its hotkey. For example, Shift-M toggles between the Rectangular Marquee(M) selection tool and the Elliptical Marquee(M) selection tool.

If you have Photoshop in front of you while you read this book, it is a good idea to play with each tool and mode as you read about it to get a feel for how it works. You can use an image you've already created, make a new one just for experimenting with the tools in this chapter, or open the image named tooltest.psd located in the folder containing the supplementary image files for this book (PS4Animators.zip, which you can download from the File Bank at http://www.mesmer.com/). Tooltest.psd is a simple image with three semi-transparent layers each containing a colored shape, which may be useful if you are unfamiliar with creating multiple layers in Photoshop (covered later).

Each of these tools has a specific purpose, and comes with a set of features that can be customized. These features are called "tool options". The tool options bar runs along the top of the Photoshop interface, directly below the drop-down menus. When a tool from the toolbar is selected, the corresponding icon will appear on the tool options bar so that you can tell what options are currently selected.

This chapter will familiarize you with a variety of the best and most often used tools and options for game and entertainment industry digital artists. The tools have been arranged into categories based on their general function. For example, all of the tools used for painting are listed together under "Painting" for ease of reference.

First, you will learn about using the brush tool and receive suggestions about how it can best be used. The brush tool is the most important tool in the Photoshop toolbox, and comes with a complex set of options that will also be described with further detail in Chapter 2. It is important to be knowledgeable about this tool because it offers a gargantuan array of creative potential for creating top-notch textures and artwork. In addition to learning about the brush tool, you'll learn how to choose a good color palette to paint with. A good palette is very important because it is primarily responsible for conveying mood, and tone, and the overall emotional concept of the stuff you're working on.

As you paint, you'll probably want to move things around, add shapes, delete other elements, and manipulate the interface and documents efficiently. This is where selections, corrections, and navigating come in. Selection tools are used for isolating, adding, and subtracting to your work. They are extremely important because they add flexibility to the decision-making process as you work. With selection tools, you can change a piece as often as needed to get the right result. Similarly, the correcting tools keep things flexible because it is so easy to repair areas of an image that are not working or are obvious blemishes.

This chapter will also address the concept of vector graphics, and how they are incorporated into Photoshop. This type of graphic is often needed for text, bold shapes and details, smooth lines, and special shapes. They often come in handy as easy solutions to tricky problems.

Lastly, how to take measurements of image files will be addressed. Occasionally, a texture will need to be painted in a precise fashion or a measurement might be needed to determine the dimensions of an image. This section of the chapter will go over the Measure Tool of Photoshop, as well as some tips on how to use other tools for measuring.

PAINTING

Brush tools represent all of the tools in the tool bar that are meant to simulate an actual brush or brushed effect from real life.

The art of painting takes many forms in the game and effects industries. One artist might be expected to hand-paint every texture from the base color up – all hand-drawn shadows, highlights and details – with the use of a brush tool. This method of painting is much more oriented towards "fine" art in that it relies on the artist being able to paint formally – with either actual paint or digital paint. Painting textures by hand is fun because there is a lot of freedom to build up form and shape just like working with oil paint.

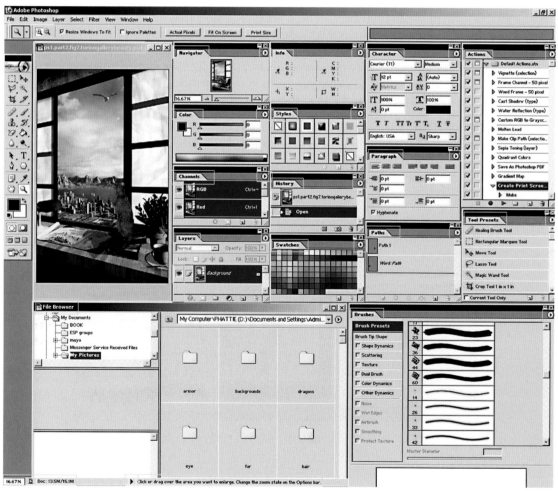

The Photoshop Interface

A second application of painting skill for a texture artist is the construction of original textures from photographs. A lot of detail, form, and even lighting might already be present in the source photographs, but successfully melding source images into a workable texture image involves painting with a brush tool.

Another artist might be assigned the task of altering a pre-made texture, HUD, or screenshot with a little more depth, contrast, and detail added via use of the Burn/Dodge tools, or the Brush tool.

PUTTING PAINT ON THE SCREEN

Painting is executed one of two ways: with the mouse, or with a stylus and a graphics tablet, such as a Wacom artpad. Painting with a stylus is without question my preferred method, as it allows for much greater precision and dexterity. Though some tools do work better when used with a mouse, the brush tools work best with the stylus and pad. Every artist should include this equipment in their workstation area.

*Brush
Button*

BRUSH TOOL

The Brush(B) is a versatile tool. Photoshop comes with its own set of default brushes, plus some other customized sets such as square brushes, shadows, textures, and finishers. These brushes can be used for many purposes such as painting lines, outlines, highlights, shadows, shapes and objects, volume, form, depth, noise, leaves, grains, surfaces, and many more. Each brush included with Photoshop is assigned a name, but don't let that dictate how you use them. It is also possible to make your own custom brushes, not only for the Brush tool, but all the other brush-type tools as well.

There are many different brushes, and there are options to create, load, reset, and save them, as you work. It is important to know how to keep brushes because it will save you the trouble of having to remember how you made them if you find you need them again. A collection of custom brushes is a fun and handy resource to have for use.

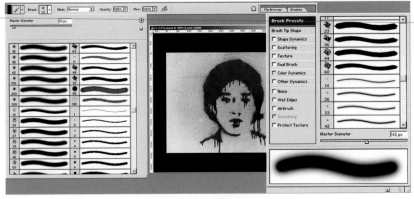

Options of the Brush tool

The first step to creating a custom brush is to set the diameter of the brush. On the tool options bar, click on the selected brush shape represented by a round black dot (or something similar) to set the Master Diameter. This area of the options bar is called the brush preset picker. Here is where other brush shapes can be chosen and the master diameter of the selected brush set. Use the slider to increase or decrease the brush diameter. You can also enter a numeric value to set diameter size. Note that if you wish to reset the tool, the fast way to do this is click on the tool icon to the far left of the options bar and right-click. As with all the other tools, you may reset just the one tool, or all of the Photoshop tools.

The other function of this button is to serve as the tool preset picker. As with the preset picker for the currently selected tool (in this instance, the brush tool), this drop-down option lets you choose pre-made brushes complete with a variety of options.

To create a new brush, reset more brushes, load them, save new brushes, or replace one set of brushes with another, go back to the brush preset picker and click the black arrow (within the circle) to the right of the brush choices. This menu also allows you to set the size and type of brush preview thumbnails. The bottom of the menu lists the available brushes. Click on these to automatically append them to the current list.

Next, back along the top options bar, you can specify which blending mode you would like to paint with. A blending mode is essentially an effect that you can apply to several of the tools, and to your layers via the Layers palette. These modes alter the way that brush strokes and other layers interact with the layers beneath them. Blending modes are very important to fine-tuning your work and can produce some really cool effects. Descriptions of all the different blending modes can be found in the next chapter, along with samples of each.

After the blending mode drop-down list comes the Opacity slider. You can paint with thick, heavy paint at full opacity, or paint with thin, transparent washes at low opacity.

The last option on the Options bar is the Flow slider coupled with the Airbrush icon. In previous versions of Photoshop, the airbrush was a tool all its own. In 7.0, however, it has been modified to provide a new effect for all of the painterly tools of the program. The airbrush option adds painted hues gradually, replicating a realistic airbrush effect. Use the Flow slider to specify how much paint you want to emit from the nozzle of the digital airbrush.

The Airbrush option, if handled with sensitivity, can yield excellent results. It is great for use with drawing tablets, too, because it can be configured for sensitivity using the tablet's software, as well as by using the Pen Pressure controls incorporated into the Brushes palette.

The options of the Brush(B) tool should be used in conjunction with the new Brushes palette, located on the top-right of the interface by default. This palette is addressed in detail in Chapter 2.

*Paint
Bucket*

PAINT BUCKET TOOL

The Paint Bucket(G) tool fills in areas with a solid foreground, background, pattern, swatch color, or value. Use this tool for filling in large shapes in the blink of a mouse click. The Paint Bucket(G) is very handy for creating the foundation hue or value you choose (within a selection) to build the rest of a texture on, such as a dark reddish hue for the beginning of a brick wall, or green for a goblin skin texture.

In addition to the power of the color fill, you can use the Paint Bucket(G) tool to fill a selection or area with a pattern chosen from the defaults, or that you created yourself. The bucket can be further customized by its ability to fill in a particular blending mode, raising and lowering the Opacity of the fill, and changing the Tolerance of the fill. With a higher Tolerance, the fill will be less particular in what it chooses to color in. For example, with a low Tolerance set for a cloudy gray sky, the fill will only cover strict values of one gray. The lower the Tolerance, the fewer values the fill will color. With a higher Tolerance, the fill will cover the initial value of gray, as well as perhaps the next lightest gray. The higher you go, the more values are included in the fill.

Keeping Anti-Alias checked will ensure your edges stay smooth and beautiful.

When Contiguous is checked, only pixels within the Tolerance range that are connected to the one you click on will be filled. When Contiguous is unchecked, pixels within the Tolerance range of the pixel you click on will be filled no matter where they are on the image.

When All Layers is unchecked, pixels outside the tolerance range "block" the fill only if they are on the active layer. When All Layers is checked, pixels that are outside the Tolerance range on any layer will constrain the fill. Either way, the bucket affects only the active layer.

Gradient

GRADIENT TOOL

The Gradient(G) tool is the Paint Bucket(G)'s alternate mode, and creates gradations of two or more colors, blending between them in one of several patterns. Gradients are an excellent tool because they're a great way to quickly simulate 3D effects on a 2D plane. Pick a foreground and background color on the tool bar, then click-and-drag to indicate the center and direction of the gradient. Gradients can be straight, radial, reflective, and diamond-shaped; experiment with the different modes until you get the effect you want.

Gradients are an excellent way to quickly suggest form and volume. In addition to the basic two-color gradient, you can select one of many pre-defined patterns using the gradient picker button. Just like the brushes, you can load, reset, save, and delete gradient patterns.

Next choose the type of gradient – linear, radial, angle, reflective, or diamond – you need for your fill. Use the blending modes and Opacity controls to further refine the effect. To reverse the order of colors in the gradient fill, select Reverse.

To create a smoother blend of the chosen hues with less banding, select Dither. Certain preset gradient patterns have transparent areas; uncheck Transparent to make those areas solid.

Smudge

SMUDGE TOOL

Ever feel like finger-painting? The Smudge(R) tool does just that. You can turn your mouse or stylus into a virtual finger to push and pull the pigment on your Photoshop canvas. I like to use this tool for touching up small areas of paint where the highlights and shadows need better blending and to quickly correct little areas of cloned or tiled textures that need breaking up. I also use this tool to create a smoother edge or surface in areas that are overly pixelated or poorly blended. This is a good tool for moving paint from one area to another quickly and painlessly and is also a great fast way to "rub out" paint that isn't working – such as dodged-in highlights. This tool works best on a smaller scale, which allows for a lot more precision.

Choose the brush size, blending mode (note that not all the blending modes are available for these tools Options), Pressure, and whether or not you want to use all the layers to alter the active layer. Lastly, you can check the Finger Painting box to simulate the effect of dragging your fingers through thick paint (or thin, depending on your settings). Play around with the pressure settings; there's a big difference between more pressure and less.

Blur

BLUR TOOL

The Blur(R) tool softens any area you paint over. Blurs can be applied to everything and anything that requires a softening, distanced, or atmospheric look. I also use this tool to create soft highlights with diffused edges, and to blend areas of color that require a softer look.

The options for the Blur(R) tool are similar to the Brush(B) tool. Choose brush size, blending mode (limited to normal, darken, lighten, hue, saturation, color, and luminosity), strength, and whether or not to use all layers.

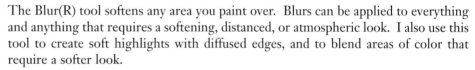

Dodge

DODGE TOOL

The Dodge(O) tool is meant to mimic the traditional photography technique of pulling out stronger highlights in the photograph. The idea is to create areas of an image that have been more exposed to light than others; this tool lightens and decreases contrast. Dodge(O) can be used for increasing highlights that will better describe form, depth, and dimensionality of painted objects. It can also be used for the general lightening of too-dark areas, or emphasizing tiny details. For example, use the Dodge(O) tool to create halos of light around street signs, or to enhance reflections on armor and add height to rivets. I also frequently use the dodge tool to apply hot highlights to hard stone and metal. This tool is a quick way to add depth and dimension to circular objects by decreasing the brush size with each click, culminating in a small hot highlight that turns a flat circle of paint in to a lit sphere. Note, however that the dodge tool doesn't work on empty layers, which means to get it to work, it has to paint directly onto an image.

First, choose a brush size. Then, select what to change in the image: Midtones affects the middle range of values, Shadows affects the dark areas, and Highlights affects the light areas. Specify the exposure for the tool: just like in traditional photography, the higher the exposure, the more lightening the effect will be. Don't let the tools options limit your use of them, however. It's possible to make creative use of applying its different functions in unconventional ways. Don't be afraid to experiment!

Burn

BURN TOOL

An alternate mode for the Dodge(O) tool, burning also comes from a traditional photography technique. However, the Burn(O) tool is the opposite: it adds darkness to the image and increases contrast. Use the Burn(O) tool to tone down lighting or to even out a summer sky that is unnaturally bright. The burn tool can also be used for details and for adding shadows.

Bear in mind, however, that burning with this tool produces black. Black is not always the appropriate choice for describing dark areas on an image. On a TV – where your game art may wind up – black looks like an empty void of nothing and tends to flatten out the rest of the image, creating deadness. Use the Burn(O) tool in moderation and for smaller detail areas where the black it produces won't be too obvious.

The options for the Burn(O) tool are the same as for dodging.

Sponge

SPONGE TOOL

Another alternate mode of the Dodge(O) tool, the Sponge(O) tool changes the color saturation of an area, either desaturating or saturating the paint. This is a great tool to use to create variations of a single hue along the surface of a painted shape. You can paint in a highly saturated version of the base color, or a similarly desaturated one. Variations of hue in textures are desirable because they break up the heaviness and monotony of large areas of paint. I use this tool often to add colorful highlights, break up paint, and occasionally to take down the saturation in small areas of a texture.

The options for the Sponge(O) tool are similar to the other painterly tools, except that you can choose between the Saturate and Desaturate modes. Unlike dodging and burning, this tool works with pressure.

CHOOSING COLORS TO PAINT WITH

Selecting the right colors to paint with is very important. There are several different methods of selecting colors to paint with, including picking from a preset palette; mixing hue, saturation, and value in the color picker; sampling colors from a different image; and even making your own palette of colors to choose from.

Foreground/ Background Swatches

FOREGROUND/BACKGROUND SWATCHES

Look toward the bottom of the vertical tool bar. There you will see two large squares, one filled with black and one with white. These are the default color settings of the foreground and background swatches. Whatever you see in top box is the color that will appear when you fill with the bucket, paint with the brush, draw with the pencil, etc. To change the foreground color, click on it once. The color picker will promptly appear. Either choose a color here, type in the color's numerical values, or click Custom to choose from the Swatches palette.

Whatever you see in the background swatch is the color that will appear when you use any tool that uses a background color, such as the Gradient(G) tool. To change the background color, click on it once to access the color picker. Choose a color, type in values, or click Custom to choose from the Swatches palettes.

These two buttons will be used frequently as you work. Note that it is always a good plan to keep track of the colors you use, so that you can later add or repair textures with the same colors they were created with. It's a good idea to save the colors you like to the Swatches palette. You can do this by clicking on the options arrow of the Swatches palette and selecting Save Swatches. Type in a name for the color palette, hit Enter, and a file now exists containing the swatches. (For more detail on how to save swatches, see the next chapter.)

EYEDROPPER TOOL

Eyedropper

The Eyedropper(I) tool is the tool used most frequently to choose palette colors from images or from the swatches palette. Simply mouse over the areas of an image you want to take a color sample from, and click. The color will appear in the foreground color box of the tool bar. From there you can paint with the sampled color, or add it to the swatches palette as needed.

The Eyedropper(I) tool has three options to choose the sample area: Point Sample reads the value of a single pixel. 3 by 3 Average reads the average value of a 3-by-3 pixel area around the cursor. 5 by 5 Average reads the average value of a 5-by-5 pixel area. I personally never bother to set any options for this tool. Just click where you like the color and call it good.

SELECTIONS

A selection is an area of an image that has been isolated from the rest of the image in order to make changes to that area. Making selections with Photoshop 7.0's selection tools is a piece of cake because the tools are well-designed and highly flexible. You will spend a great deal of time working with selections, so it is a good idea to get to know these tools well.

WHY SELECTIONS ARE USEFUL

Selected areas marked off with these tools can be filled with solid colors, patterns, photographic source images, hand painted areas of detail, and more. Almost all of the tools, operations, and filters in Photoshop will affect only the selected area, if there is one active. Selections, sometimes called "selection masks", allow you to make very specific changes, by protecting the unselected parts of the image. Selections can be used to remove detailed objects from backgrounds, and can be used to move elements of your work around the image. A selection can be applied to an entire image and then used to delete all the contents of that image with just a one-button press. Another useful application of selecting part of an image is to create an area of transparency unique to that image. These are called Alpha channels and will be detailed later in this book. It is easy to see why knowing how to make selections with these tools is important.

MARQUEES

Marquee

The Marquee(M) tool is the first selection tool on the top of the tool bar, and comes in four flavors: rectangular, elliptical, single row, and single column. This is the tool you need for creating basic geometric shapes for new fills and patterns, as well as selecting basic geometric shapes.

The Marquee(M) options cover a lot of important bases for customizing and manipulating your selections. Reading from left to right, the first option is the Marquee(M) tool icon with a down-facing arrow next to it. Right-clicking on the tool icon in the Option bar offers the option to reset that tool's options to their default, or to reset all of the tools. Left-clicking on the tool icon or down-facing arrow presents the tool presets menu, which is used for saving tool settings, or choosing a previously saved setting for the tool.

To the right of the tool icon are four buttons with different square-shaped icons on them. Hover your mouse over each to read their descriptions. "New selection" creates a new selection in the shape of the currently selected Marquee type. Add to a Selection (hotkey hold Shift) allows you to add to the currently active selection. Subtract Selection (hotkey hold Alt) removes part of the selection with the active Marquee shape. Intersect Selection (hotkey hold Shift-Alt) will create a selected area from the space that two overlapped selections have in common. For example, in Intersect mode, if a rectangular selection is drawn halfway over an elliptical selection, then the result will be a half-circle selection.

Remember to practice. Hands-on experimentation will solidify the information written here, and help you to retain it.

In the Feather field, you can specify how rounded, smooth, and blurred the edges of a selection are.

The Anti-Alias box should always be checked so that your selections end up even, smooth, and lovely instead of uneven, jagged, and ugly.

The Marquee(M) tool has three options for Style: Normal gives you whatever shape you click, drag, and release the mouse to accept; Constrained Aspect Ratio will permit selections only in the shape of a width-to-height ratio you specify; and Fixed Size lets you specify exact pixel dimensions for a selection and click once to summon a selection of that size.

LASSOS

Lasso

The Lasso(L) tools are another type of tool for making selections. These work a bit differently from the Marquee(M), having the capability to enclose much more complicated forms within their fences. Lassos have three flavors: Freehand, Polygonal, and Magnetic. You can access the different types by clicking and holding on the Lasso(L) tool in the tool bar and picking from the pop-up menu, or by pressing Shift-L to cycle through the modes until the one you want is active.

The Freehand Lasso(L) is excellent for selecting organic, reasonably complex shapes. If you are either very dexterous or have the fortune of possessing a drawing tablet, the Freehand Lasso(L) is a flexible option: just click, drag, and draw. Use this tool for encircling or specifying a more organic shape, like an oddly-shaped facial structure or an irregular tree trunk.

Options of the Freehand Lasso tool

The Freehand Lasso(L) has options very similar to those that were covered for the Marquee(M) tool. Once again, the ability to add, subtract, intersect, and create new selections is available for this selection tool, as well as the option to feather your selection. Make sure the anti-aliasing box has a check in it and, if you need to, you can reset the tool to its defaults by right-clicking on the Lasso icon at the far left of the Options bar.

Polygonal Lasso button

The Polygonal Lasso(L) tool is adept at surrounding a fairly complex polygonal geometric object with a selection. Click to create points along a shape's edge to select a precise selection. Use this tool to create or select angular geometric shapes, like the wall section of an architectural texture map, or sections of a character's weapon.

The options for Polygonal Lasso(L) are the same as those for Freehand.

Options of the Polygonal Lasso tool

Magnetic Lasso

The Magnetic version of the lasso will apply a sticky border of control points to an object's edge, for an even tighter selection. The number of points can be manipulated using the options for this tool. It can be tricky, though. Use this tool to select strong yet irregular edges quickly.

As the name of this tool implies, it behaves as if the control points created by the cursor are magnetically attracted to the edge of what you are attempting to select. You can specify the range within which the tool will detect edges to select, the strength of the magnetization, and the frequency that the control points of the selection are set.

To set the detection width for edges, enter a pixel value between 1 and 40 in the Width field. The Magnetic Lasso(L) tool will only select edges within the specified distance from the pointer. This distance is depicted by a small or large circle – depending on your settings – that surrounds the pointer.

To alter the lasso's sensitivity to edges in the image, enter a number between 1% and 100% for Edge Contrast. A higher value selects edges of higher contrast within the composition, while a lower number selects edges of a lower contrast.

To set the rate at which the lasso sets control points, enter a number between 0 and 100 for Frequency. A higher number anchors the selection border in place more quickly, leaving lots of control points along the edge.

Options of the Magnetic Lasso tool

This tool requires some practice. Experiment with making selections in the following fashion: an image with strong, defined edges can be done using a higher Width and Edge Contrast, dragging along the border quickly. On an image with less defined, softer edges, set a low Width and Edge Contrast, and drag along the border more carefully.

Wand

WAND TOOL

Like the Marquee(M) and Lasso(L) tools, the Magic Wand(W) creates selections. When you click on a pixel with the Wand(W), other pixels of a similar color are also selected: one click and an entire surface can be under your creative power. For example, you might use it to select all the leaves in an image of a tree.

Like the other selection tools, there are options for adding, subtracting, intersecting, and creating new selections with subsequent clicks. The Wand(W) selects pixels similar to what you click on: Tolerance determines how similar they need to be in order to be selected. Enter a value from 0 to 255; a low number selects colors very similar to the pixel you click, a high number to select a wider range of hues. Don't forget to check the Anti-Alias box to define a smooth edge. If you need to select areas that are next to each other, and of the same hues, check the Contiguous box. Otherwise, all pixels within the Tolerance level will be selected, no matter where they are on the image. To select colors using data from all the layers currently visible, select Use All Layers. By default, the Magic Wand(W) tool selects colors from only the active layer.

Pen

PEN TOOLS

The Pen(P) tool is the most advanced selection tool of the lot. However, it also takes the most time to manipulate, but is well worth the precise results. Use the Pen(P) tool to draw complicated shapes around an area of your work. Once the path has been completed, you can turn the path into a selection (by either right-clicking on the path to access the Make a Selection command, or clicking the Load Path as a Selection button on the bottom of the Paths palette) and save that selection. Saving paths and selections created with the Pen(P) tool will help you avoid having to outline complex selections over and over until you drive yourself nuts. Use this tool for separating and then compositing elements together, or for any complicated selection you'll need to reuse.

The Pen(P) tool comes in five variations: Normal, Freehand, Add Anchor Point, Delete Anchor Point, and Convert Point.

This tool can also be used to draw curved or special lines and borders. Simply use the tool to place points along the desired path in the texture file. Don't worry about having to close the circle of points. When you have the line you like, right-click on the path and a context-sensitive menu will appear. To turn the new path into a line, choose Stroke Path from the menu. A dialog will appear that tells you which tool will be used to stroke the path. The default tool is the Brush and the current settings of the brush will be applied to the stroke. For example, if the brush is set to a master diameter of 6 with 50% hardness, the line that appears will be 6 pixels wide and have a medium-soft edge. This line will be colored by whatever is the current foreground swatch. Then, as the final step, right-click again and click Delete Path from the menu. This is a great technique for creating unbroken, complex lines quickly and efficiently.

The options for the Pen(P) tool are as comprehensive as the tool itself. Choose between Create New Shape Layer and Create New Work Path. Creating a new shape layer will insert a new layer into the layer stack. As you add anchor points on the new shape layer, a fill will appear that fills in the shape as you click. A new clipping path layer will also appear in the paths layer stack. In the Create New Shape Layer mode, you are also able to apply a style to the layer. Click on the style you want and drag it onto the appropriate area on your image. The image will automatically update once you release the mouse.

Create New Work Path will place anchor points everywhere you click, on the layer that is selected. If you do not release the mouse once a point has been created, you can drag to activate Bezier handles for that point. Bezier handles are an even deeper refinement for creating accurate shapes and selections. Experiment with them.

Next, you can select a blending mode as well as Opacity for the layer. To see what is happening with your path, use the Rubber Band to preview path segments as you draw. After you define at least one anchor point for a path, Photoshop displays the next proposed segment as you move the pointer in the image. The segment doesn't become permanent until you click.

Click the Auto Add/Delete box to automatically add or remove anchor points from a path while drawing with the Pen(P) tool.

With this tool, you can also select which type of selection you would like to make, as you have done for the Marquee(M) and Lasso(L) tools: add to selection, subtract from selection, intersect selection, and exclude overlapping shape areas.

Click the check mark at the end of the Pen(P) Tool Options bar or hit Enter to finalize the path. Press Esc to cancel.

The Freehand options are the same as above except for one interesting difference: you can convert the Freehand Pen(P) tool into a magnetic pen, just like the Magnetic Lasso(L) tool.

Enter a number in the Curve Fit field to control how responsive the path is to the movement of your mouse or graphics tablet pen. Higher values entered into Curve Fit will create a simple path with few anchor points.

The Magnetic Pen(P) tool also has its own drop-down options menu. For Width, enter a pixel value between 1 and 40. The magnetic pen sees edges only within the specified distance from the pointer, as indicated by the circle around the tool. To set the Contrast, enter a percentage to set the contrast needed between pixels to be considered as an edge. Use a higher value for low contrast images. Frequency determines how many anchor points are added to the magnetic selection. This tool is really not much different than the magnetic version of the lasso. However, it has many more options having to do with paths, which the lasso tool does not offer.

The Add Anchor point tool places new control points along a path. New anchor points can make a curve smoother, change a curve into a sharp corner, or help to create a whole new shape. There are no options for this tool.

The Delete Anchor Point Tool removes unwanted control points from your paths. Use this tool to simplify paths. There are no options for this tool.

The Convert Point tool changes smooth points placed along a path into corner points. Smooth points are points that morph into curves when the Bezier handles of that point are clicked and dragged. Smooth points have uniform Bezier handles. Corner points are points that create a sharp angle when the Bezier handles for these points are manipulated. Corner points have broken handles. There are no options for this tool.

Edit Modes

QUICK MASKING

Directly below the foreground/background swatches on the tool bar, there are two rectangular buttons with circles in them, which change the edit mode of Photoshop. There are two primary edit modes for making changes to your work. Standard mode is the first and the default mode, and enables you to make changes directly to the content of your layers. Alterations made in this mode will be applied straight to the layers' content, without adding a protective mask or overlay to the imagery.

Quick Mask mode can be turned on by depressing the edit mode button on the right. I use Quick Masks to create special selections called Alpha channels (to be detailed later in this book) that turn the backgrounds of some textures transparent, saving and preserving the main subject. Using Quick Mask is not the same as drawing a selection with a lasso or a pen. The difference between using this mode versus a selection tool to create a selection, is that Quick Mask Mode uses paint and a brush to fill in an area that is to be saved, instead of placing points around the border of an area that is to be saved. I use Quick Mask mode to create transparent areas around a subject because sometimes it's much faster to paint in a solid shape, instead of placing careful points with the lasso or a pen. Quick Masks and Alpha channels are covered in greater detail later.

IMAGE CORRECTION

Some of the most common problems that will come up are matching up edges, tiling seamlessly, reproducing areas of an image, repairing areas of an image, or just plain taking things out. Photoshop provides a nice variety of correction tools and options that cover most of the problem solving territory, and then some.

These tools specialize in being able to match areas closely with other areas of the image, where needed. The Clone Stamp(S) tool is the most well-known of these tools, famous for its ability to blend textures together, duplicate elements of an image with perfection, and for tiling seamless textures. Pattern stamping lets you select a preset pattern to use within an image or selection. The Healing(J) tool, a new addition to the tool bar, is very similar to cloning, but focuses on matching lighting on the target area – handy for removing unwanted details. It can also be used in conjunction with the Clone tool to create seamless tiles twice as fast as before. Using a selection marquee, the Patch(J) tool repairs selected areas of an image. The Crop(C) tool is convenient for a vaiety of reasons, but its purpose is to cut away or reframe the borders of an image.

Clone Stamp

THE CLONE STAMP tool

The Clone Stamp(S) tool is the ultimate time-saver. It duplicates elements of your work exactly, from one part of the image to another. Sample an area of an image by Alt-clicking, and paint anywhere on the image to copy the information from the sampled area. This tool is indispensable for replicating information in areas of your image that would otherwise take forever to paint or draw by hand. You can also eliminate unwanted information by painting over the bad areas with information from the good areas.

This tool is also frequently used for creating seamless texture tiles. This is the process of creating , say, a brick texture that can be repeatedly applied to an environment without any visible borders. For large areas in game environments, this is a crucial technique to learn well as it can be used to create walls, terrains, and skies.

Use this tool to add new grass that looks just like the old grass to a field texture, or remove blemishes from a digital photograph of skin, or to take the seams out of texture tiles.

The Clone Stamp(S) tool works well in conjunction with the Healing(J) tool and the Patch(P) tool.

Like the Brush(B) tool, the Clone Stamp(S) tool has brush, blending mode, and opacity options on its tool options bar.

The Aligned option, when checked, will cause the cursor point used for sampling to stay parallel with the cloning brush, wherever it is moved around the image. This option is useful when you want to use different-sized brushes to paint an image, or you want to clone a linear pattern across a composition. You can also use the Aligned option to duplicate two halves of a single image and place them at different locations. If Aligned is deselected, the sampled area is applied from the initial sampling point each time you stop and resume painting. This option is good for applying multiple copies of the same part of an image to different areas.

When Use All Layers is checked, all the layers will be taken into consideration when you sample and paint. When it is unchecked, only information from the active layer will be copied.

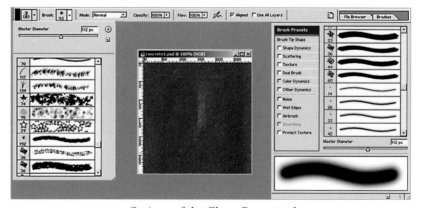

Options of the Clone Stamp tool

*Pattern
Stamp*

THE PATTERN STAMP TOOL

Pattern Stamp(S) is an alternate mode for the Stamp tool that paints patterns instead of parts of the image. Use this tool to select preset Photoshop patterns or apply custom patterns into your textures.

The Pattern Stamp(S) tool has brushes, blending modes, Opacity settings, and an airbrush mode.

Choose a pattern from the drop-down list in the Options bar. To load additional pattern libraries, click on the circular options arrow of the presets palette to access the options menu and select a library name – such as Artist's Surfaces – from the list menu. Another option for adding more presets is clicking the Load Patterns Option and navigating to the folder where the library is stored. Select Aligned to repeat the pattern as contiguous, uniform tiles, aligned from one paint area to the next. If Aligned is unchecked, the pattern is newly centered on the pointer each time you stop and resume painting. Last, check the Impressionistic box to paint a more abstract, blurred version of the pattern you have selected.

Rock wall pattern

Clouds pattern

Gravel pattern

Water pattern

Bark pattern　　　*Weave pattern*

Denim pattern　　　*Daisies pattern*

Healing

HEALING BRUSH

The Healing(J) tool is similar to the more conventional Clone(S) tool (described above) in that it is like a paintbrush that paints another part of the image onto the area you are clicking and dragging on. However, unlike cloning, this tool attempts to match the hue and lighting of that area. For example: a character's face texture has some artifacts from JPEG compression, blotching the cheeks here and there. Select the healing tool and Alt-click to select (sample) an area of skin without artifacts, even if that good skin is about five values too dark, and paint over the damaged area. A "healed" area will appear, devoid of artifacts, matching the value of the target area of the image. Use this tool for getting rid of artifacts, flaws, wrinkles, seams, etc.

This tool can also be used to create seamless texture tiles fast. Paired with the power of cloning, this tool will assist the tiling process by more closely matching the light and hue of the image to be tiled. A good technique to use that will be detailed further later on is to use the Healing(J) tool to patch up the edges of a tile, then use cloning to refine the areas.

Options of the Healing tool

Click on the brush button to access the options for Healing(J). You can adjust the diameter, hardness/softness, angle, roundness, and spacing with this dialog. Specify a blending mode from a limited list, and click on either Sample or Pattern to choose what source the tool will work from as its reference point. Sample is an area of the image you choose by Alt-clicking, Pattern is a texture from the Photoshop presets menu.

The Aligned option, when checked, will cause the cursor point used for sampling to stay parallel with the healing brush, wherever it is moved around the image. If Aligned is unchecked, the sampled area is applied from the initial sampling point each time you stop and resume painting.

PATCH HEALING

Patch

The Patch(J) tool is an alternate mode for the Healing(J) tool, accessed by clicking and holding on it in the toolbar. Patch(J) is very similar to the Healing(J) tool, only it makes use of selection marquees to specify which areas of an image need to be amended. Draw a selection around a damaged area of an image. Then click and drag the marquee to a location on the image that will repair the damaged area nicely. (This action can also be performed in reverse.) Once the mouse button is released, the selection will be filled in with the information from the second area specified by the mouse release. Use this tool for correcting large, problematic areas of your imagery.

With Source checked in the Options bar, create a selection around an area you need to have repaired and then drag the marquee you want to sample from. When you let go of the mouse button, the first area that was selected is patched up from the second area you dragged to. Destination is the opposite: create your selection in an area that is just fine, then drag that selection to an area that needs some repair work. Release the mouse button and voila! All fixed up.

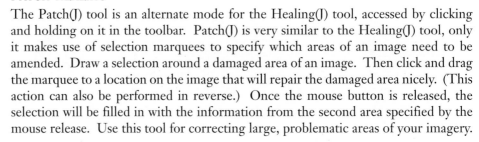

Options of the Patch tool

ERASER TOOL

Eraser

The Eraser(E) tool erases pixels, functioning like a brush tool. In fact, one way to look at the Eraser tool is that it's good for painting away paint. When used on the background layer, the Eraser(E) changes pixels to the background color selected in the tool bar. When used on any other layer, it makes pixels transparent.

In the Mode option you can choose between Brush, Pencil, and Block, which will each yield different results. Use brush to paint with the eraser, pencil for defined lines and areas, and the block tool mode for square areas. Depending on which mode you choose for erasing, some of the other option boxes and fields may or not be available. For example, if you are working with the Brush mode, the Opacity and Airbrush options are available. However, working with the Block tool mode will disable them. To erase to a saved state or snapshot of the image, select a state or snapshot, then check the Erase to History box.

*Magic
Eraser*

MAGIC ERASER TOOL

The Magic Eraser(E) tool works like the Magic Wand(W) tool, except that it erases instead of creating a selection. When you click on a pixel with this tool, pixels of a similar color are also erased. I use the Magic Eraser a great deal to dispense with unwanted backgrounds of solid colors. One simple click and the black background of a render is completely gone. This also works well to erase the backgrounds from UV maps, if necessary. However, this tool tends to leave a 1-pixel fringe of the background color along the edge of the subject to be retained. To fix this, usually executing a 1-point Defringe command works just fine.

Like the Wand(W), Tolerance determines how similar a pixel has to be to the pixel you clicked on for it to be erased. Anti-Aliasing smoothes the edges of the area you erase. If Contiguous is checked, the Magic Eraser(E) erases only similar pixels adjoining the one you click. If it is unchecked, similar pixels are erased irrespective of where they are on the image.

Select Use All Layers to erase from the entire image. (Although the layers you have invisible won't be affected.) Opacity dictates the strength of the erasure. An Opacity of 100% erases pixels to total transparency.

Options of the Magic Eraser tool

Crop

CROPPING

Most of the time, the Crop(C) tool won't be used to resize an actual texture PSD, because texture images come in predetermined dimensions already. 512x512 , 256x256, 128x128 pixels are examples of this. However, it is often useful for cropping down screenshots, or source images copied from the Internet. This tool is also great for chopping off borders of photographic elements you may be importing into the texture at hand.

Use the Crop(C) tool to pare away parts of your image you don't want or need. Bear in mind that the Crop(C) tool deletes whatever winds up outside of its bounding box borders.

When you select the Crop(C) tool, the first options that appear are those that have to do with its bounding box. You can specify the resolution of the final crop, as well as how the crop is to be measured: pixels per inch or pixels per centimeter. If you don't specify a resolution, the area you draw with the Crop(C) tool will be the size of the image after the crop operation. If you specify a resolution, the area you draw will be scaled to fit that resolution as part of the crop operation. Clicking Front Image selects the width and height of the current image as the resolution. Clear will delete whatever width and height measurements you have selected.

Once the Crop(C) tool has been clicked and dragged around the area you want to isolate, a different category of options will appear along the Crop(C) Tool Options bar. This set of options has to do with framing the image. For instance, if you have the Shield Cropped Area box checked, then all of the area of the image not included within the Crop(C) tool bounding box (everything that will be cropped off) will be obscured by a shield of darker color. You can specify the color and opacity of the shield. Finally, if you put a check in the Perspective box, you can skew the Crop(C) tool bounding box points into a polygonal shape.

Once you have defined a crop area and set the options, execute the operation by hitting Enter, clicking the checkmark icon in the Options bar, or double-clicking within the crop area. To cancel a crop without executing it, click on the X in the options bar or press Esc.

NAVIGATING PHOTOSHOP

As your skills with Photoshop grow stronger, you will want to work faster. This is where Photoshop navigation comes into the picture.

It'll be impossible to execute both minute and large-scale tasks in the standard view an image is presented in upon opening. The need to zoom in and out will make itself apparent early on, as will the need to move around an image that has been magnified. Sometimes, it'll be a better idea to isolate the image so that nothing else is visible on the display, including menu commands and other open documents. The Magnifying Glass, the Hand, and the Screen Modes are awesome tools for navigation. The most important and powerful of all the navigation tools is the Move(V) tool, which can move entire layers, selected elements, and even duplicate parts of an image.

Move

MOVE TOOL

The Move(V) tool moves things, specifically: selections, the contents of layers, or the layers themselves. The Move(V) tool is also used to duplicate layers quickly: hold down Alt while clicking and dragging with the Move(V) tool. This technique works great for covering a large area that needs to be filled with a seamless tile, such as a brick wall.

Note: in order to help prevent accidents from happening – and they will – make the effort to activate the Move(V) tool whenever you are not actively working with any of the other tools. This will help you avoid things like accidental brush marks that go unnoticed until it's too late.

There are a lot of useful options for the Move(V) tool. As with all the tools, you can reset by right-clicking on the icon for the tool on the Options bar. To save tool settings, or choose a previously saved setting for the Move(V) tool, left-click to access the tool presets dialog.

Next comes the most important option: Auto Select Layer. When you click on part of an image with the Move(V) tool with this box checked, the layer that contains the part of the image you click on will become active. This prevents having to click on separate layers in the Layers palette over and over again to select them. However, the Auto Select Layer tool does not do well with layers that are not of 100% Opacity. It does not have a Tolerance control of its own, so you must be careful. If not, things will get moved that you do not want moved. If you use Auto Select often, I recommend locking down the position of layers you don't want moved.

Another very easy, efficient, and fast way to select layers with the Move(V) tool while you work is to simply right-click on the image. Depending on where the cursor is located, a dialog (context-sensitive menu) will appear with the names of all the layers located in that area of the work. Try it out by right-clicking over an area of the image that has only one layer, and then repeating the process over an area that you know has several layers. Then, to make a selection, simply click on the layer you wish to select and it is highlighted on the Layers palette.

There is also a checkbox on the options bar to show a bounding box around the contents of your active layers and selections. When the bounding box is visible, you can access Transform mode while using the Move(V) tool by clicking on a control point (the small squares) at the edges and corners of the bounding box. The Move(V) tool deactivates, and the Option bar changes to show the Transform options. While in Transform mode, click-and-drag on the control points to scale (reduce or enlarge) the image, click-and-drag outside the bounding box to rotate the image, and click-and-drag inside the bounding box to translate (move) the image. You can also specify exactly the transformations you want by entering values in the numerical entry boxes in the option bar.

Experiment with holding down the Shift, Alt, and Ctrl/⌘ keys, separately, while you use the transformations. The Shift key constrains the proportions of the image while scaling, and constrains the image to travelling in a straight line (at a 45-degree angle) when moving. Holding the Alt key will scale the image relative to its pivot point (the circle and crosshairs, in the center of the bounding box unless you move it). The Ctrl/⌘ key will change the control points to distort rather than scale. To finalize the transformations, either click the checkmark icon in the option bar, hit Enter on the keyboard, or double-left-click inside the bounding box area. To cancel the transform and revert to where you were before you started dragging on the control points, click the X icon on the option bar or press the Esc key on the keyboard.

HAND TOOL

Hand

The Hand makes cruising back and forth within a magnified image the height of simplicity. By holding down the Space bar, then clicking and dragging with the mouse, you can navigate back and forth. Keep an eye on the Navigator palette to see where the mouse arrow is located at any given time.

You can click on one of the three automatic zoom options for the Hand(H) tool, which actually correspond with commands in the drop-down menus. Click on Actual Pixels and the image will be presented on your monitor in its pixel size (100% zoom). Fit on Screen will enlarge the image to the size of your screen while retaining its proportions. Hit the Print Size button to determine what the dimensions will be for output to print.

MAGNIFYING GLASS TOOL

Magnifying Glass

Need to get in close quickly? Hit Z on the keyboard and keep clicking until you're at the level of detail desired. Need to get back out just as fast? Hold down Alt (or Option for Macs) and click again to zoom out. This is the Magnifying Glass(Z) tool, universally used to jump in and out of your images fast.

The options for the Magnifying Glass(Z) are pretty much the same as Mr. Hand's. In this case, however, you can turn on the Resize Windows to Fit option and the window will then increase or decrease to accommodate your image's size after zooming. This is helpful because it makes it much easier to keep your reference point in view. I never work without this option checked because it is a serious pain to have to manually resize the image windows every time I zoom in or out.

Options of the Magnifying Glass tool

*Screen
Modes*

SCREEN MODES

The screen mode buttons located directly underneath the edit mode buttons on the tool bar. Each of the three rectangular buttons represent a way of viewing image documents and each has a quick reference icon on the button. The first on the left is a bar with windows (Standard), the center screen mode is a bar only (Full Screen with Menu Bar), and the right button has no bar (Full Screen). Screen modes affect how an image file is presented on the Photoshop display screen. Depending on which mode is selected, your texture image may be seen floating in an image window, centered in a grey screen, or placed in the middle of a black screen. I use these modes to check the accuracy of renderings created by my 3D package and to work on details in highly magnified areas with more space.

Standard Screen Mode is the default mode for viewing image documents. Standard Screen Mode provides you with opened image files tidily placed within floating image windows that can be dragged and scaled. This mode allows you to freely move the image around the Photoshop interface, which is handy when all of the palettes are open and visible, as well as when you are working with multiple images.

Activating Full Screen Mode with Menu Bar expands the image window of a selected file to cover the entire screen, isolating it against a background of medium grey. This mode is great if you need more space, or if you don't want to see any other image files as you work. Notice that the border of the interface has been pared down to add space. In this mode, however, it is no longer possible to move the image freely around the interface, as it is positioned in the center of the monitor

Full Screen Mode (without menu bar) takes the previous mode one step further, filling the screen with the image and causing the drop-down menus to disappear. Don't fret – look at the top of the tool bar. See the tiny black arrow? That is where your drop-downs can now be found.

The background of this mode is a default black. To hide the Photoshop palettes from view in order to see your entire image, simply hit the Tab key. To get them back, hit the Tab key again.

To change the color of the background in all three modes, choose the desired color as a foreground color, select G (for the Paint Bucket), depress Shift, and click in the border area. The background color will now match the currently selected foreground color.

VECTORS

Whereas most of the tools in Photoshop create and edit bitmap graphics where the color of each pixel is specified, vector graphics are defined by curves, which result in a smooth edged line or shape easily moved and transformed without loss of resolution. The Vector(U) tools create various geometric shapes, lines, and custom preset shapes, each of which has different options. These special tools have been greatly improved, and are a welcome addition to the arsenal of flexible tools the program has to offer.

WHY VECTORS ARE USEFUL

Bitmap images are comprised of single pixels, each assigned a single color and value. This are the type of graphic Photoshop was originally designed to deal with. Enter vector graphics, more commonly associated with illustration and web design programs. Vector graphics are useful because they use curves that don't decay after several transformations, unlike patterns of pixels. They provide an easy way to add text and special shapes to work (especially on a small scale that would be impossible to do with a bitmap), and they are useful for creating interface elements like heads-up displays. The vector graphics of Photoshop can be used with plenty of different fonts, and it's possible to turn any bitmap shape you create into a custom vector graphic.

FREEFORM SHAPES

Custom Shape

Mouse over the tool bar to find the Rectangle(U) tool (located under the Text(T) tool), click, and hold. The menu for this button will drop down, revealing all of the tool choices available for creating vector shapes and lines. These choices come in basic shapes, and they can be added together to form more complex shapes.

Choose any one of the shapes listed in the shapes button menu of the tool bar. Now look to the top options bar for the chosen tool and click on the Pen Tool, Freeform Pen Tool, Rectangle, Rounded Rectangle, Ellipse, Polygon, Line, and Custom Shape buttons along the bar. Then click on the inverted arrow button at the end of the row to view the option settings for each vector shape tool. These options let you use any of the shape and line choices without having to scroll up and down in the shapes menu on the tool bar.

FUNCTION BUTTONS

The function buttons are the first three to the right of the Tool Preset Picker button at the top-left of the options bar for each vector shape tool. Function buttons tell Photoshop how to add vector shapes and lines into your work. Is the function to create a mask layer, or a new path, or a fill?

Select one of the shape tools from the tool bar menu and then look up to the options bar. Use your mouse to roll over the top-left square button that looks like it has points on each corner to find out the name of the button. This is the Shape Layers button. Click it to automatically create new layers that contain the vector shapes you create as you work. This function allows you to add vector assets without affecting the original image, and all of Photoshop's tools and goodies can be applied to them separately.

The next button over is the Paths button. Depressing the Paths button before you begin will generate a path outline (without anchor points) directly on the image, which can then be treated exactly like a path drawn with a pen tool. This option is available for all of the vector shapes tools, including all of the custom shapes. Right-click on a path created with this tool to access options like defining a custom shape, applying blending options, or creating a selection.

The third button of the first trio is the Fill Pixels button. When you use the vector tools with Fill Pixels mode selected, a filled-in shape is added directly to the active layer. Click and drag to place solid shapes and lines, which will be filled with the currently selected foreground color.

CURVES

The next group of buttons are the options used to add shapes, paths, lines, and custom graphics to an image.

The first of these is the Pen(P) tool, an incredibly flexible tool for creating drawings and shapes. It can be used in conjunction with the Shape Layers and Paths function buttons. Fill Pixels is not available for this tool.

The Freeform Pen tool defines shapes and paths without anchor points, that can then be further manipulated using the right-click context-sensitive menu, or the tools of the Paths palette. Fill Pixels is not available with this tool.

GEOMETRIC SHAPES

The next button option, the Rectangle Shape tool, creates hard-cornered square and rectangular vector shapes. You can access its options by clicking the inverted black arrow to the right of the shapes buttons. The options below are the same for the Rectangle, Rounded Rectangle, and Ellipse vector shape tools.

Select the Unconstrained option to create freeform rectangles by clicking and dragging however you wish. The Square option constrains a rectangle to always have sides of equal length. Fixed Size creates a Rectangle, Rounded Rectangle, Ellipse, or Custom Shape at a specific size based on the numbers you enter into the Width and Height fields. (Remember the Marquee(M) tool.) Click once and the shape is made. The Proportional option lets you draw a shape of any size, but constrains it to the width-to-height ratio you set in the fields of the same name. The Snap to Pixels option causes the edges of Rectangles and Rounded Rectangles to stick to bitmap pixels as if they were a grid.

The Rounded Rectangle tool option produces the same general shapes as the rectangle tool, only the corners are rounded. The options for this tool are exactly the same as those for the Rectangle tool, with the exception of Radius. The Radius option specifies the amount of curvature at the corners.

The Ellipse tool makes circles and ellipses. It shares options with the Rectangle and Rounded Rectangle tools, with the exception of the Circle option, which keeps the ellipse round.

The Polygon shape is a basic five-sided polygon. The Radius option specifies the distance from the center of a polygon to the outer limits. The Smooth Corners or Smooth Indents option creates polygons that have obvious curves between points. Use this option to create star shapes that are soft instead of angular. The Indent Sides By/Star option will turn a polygonal shape into a star. You can choose a Percentage of how star-like you want the shape to look. A higher Percentage will indent the inside points further towards the center of the shape. Sides specifies the number of sides in the polygon.

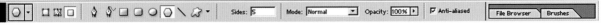

Options of the Vector Shapes tool

LINES

The Line(U) tool comes in handy a lot for things. Once a line is drawn, it can then be added to with the layer effects to add dimensionality and texture. It's useful enough to include its very own spot in the sun. Use this tool for bars, patterning, hair textures, or anything else that involves linear elements.

The Arrowheads Start and End options create a line with an arrow on one end or the other. Choose Start, End, or Both to decide at which end of the line arrows are generated. Enter numbers for Width and Length to set the dimensions of the arrowhead. Choose a number for the curvature of the arrowhead: the Concavity value determines the amount of angle on the arrowhead, where the arrowhead meets the line. Weight determines the pixel width of a new line.

CUSTOM VECTOR SHAPES

Photoshop comes with a collection of preset, common shapes. Click on the round arrow button of the Custom Shapes drop-down menu to access more preset menus. To create your own iconic language, you can use this tool. The options for the Custom shape tool include the previously discussed Unconstrained, Fixed Size, and From Center options, as well as its own Defined Proportions and Defined Size options.

CHANGING PATHS AND SELECTIONS

The last buttons on the options bar for the vector shapes tools are the Add, Subtract, Intersect, and Exclude selection assistants. Use these tools with the vector shape options to alter the boundaries of paths and selections.

Text

TEXT

Choose the Text(T) tool and click on the image. Automatically, a new layer designated for text will appear in the Layers palette.

The Text(T) tool is very similar to the text tools for other programs you may be familiar with: you can use whatever fonts you can get your mitts on, specify color, font, leading, and kerning. The Text(T) tool also has a great deal in common with word processing programs: you can set margins, align text, warp text, and change its formatting. In the tool options bar you can choose to create new text or a text mask. You can choose which direction the text reads in (left-to-right or up-to-down), select a font, and select a font style. You can type in any value in the Font Size field, specify which anti-aliasing mode best fits your typography (different fonts and font colors anti-alias differently, especially depending on their resolution), and even warp text.

The last button on the option bar is the Palettes button. Click this to show the Character and Paragraph floating palettes. Just like the Brush and Gradient pop-up palettes, the Character and Paragraph floating palettes have a round arrow options menu.

MEASURING

Unfortunately, it is still often a requirement to deal with numbers and basic calculations when creating textures. Fortunately, though, Photoshop makes it easy to figure out how tall and wide things are, figure out distances between elements, and more.

One reason to use a measurement tool is to figure out how well a source photo image destined for your texture will work with that texture. If you were creating a photo-realistic car, for example, and had copied a great side view of a flaming GTO, with the intent of using it as your texture, it would be necessary to make sure the image was large enough to be a good source. Anything too small wouldn't work, because scaling it up would compromise the image.

Another reason to use a measurement tool might be to add a precisely sized element to your texture image. Since it's possible to set one of these tools exactly, you can place solid fills or patterns in specific dimensions anywhere within the image.

Perhaps the simplest reason to use a measurement tool is to figure out the distance between point A and point B in an image. I also often use the tool to refresh my memory on the dimensions of a texture file or screenshot.

Measure

MEASURE TOOL

The Measure(I) tool is used to figure out the distance between two points in an image. This tool measures angles, locations, and distances . Click on one point and drag to another in order to measure a distance. Reading from left to right along the option bar for this tool will give you the following information: the starting location of the ruler (X and Y), the horizontal (W) and vertical (H) distances traveled from the starting location, the angle (A) relative to the starting point, and the total distance between the two points (D1).

To convert the Measure(I) tool into a protractor, hold down Alt and drag at an angle from one end of the measuring line, or double-click the line and drag. Hold down the Shift key to constrain the tool to multiples of 45 degrees. When using a protractor, you can see two distances traveled (D1 and D2).

TIPS ON HOW TO MEASURE WITH OTHER TOOLS

It's never a good idea to let the formal definitions of Photoshop stand in your way. Always being creative with the use of tools will open up lots of doors.

In my opinion, Photoshop seems to have a less comprehensive and coherent measuring system when compared to some of its other thorough features. In version 7.0, the tools used to take measurements are still unwieldy and even downright annoying.

One of my favorite techniques for measuring is applying a rectangular marquee around the border of an image. With a quick glance at the Info palette, I can see exactly what the size of the image is. The Elliptical version of the marquee can be used to perform the same function measuring the height and width of circles.

Note that this trick works best using the keyboard shortcuts to execute the marquee selection commands. These shortcuts are Ctrl/⌘ + A to select the entire image, and Ctrl/⌘ + D to deselect once the measurement has been taken.

The Rectangular Marquee has an option that also makes it useful for taking measurements or adding specifically-sized shapes to your work. Simply select Fixed Size from the options bar for this tool, enter in the correct numeric values, and click once. You can find out whether or not the imagery is sized correctly, or how it needs to be sized in order to work. Use this technique to determine shapes and sizes relative to other elements of the image. The fixed size marquee is also great for adding sized fills, patterns, or painted areas into the image.

Using the Crop(C) tool to ascertain dimensions while working with sizing textures is another great way to measure things. This tool, when dragged around an image, not only provides the dimensions of the crop in the Info palette, but covers the rest of the area of the image over with an opaque shield that can be made transparent so that it is possible to see how the crop relates to the rest of the image.

I use this method of measuring for two reasons. The first is as a way to see how I can reduce the size of a photographic source image or photographic texture image. These often need to be cropped and measured at the same time to make them more efficient to work with. The goal is to find a way to crop a large image while making sure to keep the composition useful and of an appropriate dimension. The second reason I use this tool is to check the composition of my image. Sometimes, when working on a composited Photoshop document, I decide that there are areas not needed or not successful and they need to go away. However, if I crop away too much, I may wind up with the wrong size for the image. The Crop(C) tool as a measurement device makes it hard to make a mistake with image size, since you can see the exact dimensions of the crop in the Info palette.

CONCLUSION

That's the tools in Photoshop! Take a good amount of time to mess around and experiment with the tools you don't know. Test out their options. You'll know more about Photoshop than ever before, and can mentally file away the tools that interest you the most for further exploration and use.

You should now have an excellent idea of how the Photoshop interface is laid out. You can move around the interface , choose and use the tools, and specify options for those tools. You have an extensive arsenal for painting, selecting, correcting, navigating, creating vector, shapes, and taking measurements.

QUIZ

1. WHICH TOOL IS BEST USED FOR SELECTING GEOMETRICAL SHAPES OF MEDIUM COMPLEXITY?
   a. The Wand tool set with a higher tolerance
   b. The Polygonal Lasso tool
   c. The Freehand Lasso tool

2. WHICH TOOL CAN BE USED TO ALIGN LAYERS WITHIN AN IMAGE?
   a. The Marquee tool
   b. The directional arrows
   c. The Move tool

3. IF YOU NEED TO DELETE A BACKGROUND FAST, WHICH TOOL WOULD BE BEST TO USE?
   a. The Eraser tool
   b. The Magic Eraser tool
   c. The Wand Tool

4. WHICH TOOL WOULD YOU USE TO CREATE A VECTOR SHAPE?
   a. The Custom Shape tool
   b. The Polygonal Lasso tool
   c. The Marquee tool

5. WHICH TOOL HAS OPTIONS FOR CUSTOMIZING BRUSH SHAPE, ROTATION, AND DIAMETER?
   a. The Brush tool
   b. The Clone Stamp tool
   c. Both A and B

6. WHICH TOOL SHOULD YOU USE TO CHANGE THE DIMENSIONS OF AN IMAGE?
   a. The Marquee tool
   b. The Crop tool
   c. The Zoom tool

7. WHICH OPTION CONTROLS HOW QUICKLY PAINT IS APPLIED TO AN IMAGE?
   a. The Brush tool
   b. Flow
   c. Wet Edges

8. WHAT ACTION ACTIVATES QUICK MASK MODE?
   a. Clicking the Edit in Quick Mask Mode button
   b. Using the Text tool Create a Mask button
   c. Creating a Shield with the Crop tool

9. WHICH TOOL WOULD YOU USE TO SELECT A COMPLEX SHAPE?
   a. The Wand tool set with a high Tolerance
   b. The Marquee Selection tool
   c. The Pen tool

10. IF YOU NEEDED TO COPY A PART OF AN IMAGE TO ANOTHER AREA OF THE IMAGE, WHICH TOOL WOULD BE THE BEST CHOICE?
   a. The Pattern Stamp tool
   b. The Clone Stamp tool
   c. The Fill tool

2 THE FLOATING PALETTES

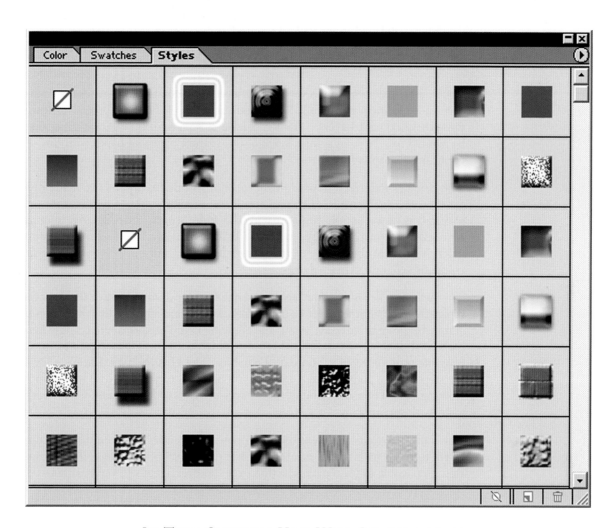

IN THIS CHAPTER YOU WILL LEARN ABOUT:

- Making the most of the powerful Layers palette
- Creating your own brushes, mixing colors, and saving swatches
- How to apply special effects and enhancements to layers
- Using the Channels palette for seeing and saving Alpha channels
- Using action scripts to automate repetitive tasks
- Using the History palette to undo multiple steps
- Using the Paths palette to create selections
- Keeping track of file information with the Info palette
- Where to manage custom tools and your image files efficiently

INTRODUCTION

While learning how to use the tools and tool options, you probably noticed several free-floating dialog boxes lined up along the right side of the Photoshop interface. These are known as "floating palettes", and are the movable menus that support the tools in the tool bar.

Each palette has a tab at the top of it that is titled in black with the name of the palette: the Layers palette says "Layers" at the top, and so forth. The palettes can be dragged anywhere on the interface by clicking and dragging on their top. It's also possible to click and drag on the bottom-right corner of each palette to resize them up or down. Some palettes are more important than others, but it is helpful to be familiar with all of them.

The floating palettes contain yet another level of executable commands for you to get even more refined and detailed with your artwork. The most crucial to learn are those that deal with Layers. Think of a layer as a piece of transparent paper that can be painted on. Now imagine a stack of transparent pieces of paper with lots of different details painted on them.

The Brushes Palette, a new addition to Photoshop 7.0, houses the many options for customizing brushes. The most important new feature of the Brushes palette is that it is now possible to paint with the style presets, introducing an amazing new level of control. Paired with the Brushes palette, the Color and Swatches palettes provide the ability to mix colors digitally, and options for saving mixed colors as separate artist palettes.

The Actions palette lets you record a sequence of commands, save them, and then replay them on another layer or image file. Actions are an incredibly helpful tool for automating repetitive tasks, saving and applying complex special effects, and saving a great deal of time. By default, this palette lives with the History palette, an indispensable tool for keeping you out of trouble. The History palette keeps a list of all the steps you've gone through and lets you undo all of them in case something isn't working out. The main point of these two palettes is to let you add or subtract from your work very quickly.

The Paths palette is an extension of the powerful Pen(P) tool, and displays separate layers for each path that is created, storing them within the image file. Because of this, it's possible to use a path selection over and over again without having to redraw it. This palette is another time- and frustration-saver.

Finally, Photoshop offers a trio of important palettes that enable you to manage your work and the tools you work with easily and efficiently. These are the Info, Tool Preset, and File Browser palettes. This chapter will go over how to read and customize the Info palette, how to use the Tool Presets to store your customized tools, and how to view and open files with the File Browser.

If the palettes are not showing or are randomly placed all over the interface, mouse up to the Window menu drop-down and check Show for everything that is hidden. It's even faster to do a Window→Workspace→Reset Palette Locations, which will restore all of the palettes to their default locations. Now you have all the palettes. Ready? Ok.

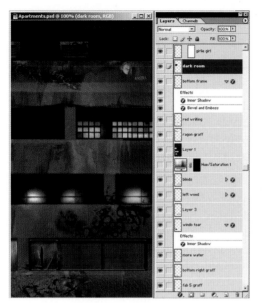

The Layers palette

USING LAYERS

Layers are unquestionably the most important concept for a new user to learn. A layer is a virtual piece of paper with nothing on it. Not only is there nothing on the paper, but the sheet is totally transparent. The idea is to be able to stack as many "sheets" of virtual paper as you need to create artwork. If you keep each detail on a separate piece of digital paper, it becomes very easy to simply toss the sheets of you don't like and keep the ones you do. It's also simple to change the contents of a layer, or add special effects to them.

LAYERS PALETTE

Making use of multiple layers will keep your work organized and allow it to be easily edited. You have the freedom to place every single separate brush stroke on a separate layer, which can be edited or deleted without affecting the rest of the image. Though that's taking things a bit too far, use as many layers as you need to keep the different elements of your work separate, so they can be freely exchanged.

Keep in mind, however, that using a lot of layers means Photoshop will behave more and more sluggishly. The best thing to do is pack your system with as much RAM as possible. Or deal with memory drain by increasing scratch disk space (see Assigning Scratch Disks in the Photoshop Help menu). You can also change the thumbnail size of the layers. Go to the Layers palette options via the round black arrow at the top right corner of the palette and click. Select Palette Options→None. Hit ok. Another thing to keep in mind is that the layer styles and blending options also drain memory. Use in moderation if you have a slow system.

There are also some work habits to keep in mind. For instance: always name your Photoshop layers. The purpose of assigning titles to all layers in the layer stack is to avoid confusion as to what is on those layers in the future, and to extend a professional courtesy to others who may need to revisit your work. Naming layers will also help you to be organized and will help avoid the frustration of trying to figure out what's on a layer (especially if the thumbnail previews are absent). Make it a habit to name all your layers.

CREATE A NEW LAYER

To create a new layer, click on the New Layer icon in the lower-right corner of the Layers palette, which looks like a stack of paper with one corner turned. If you right-click (Alt-click on a Mac) the New Layer icon, you will be presented with a dialog that lets you name the new layer while you add it, a fast and efficient method that I'd recommend. Hit Enter, and a brand new clean sheet of virtual layer will appear in the stack, directly above the layer previously selected.

Use this icon to quickly add layers to the Layer stack.

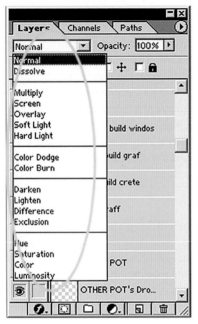

Photoshop Blending Modes

LAYER BLENDING MODES

At the top of the Layers palette, there is a drop-down menu that specifies the blending mode of the layer that is currently selected in the stack. Each new layer added to the layer stack will be set to Normal mode, by default. I use the layer blending modes to achieve an amazing array of effects. For example, I use Multiply for shadow layers, Screen for highlights, Color for solid color overlays, and Overlay to merge details with backgrounds. Usually, the only layers I set to Normal are the background layer, and layers that have blending options (special effects) assigned to them.

To choose a layer blending mode, select a layer, click on the drop-down that says Normal, and scroll down the list with the mouse (or down arrow key) to find the right mode. The mode you choose affects the currently selected layer only. Use blending modes to overlay details onto textures, create burned and dodged effects, create interesting lighting effects, composite elements of signs together, darken corners, add graffiti to textured surfaces, or add water stains to moldering concrete walls.

BLENDING MODE TYPES

As mentioned in the Brush tool section of the previous chapter, many of the tools in Photoshop have the option of selecting a blending mode. These modes alter the way that layers, paint, or effects interact with the layers beneath them. Read the descriptions and view the illustrations below to get an idea of what different blending modes can do. Note that some blending modes will only show up if there is something behind the effect or layer for it to interact with.

The way that I use blending modes is the way most people do: when a layer needs to blend with the layers under it, I scroll down through the blending mode menu looking at each effect until I arrive at the one that looks best for the situation. Rarely do I ever think to myself, "Well gee whiz, now I'm gonna apply a Black Light mode to this layer because it calculates the base color with the highest brightness value then inverts that to create a harder contrast and darker lighting effect, which is precisely the result I'm looking for." Experiment, experiment, experiment!

Normal mode

NORMAL MODE

Normal is the default mode. If you do not want the look of your brush strokes or stacked layers to change, keep the blending mode set to Normal. Layers and effects set to Normal will interact with the layers below just like their Opacity, color, and other options say they will.

Dissolve mode

Darken mode

Multiply mode

DISSOLVE MODE

The Dissolve blending mode will add a pixelated effect to paint and blended layers. This mode is best used with images of larger dimensions, as it does not anti-alias the pixelated look added to the layers. Use Dissolve to create noise effects and break-up.

BEHIND MODE

Behind mode works only on the transparent part of a layer. You can paint with this mode as you would with any other mode, but whatever you paint will only show up in areas that don't have any content. Effects executed with the Behind blending mode behave as if they are at the bottom of the layer stack.

CLEAR MODE

The Clear mode is available for the Line(U) tool when Fill is selected, the Paint Bucket(G) tool, the Fill command, and the Stroke command. When you are in this mode, whatever drawing or painting you do will erase the shape your tool creates to 100% transparency. Clear mode works pretty much just like an eraser.

DARKEN MODE

Use this mode to darken the overall values of an image. I rarely use this mode, as it has a tendency to flatten colors in an image. Instead, I use Multiply to add darkness when I want it.

MULTIPLY MODE

Multiply mode is often used for adding shadow passes to images. It is excellent because it results in a nice, rich darkness, without making the colors beneath the shadows look flat.

Here's a tip on shadow color: a good shadow color has to do with the concept behind the project. For example, a horror game with a great deal of darkness might do well with black shadows, because they create void-like areas. However, in other contexts, black shadows also have a tendency to flatten the areas of your image, reducing the sense of dimensionality. In cases where black is not conceptually sound, a low contrast purple or dark blue is a great choice. These are cool colors, and won't take away from the rest of the image.

Color Burn mode

COLOR BURN MODE

The Color Burn mode darkens pixels, increasing their contrast. I don't use this mode very often because the effect is usually too hard and pixellated for my work, but you would use this mode to achieve results for high contrast, highly saturated imagery.

Linear Burn mode

LINEAR BURN MODE

This mode is similar to Color Burn mode. However, Linear Burn mode darkens pixels by simply decreasing their brightness, instead of increasing their contrast. Use this mode for an effect similar to Color Burn, but more subtle.

Lighten mode

LIGHTEN MODE

Lighten mode produces the opposite effect of Darken mode, lightening pixels. Use this mode to generally lighten the underlying image. To my eye, this mode has a tendency to wash things out in an image, like Darken. For 3D texture work, it's a good idea to maintain great contrast and color.

Screen mode

SCREEN MODE

Screen mode is a good mode to use for adding highlights to a texture. This is the mode I set all my highlight layers to by default. What I like so much about Screen mode is that I can paint with the same base color of the main object, and not have to go to the trouble of selecting the right highlight hue. With screen mode and a single color, I know I'll get an accurate highlight every time, without wasting any time.

Color Dodge mode

COLOR DODGE MODE

Color Dodge mode is the opposite of Color Burn, brightening pixels by decreasing their contrast. This blend mode comes right from traditional photography and I like it because it is helpful for creating shiny highlights on metal. It can also be used as a way to brighten highlights painted on a Screen Mode layer. Use this tool to create bright light and an overexposed effect.

Linear Dodge mode

LINEAR DODGE MODE

Linear Dodge mode is the opposite of Linear Burn, lightening pixels by increasing their brightness – a lot. Use this mode to create simulated bright light and an overexposed effect. Linear Dodge creates effects slightly lighter than the Color Dodge Mode, and I sometimes use it for brighter highlights.

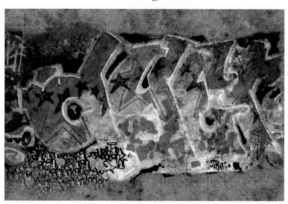

Overlay Mode

OVERLAY MODE

I use Overlay all the time for getting photographic textures to mesh with my main image. For instance, this mode works very well for putting a photo of graffiti on a hand-painted texture wall. This mode contributes enormously to a realistic look to Photoshop-made images, and I would be lost without it!

Use this mode for getting realistic texture effects, like graffiti on a wall, dirt on pavement, or worn decals on the T-shirts of your characters.

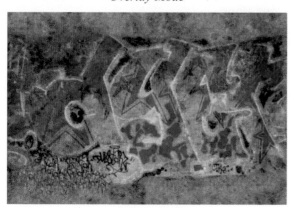

Soft Light mode

SOFT LIGHT MODE

The dark areas of a layer set to Soft Light darken the colors beneath them, and the light areas lighten anything beneath them. Soft Light creates a very nice effect that is often of lower brightness and contrast, resulting in a more diffused look. Some artists use this mode for highlights, creating a more natural, subtle look. It helps to have the correct highlight color chosen, however, and this often takes some experimentation unless the highlight and shadow color palettes have already been sorted out and provided for you in advance.

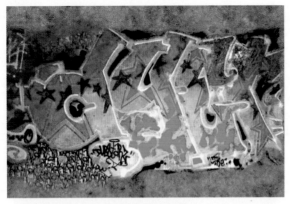

Hard Light mode

Vivid Light mode

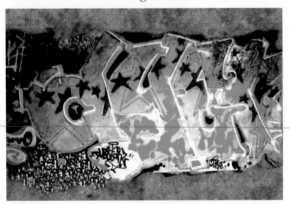

Linear Light mode

Pin Light mode

HARD LIGHT MODE

The effect of Hard Light mode is similar to Soft Light, except instead of lightening it dodges, and instead of darkening it burns. It ends up looking a lot like Soft Light, but more pronounced.

VIVID LIGHT MODE

Vivid Light is similar to Soft and Hard Light, but brightens by increasing contrast and burning, and darkens by decreasing contrast and dodging. I can't think of a single time I've used this mode, but I'm sure it works for something.

LINEAR LIGHT

Linear Light is similar to Vivid Light, except that it simply raises or lowers the brightness of the colors it's lightening or darkening, instead of burning or dodging them.

PIN LIGHT MODE

Pin Light mode is, in my opinion, the most beautiful of the blending modes. It reminds me of a delicate version of the Overlay mode. Use this mode to add details that work with a more randomized representation, or subjects that are abstract, varied, and brightly colored.

Difference mode

Exclusion mode

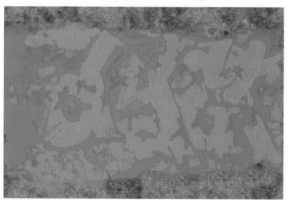

Hue mode

Saturation mode

DIFFERENCE MODE

Difference mode produces hues that are the opposites of the hues in the layer. To determine what a difference mode might do, you can select the mode, and then look at your color wheel to see how the change works. Difference mode usually results in bright colors and high contrast. Use this mode for strong color effects.

EXCLUSION MODE

The Exclusion mode works almost identically to Difference, but generally tones down those intense colors. Use this mode for effects similar to yet more subtle than Difference.

HUE MODE

When a layer or paint stroke is set to Hue mode, it transfers only its hue, using the saturation and brightness of the color beneath it. This mode works a lot like the color mode, or at least looks a lot like the Color mode. I don't think it works as well, though, so I use Color mode instead.

SATURATION MODE

Saturation mode is similar to Hue mode, but combines the saturation of the active layer with the hue and brightness of the layers beneath it.

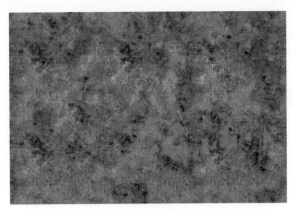

Color mode

COLOR MODE

Color mode is one way to add a fast and convincing color overlay. It works well for adding a color over the top of a monochromatic image to change its appearance. I once used it to turn a single silver Caddy texture into a fleet of different-colored cars for a driving game.

Luminosity mode

LUMINOSITY MODE

Luminosity mode is the exact opposite of Color mode, and combines the brightness of the blending layer with the hue and saturation of the layers below it.

OPACITY SLIDER

To the immediate right of the layer blending modes drop-down is the Opacity slider. The Opacity slider controls the visibility of the contents and effects applied to a layer. Reducing Opacity of a layer reveals more of the layers below, while fading the overall detail and contrast of the current layer. If you are looking for just a hint of a shape or effect, use the Opacity slider to make that layer more transparent.

FILL SLIDER

Similar to the Opacity slider, the Fill slider works by increasing the transparency of something contained in a layer. However, unlike the Opacity slider, the Fill slider only affects the actual paint of the layer. It does not have any impact on layer styles applied to the layer.

I prefer to use the Fill slider for most subject matter that needs transparency because it leaves the special effects of the layer untouched. By leaving them 100% opaque, I often get an interesting blend that still retains contrast, depth, and patterning.

LOCKS

Sometimes it's important to make sure the layers of an image don't get accidentally marked or moved. Photoshop answers this need by providing four types of blocking options, or locks. Locking prevents painting over an area of a layer, moving an area of a layer, or both.

The locking options can be found below the blending mode options, and look like a small checkerboard, brush, crossed-arrow icon, and padlock, which respectively correspond to Lock Transparent Pixels, Lock Image Pixels, Lock Position of an entire layer, and Lock All of an entire layer. To lock a layer, select it, and then click on the appropriate icon. A small padlock will appear next to the layer, indicating at least one function has been blocked. If you try to fill, paint, move, or manipulate the locked layer, warning boxes will appear. Another way to tell when a layer is locked is to mouse over it. If you are trying to paint, for example, the cursor will turn into a circle with a bar through it – the universal symbol for "No".

I often use these features to lock layers in order to protect what I've done. I find this is also convenient when others are opening and working with my files. Locking layers serves as a polite hint not to mess with what's on that layer.

LAYER STACK

Underneath the lock Options is the list of layers. You can open the tooltest.psd file from Chapter 1 to experiment with the layer options below, or create your own new file (File➔New) and add some layers.

The eyeball icon next to a layer means that layer is visible. Click on the eyeball and the contents of that layer will disappear, because you have just made it invisible. The brush icon indicates what mode you are editing in. If you were to be painting in quick mask mode, the layer would turn light gray and the brush would disappear. Try this out. (You can get into quick mask mode by hitting Q on the keyboard.) Masks are used for obscuring other parts of the image and can also be used for isolating certain aspects of your work. Some people find them very helpful, others find them unnecessarily time consuming. You can experiment with masks and decide for yourself.

The options for this palette can be found by clicking on the small black arrow within a circle, on the top-right of the palette. Here you have fast access to most of the drop-down menus for the Layer menu. You can choose to create new layer sets, delete them, select layer properties and blending options, merge layers, and at the bottom, choose how you would like the thumbnails to appear on the Layers palette. Experiment with them, but bear in mind that large thumbnails do take up memory. When you have 100 layers or more to work with, this can become a problem.

Note that you can also access options for all aspects of a layer by right-clicking on what you wish to change. For example, if you want to make a change to a mask while in mask mode, right-click on the mask to get more options. Repeat this for the layer image icon, the brush icon, and the eyeball icon. Each has a drop-down menu you can use to manipulate your work faster, and more effectively.

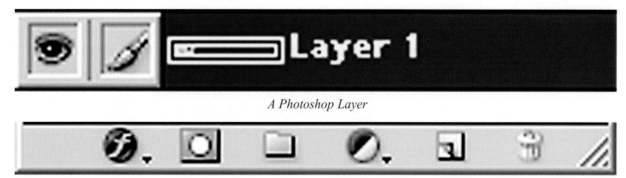

A Photoshop Layer

Layers Palette button shortcuts

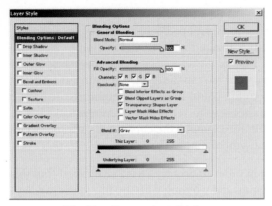

The blending options Dialog

BLENDING OPTIONS

Blending options are not the same as blending modes, so don't confuse them. The blending options dialog box is the tool that is used for creating layer effects – also known as layer styles – like drop shadows and beveling effects. You can access the blending options dialog by either right-clicking on the relevant layer and choosing Blending Options from the pop-up list, by double-clicking in the empty space of a layer, or by clicking on the Add Layer Style button on the bottom-left of the Layers palette. This menu allows you to choose either a specific style (combination of layer effects) to apply to your selected layer, or you can simply choose Blending Options to take you right to the default dialog box.

When a layer has a style defined, in the layer stack it will have a small icon that looks like a white script "f" in a black circle. Click on the small arrow to the left of those icons and you'll see those effects drop-down from the layer. Layer styles each get their own sub-layer to reside upon within the Layer stack, under the selected layer. Just as with any other layer, the eyeball indicates the visibility of the layer effect that has been added. Click on the eyeball and the layer style will disappear from your image. Click on the eyeball next to Effects and all the effects will become invisible.

To re-access the Layer Style dialog box to adjust your layer styles, double-click on the effects icon visible on the main layer. This will launch the Blending Options dialog box to its default state, with all of the effects listed to the left. If you only want to change the settings of a particular effect, such as a drop shadow already applied to the layer, double click on the effects icon located on the Drop Shadow layer. The blending options dialog box will launch to the Drop Shadow controls, and you can make your changes from there.

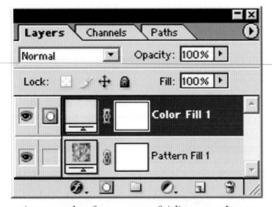

An example of two types of Adjustment Layer

ADJUSTMENT LAYERS

Sometimes it is not a good idea to make major alterations directly to layers in your layer stack. In such a case, an Adjustment Layer can be used. Adjustment Layers add a new layer to the stack that has a built-in effect such as Hue/Saturation or Brightness/Contrast. Adjustment Layers alter the overall look of all the layers located beneath them in the layer stack.

The menu for Adjustment Layers can be accessed by clicking on the Create New Fill or Adjustment Layer button on the bottom of the Layers palette (the black and white circle icon split diagonally in half). You can also add an Adjustment Layer via the Layer drop-down menu located at the top of the Photoshop interface. Click on that button and select which type of adjustment you would like to make. Note that some of these layers are technically fills, but still behave in the same fashion as the Adjustment Layers.

After you have selected the appropriate Adjustment Layer, a dialog box will pop up that contains the controls for that particular type of layer. If you choose a Brightness/Contrast Adjustment Layer, then the dialog box for that command will appear containing the sliders for Brightness and Contrast. Then you can mess around with the controls until you see what you like happening in the image, then press Enter to finalize (or Esc to cancel), and a brand new layer will appear in your layer stack. From there, to make further adjustments, simply double-click on the layer thumbnail that contains the slider icon for the layer and the controls dialog for it will reappear.

Don't forget that if you want to delete the Adjustment Layer, just click and drag it onto the trashcan button on the bottom of the palette. I use Adjustment Layers to add atmosphere to environmental scenes, to darken the lighting of a city that is not dark enough, or to change the color of a texture, like the grain in wood. These layers also come in very handy for creating color overlays quickly. My recipe is a Solid Color Adjustment layer set to the Color blending mode. It works every time!

USING LAYER STYLES

Layer Styles are combinations of blending options (or special effects), such as Drop Shadow, Glow, Emboss, Overlay, and Stroke, that can be applied to layers in various ways to get some really cool and creative results. The Styles palette works in partnership with the Layers palette and the blending options command that you can choose there to create all kinds of textures: wood, glass, plastics, bump maps, hair, stone, sunsets, shadows, enamels – just about anything.

For inspiration, you may want to experiment with the preset Layer Styles. Various libraries of style types can be loaded from the Style palette options.

Just like Layers and Swatches, it is possible – and recommended – to assign names to all of the new styles that you create and save. Sometimes even adding the date to a name or number is an excellent way to keep track of styles you create, particularly if you have several that are similar.

I concoct Layer Styles for a lot of different purposes. I use them for reflective surfaces, ground textures such as grass and sand, rivets and nail heads, beveled edges, stones, concrete, and whatever else needs a good simulation of surface tactility. I encourage you to experiment and play with creating Layer Styles as often as you can. They come in very handy for a lot of the art tasks that will be sent your way.

CREATING A NEW LAYER STYLE

To create a new style, select a layer other than the background, and either double-click on it in the Layers palette or click on the black-circle-"f" effects button at the bottom of the Layers palette. Choose blending options and the Layer Style dialog box will appear, giving you all the options for adding effects and creating a style. Follow the short exercise in the next few paragraphs for a tour of the Layer Style dialog box.

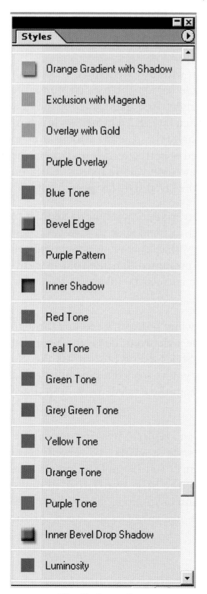

The Styles palette

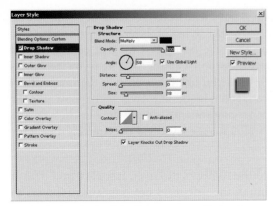

The Layer Styles blending options dialog box

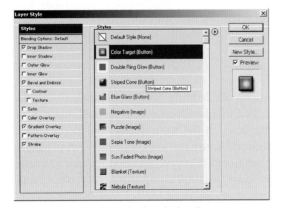

The Layer Styles dialog box

Check the Drop Shadow field and click on the Drop Shadow layer to activate it. The Drop Shadow settings will appear. Click and drag on the image to position the shadow. It will move as your mouse moves over the interface. (This is a shortcut to having to position your shadow with the Angle dial.) Next put a check next to Texture and click on the Texture layer. Now you will want to click on the arrow next to the Pattern thumbnail to access the Options menu. Remember that a black arrow in a circular button is the way to the options! Click Reset Patterns and the defaults will be restored. Next, select the Metal Landscape pattern (you can find out the names of the patterns by holding your mouse over them to view the label of the pattern). The effect of choosing this pattern should be visible. If not, mess with the Scale and Depth sliders of the Texture Options. Once you have an obvious effect happening, slap on an Outer Glow by putting a checkmark next to it, then select the Outer Glow line to see its options to the right, and change the color of the glow to something bright.

There is enough going on with this style so far to warrant saving it: click on the Style bar on the top-left, press the New Style button to the right, type in a name for the new style ("teststyle" is fine), then hit OK. The new style is now visible at the bottom of the Styles palette. Mouse over to make sure you have named it correctly. Now click on the No Style button. The new style will disappear. Click on the new teststyle button; the saved style has been reapplied.

You can make very complex effects, turn it into a Layer Style, and quickly apply it to any layer of any image, any time. The last step is to remember to save your new styles. Do this by accessing the options for the styles (black arrow in a round button to the right) and selecting Save Styles. You will be prompted to name your new category and they will automatically be saved in to the correct file folder for the styles, easily accessible from the same place at a later date.

To undo a Layer Style applied, simply click on the white box with a red line through it. This is the No Styles button and it will clear the style from the layer. Note that Ctrl/⌘ + Z (Undo) doesn't work from the Layer Styles dialog box, so use the No Style sbutton. If you don't see a No Styles button, you've loaded a style library that doesn't include it; choose the Reset Styles option from the circled arrow drop-down to return to the default.

The Styles palette options let you reset, load, save, and replace styles in your palette. There are also several different choices for how style swatches are viewed: small thumbnails, large thumbnails, or a text list. The Small and Large List options have the added benefit of being able to see the names of the Style swatches at all times. Otherwise, to see the names of the swatches in thumbnail mode, hover the mouse over the swatch and the name will pop up, just like every other aspect of the Photoshop interface.

*Darkcity before Adjustment Layers were added,
original version*

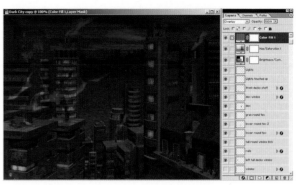

*Darkcity before Adjustment Layers were added, solid
version*

The adjusted Darkcity with a grid Pattern layer

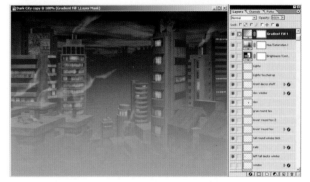

*The adjusted Darkcity with a gray to transparent
Gradient*

*Darkcity with a second Adjustment Layer –
Hue/Saturation*

*Darkcity with the first Adjustment Layer –
Brightness/Contrast*

The adjusted Darkcity with a Levels Layer

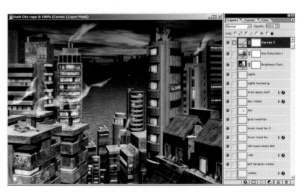

The adjusted Darkcity with a Curves Layer

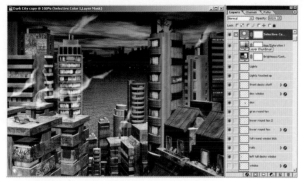

The adjusted Darkcity with a Selective Color Layer

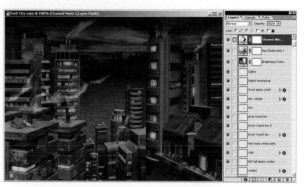

The adjusted Darkcity with a Channel Mixer Layer

The adjusted Darkcity with a Gradient Map Layer

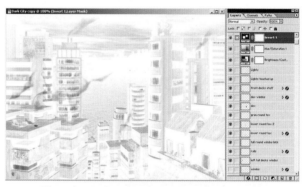

The adjusted Darkcity with an Invert Layer

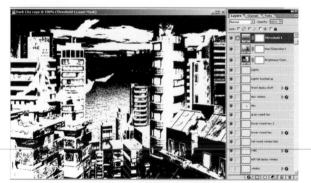

The adjusted Darkcity with a Threshold Layer

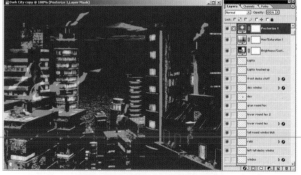

The adjusted Darkcity with a Posterize Layer

CREATING TEXT EFFECTS

Layers Styles are often applied to Photoshop text layers, as well as paint layers. When you select the tool for creating text from the tool bar and click in the image, Photoshop automatically generates a new layer in the Layers palette that stores what you type in. You can tell which layers are text layers because a letter "T" appears in the place where the thumbnail would normally be.

I use the Text(T) tool in conjunction with the Character and Paragraph palettes to create decals for vehicles, signs of all shapes and sizes for roads and buildings, and to create HUD elements and menu screens. I can align my text, warp it, apply styles to it, transform the text, and kern it, all of which are supported by the text-oriented floating palettes.

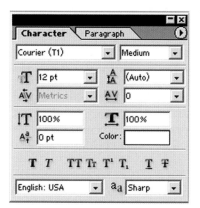

The Character palette

The Character Palette Options

CHARACTER PALETTE

To find the Character palette, hit T on the keyboard for the Text(T) tool and look up to the right of the options bar. You will see a button that looks like a square paper with bullets on it. This is the button to click for access to the Characters palette.

The Character palette is there to be used in conjunction with the Text(T) tool . Here you can specify the font, font style, color, kerning, leading, and size of the type you work with. It's also possible to choose a different language or punctuation system to type with, and the anti-aliasing options can be found in the bottom-right corner. Anti-aliasing options are good to know because they determine how the edges of your text will look on screen. Some text colors don't anti-alias well by default, so it's often necessary to choose a different anti-aliasing mode for them. An example of frequently rough-edged color would be chartreuse or bright yellow. Use a crisp or a smooth anti-aliasing style for these.

The options of the Character palette add even more depth to creating text. Click on the palette options arrow in order to get to some more goodies for the Character palette and Text(T) tool. You can set text to bold, italic, underline, and strikethrough. My favorite options are those that let me change the text to all caps or small caps.

As always, play and experiment with the options and features of the Characters palette. Remember to never let the official definition of any tool dictate what you do with it.

PARAGRAPH PALETTE

The Paragraph palette can be reached by clicking on the same button of the text options bar as for the Character palette. This palette lives underneath the Character palette by default. You can use the Paragraph palette to set formatting options for a single paragraph, multiple paragraphs, or all paragraphs in a type layer. I have used it to create documents used as props or background assets on several occasions. My favorite use was to align the text paragraphs on a series of "Wanted" posters I did for a recent project. I've also used the features of the Paragraph palette to create menu screen text for 3D games. It is a very handy tool, and a real pain not to have. Fortunately, you no longer have to endlessly nudge text paragraphs with the Move(V) tool.

As with the rest of the palettes, the Paragraph palette has its own set of options commands. Here you will find the commands that will assist the layout of your text. You can specify leading, hyphenation, and justification. If things go wrong, click the last command, Reset Paragraph, to start over.

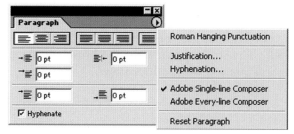

The Paragraph palette

CUSTOMIZING BRUSHES, COLORS, AND COLOR PALETTES

The second most important thing to know about how to use Photoshop, after the concept of layers, is how to use brushes with the new Brushes palette.

In my mind the most exciting thing about this new extension of the painting engine of Photoshop is the ability to paint with preset textures and your own textures. However, there are tons of other new settings you can choose and configure; there really isn't a limit on the shape of a brush tip, or the way it applies paint to a digital canvas.

Of course, the brushes wouldn't be nearly as effective if the colors you paint with weren't fully customizable, too. Though no new major developments have occurred in how colors are mixed and saved into palettes, the whole process of preparing to paint has been made much easier all around.

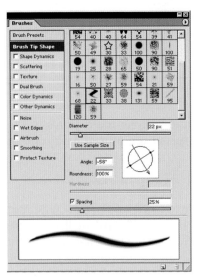

The Brushes palette

BRUSHES PALETTE

Look to the top-right of the interface and you will see two tabs, one of which is labeled Brushes. Click on this tab and the palette will drop down.

Virtually any sort of brush stroke can be reproduced: there are calligraphic brushes, dry media brushes, natural brushes, special effects brushes, thick heavy brushes, and wet media brushes. Augmenting the selection of brushes are the Brush presets, a list of specialized settings that give fine control over the properties of a brush, such as tip size and shape, how it interacts with the canvas, whether or not it scatters paint, paints with a texture, and more. Click on the names of the categories below to access their options.

BRUSH PRESETS

Brush presets list all of the brushes currently loaded into the palette with a brush tip preview, a stroke preview, and the default Master Diameter of the brush. Manipulate the Master Diameter beneath the preview list and watch the brush stroke change.

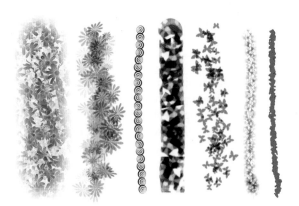

Examples of Photoshop brushes

BRUSH TIP SHAPE

Previously, the option to change the diameter and the shape of the brush tip were located in the options bar. Now they are included in the Brushes palette, and even more refined. Manipulate the Diameter slider to increase or decrease brush size, click and drag to alter the angle and rotation of the brush, and experiment with the hardness/softness and spacing of a chosen brush. Spacing controls the amount of space between each dab of paint as you draw; for instance, you could make a dotted line with one stroke by increasing the spacing. The stroke preview for the brush tip shape changes as you edit the brush's settings.

SHAPE DYNAMICS

The options for Shape Dynamics are all about randomizing the look of the brush stroke. Size Jitter randomizes the size of the brush tip as you paint, between its Master Diameter and the Minimum Diameter option below Size Jitter. Tilt Scale controls the scale of the stroke when your pen tip is angled, configurable with a graphics tablet. Angle Jitter and Control randomizes the angle of a non-round brush. Roundness Jitter varies how round the brush tip is, between a maximum of the Roundness set in the Brush Tip Shape tab and the Minimum Roundness below Roundness Jitter.

SCATTERING

Scatter causes the brush tip to be dispersed randomly along the stroke. So, a soft round brush, when scattered, will result in a stroke comprised of lots of little, soft round dots. The higher the Scatter, the further apart these dots will move. Check Both Axes to scatter the stroke in all directions. Some uses for this feature might be adding dirt to something, creating a pattern, or adding freckles to the nose of a character. I also use it to create painted color variations on terrain tiles because I can cover a lot more ground with one scattered stroke than I could with just one standard stroke.

TEXTURE

The ability to paint with a texture is an awesome option for your brushes! Take those pattern presets and apply them to your painted work. Simply click on the texture swatch at the top of the palette to reset, load, save, or replace the texture you need, then manipulate the sliders to get the stroke you want. Scale will determine the size of the texture within the stroke. Then choose a Mode that will determine how the paint color of the brush interacts with the texture. The Depth slider specifies how dimensional the stroke is meant to be, by changing the amount of blending of the texture in the paint stroke. Depth Jitter randomizes that blending between Depth and Minimum Depth. The Texture option can be a fast and easy way to add pattern, depth, and dimension to your painted surfaces. I use it to paint ground surfaces quite often, such as setting a grass texture to a brush, or painting with a noise texture to simulate sand. I also love it for adding abstract detail for surfaces such as concrete walls or asphalt.

DUAL BRUSH

Dual Brush lets you use a brush within a brush. That is, the regular Brush settings set the shape of the outer edge of the stroke, and the Brush settings in the Dual Brush tab affect the pattern within the stroke. (The results are most visible when using one of the "special effect" brush shapes, like the stars or leaves, for the second Dual Brush tip.) Set the parameters for the first brush tip in the Brush Tip Shape section of the palette, then place a checkmark in the Dual Brush box to activate, choose, and configure the second tip with which to paint. Adjust the diameter, spacing, and scatter of the inner stroke with the sliders below. The last slider, Count, specifies how many inner brush strokes are included within each larger stroke.

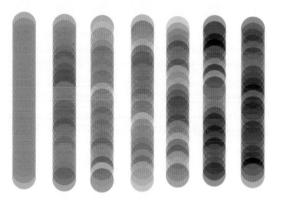

The Color Dynamics of the Brushes palette

COLOR DYNAMICS

Color Dynamics vary the color of a stroke. Foreground/Background Jitter randomly shifts the hue of the stroke toward the Background swatch from the Foreground swatch, with the Percentage slider controlling how far the hue shifts. Hue Jitter is like Foreground/Background Jitter except the hue is varied randomly instead of toward the Background swatch. A higher value opens a wider range of possible hues. Saturation Jitter and Brightness Jitter randomize the Saturation and Brightness of the color being painted. Purity controls how much the various colors that get used in a stroke blend together (maximum Purity results in the colors being very vibrant but separate, while a lower Purity blends the colors more but is desaturated).

OTHER PAINT DYNAMICS

Opacity Jitter varies the transparency of the paint over the course of each stroke. Flow Jitter varies the flow of paint in the stroke, up to the Flow set in the options bar for the tool you're using.

NOISE

Unlike the options above, the next set of options in the Brushes palette don't have any additional controls: they're either on (checked) or off. Noise adds a pattern of pixellation to a brush stroke, and can be a quick and easy way to add grit to parts of a texture without resorting to selection masks and the Noise filter. I love this option because it is so much easier to make the details of a gritty image work together and seem like they belong to the same world. It's a simple brush effect, but it works.

WET EDGES

Wet Edges simulates a brush being used with a wet medium: watercolor, gouache, acrylics, sumi ink, etc. When checked, a border along the edges of your strokes will appear to be less faded and more saturated than the pigment in the center of the brush. This effect yields an extra bit of realism for scenes and surfaces that require a wet look. I rely on this tool for adding water damage to my environments.

AIRBRUSH

The Airbrush feature adds the sensibilities of an airbrush to the brush, letting you build up paint with successive strokes. An airbrush works like a miniature garden sprinkler, spraying consistent and even amounts of pigment onto a surface with varying amounts of pressure and radius.

SMOOTHING

The Brushes palette Smoothing option smoothes the curve of your brush strokes, which can be jittery even when you draw with a stylus, let alone a mouse. Smoothing has obvious advantages, but the disadvantage of your brush strokes not being in the precise shape you drew them, which is sometimes necessary.

PROTECT TEXTURE

With Protect Texture checked, every brush that has a texture will use the same pattern and scale, which is useful if you want to paint the same texture with brushes of different sizes and shapes.

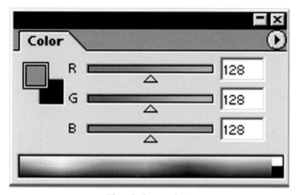

The Color palette

COLORS PALETTE

By default, the Colors palette can be found to the right of the Photoshop interface. It is the topmost of the Colors, Swatches, Styles palettes, positioned right above the History/Actions/Tool Presets palettes.

The Color palette is handy for quickly choosing foreground and background colors with just a click of the mouse. First select either the foreground or background swatch on the palette, by clicking. These two swatches are represented by icons that look exactly like the foreground/background swatches on the tool bar. Once a swatch is selected, click on the multicolored spectrum bar running along the bottom of the palette and the selected hue will replace the selected swatch. This palette is also used for mixing colors to add as new swatches to the Swatches palette. You can use the color bar slider to select your color, or you can enter values directly into the available fields. If you need to use a color mode other than RGB, you can select color sliders for all the most-used color modes.

Click on the options arrow for the Color palette to access a number of options based on color profiles for print and the web. The sliders are RGB (Red/Green/Blue; useful for computers) by default, but can be changed to HSB (Hue/Saturation/Brightness; useful for humans), CMYK (Cyan/Magenta/Yellow/blacK; useful for print), Grayscale, and more.

SWATCHES PALETTE

The Swatches palette can be thought of as your paint box. You can add your mixed colors from the Color palette as new swatches, creating your own palette of colors for your project. There are shortcut buttons at the bottom of the Swatches palette to Create New Swatch of Foreground Color, and to Delete a swatch.

You can choose a foreground or background color from the Swatches palette, or you can add or delete colors to create a custom swatch library. You can also save a library of swatches and reload them for use in another image. Although you can add many colors to the Swatches palette, you should manage its size and organization. You can load, save, and manage libraries of swatches using the Preset Manager. Right-click on swatches to create new, rename, or delete swatches.

New Swatch...

Reset Swatches...
Load Swatches...
Save Swatches...
Replace Swatches...

✓ Small Thumbnail
Small List

ANPA Colors.aco
DIC Colors.aco
FOCOLTONE Colors.aco
Pantone Colors (Coated).aco
Pantone Colors (Process).aco
Pantone Colors (ProSim).aco
Pantone Colors (Uncoated).aco
TOYO Colors.aco
TRUMATCH Colors.aco
Hair.aco
Illustrations.aco
Lizard Orc.aco
Mac OS.aco
Skins.aco
VisiBone.aco
VisiBone2.aco
Web Hues.aco
Web Safe Colors.aco
Web Spectrum.aco
Windows.aco

The Color Palette Options Menu

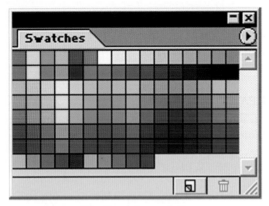

The Swatches palette

I make sure to always customize and save the palettes I use via the Preset Manager option. Each project I do has its own collection of colors and I use the Preset Manager to keep the swatches organized in order of their hue. I also make sure each has a title assigned to it so that when I'm looking at a list of 50 swatches, I can quickly find what I'm looking for. Keeping separate palettes for each project, instead of a huge hodge-podge of randomly chosen swatches, is also a great way to keep track of what decisions you've made as you paint, and makes reusing successful palettes a piece of cake.

AUTOMATING TASKS

The next order of important business when negotiating Photoshop is how to work faster and more efficiently. Actions are the solution to the problem of having to do the same set of steps over and over again. Tasks like adding the same layer style, creating a certain size document, cropping several images to the same size, converting them all to another file type, or creating a complex selection are examples of things it's a pain in the rear to keep redoing. All of these and more can be automated by using the Actions palette.

ACTIONS OVERVIEW

An "Action" in Photoshop is a saved sequence of steps that you make as you work. For example, you may make five brush strokes, switch to the fill tool, then back to the brush, and so on. Each application of paint you make to the image is a step listed in the Actions palette. To save this list and make it reusable, create a new Action with the button on the botton of the Actions palette, then simply press the Record button, perform all the steps you need to, then hit Stop. Photoshop has just recorded all of the steps and it's now possible for you to apply those steps to something else in your work with just one click of the Play button.

Use the Actions palette for programming Photoshop to do what you want quickly and efficiently. Don't torture yourself trying to memorize how you arrived at a certain result and then re-apply those steps over and over again manually: save them as a new Actions Set! Save that flame effect you love so much as an action and use it over and over again until all your work is on fire!

RECORDING AND USING ACTIONS

The Actions palette and all its handy features are located to the right of the screen, beneath the History palette. Click the Actions tab to bring the palette to the top of the stack.

The Actions palette

New Action...
New Set...
Duplicate
Delete
Play

Start Recording
Record Again...
Insert Menu Item...
Insert Stop...
Insert Path

Action Options...
Playback Options...

Clear All Actions
Reset Actions
Load Actions...
Replace Actions...
Save Actions...

Button Mode

Commands.atn
Frames.atn
Image Effects.atn
Production.atn
Text Effects.atn
Textures.atn

The Actions Palette Options Menu

The History palette

To create your own Action, click the New Action button at the bottom of the palette. When the dialog comes up for new Actions, type in a title and click Record or hit Enter. Once the Record button is activated (it depresses and turns red), begin executing the steps you want to record. After you have completed the final command of the sequence, click the square Stop button to complete the new Action. The last step is to test out what you have just recorded. Select the first step of the new Action and click the Play icon button at the bottom of the palette. If you did it correctly, the action will play and Photoshop will perform the operations you recorded.

The Actions palette records, plays, edits, and deletes individual actions. This palette also lets you save and load action files.

In Photoshop, Actions are grouped into sets, and you can create new sets to better organize your Actions. By default, the Actions palette displays Actions in list mode, in which you can expand and collapse sets, Actions, and commands. However, you can also choose to display Actions as buttons in the Actions palette that play an Action with a single mouse click. Photoshop also has a small stash of preset texture Actions you can use or experiment with. Create a new document and apply some of them to see what they do. (Since you can see what steps the Actions are composed of within the History palette, Actions are an excellent resource: you can learn a great deal from simply studying them.) There are things like parchment, bricks, and different types of wood. As you work through them, sometimes you will be prompted to go find the Photoshop 7.0 Texturizer folder and load a file from there. Don't forget this: it's another good place for some bumpy kinds of stuff and you will learn more about it soon.

BACKTRACKING WITH THE HISTORY PALETTE

The History palette is located at the top of the History/Actions/Tool Presets palette trio. As usual, you can tell it's the right palette because it says so at the top. Click on the History tab to activate the floating palette. You will see a list of whatever you've done with your work beneath the image thumbnail at the top.

The History palette is indispensable for fixing mistakes. This is the palette that lists all of the steps that have been performed on the image file in chronological order: Brush, Brush, Brush, Pencil, Pencil, New Anchor Point, New Anchor Point, New Anchor Point, Brush, Pencil, Fill. Get the picture? If not, check out what happens to the stack in the History palette as you use the tools. This palette is very useful for undoing mistakes you made several steps in the past. You can even set how many steps back the palette will go to delete steps, or "states". This palette is also handy for creating workable duplicates of the same document and allows you to store alternate versions of the piece within the original PSD file.

HOW THE HISTORY PALETTE CAN SAVE YOUR BACON

Have you overworked your image? Are you completely dissatisfied with a direction the work is taking? Do you want to revert to the image as it was a half-hour previously? Then look to the History palette. The History palette lets you erase an unlimited number of steps. By default, the number of steps Photoshop will save is 20. However, you can reset this number by doing a Ctrl + K to bring up the Preferences dialog and typing in a new number in the History States box. Keep in mind, though, that the higher the number, the clunkier Photoshop will be as its memory is sapped by all those stored history states.

Click on the Create New Document from Current State button, and note that the title of the new document is actually the current action that was selected in the History layer stack. You now have a separate document that has preserved the step highlighted in the History palette when you created a new document from its current state.

The Create New Snapshot button saves the current state of the image, and its history, as a "snapshot" within the original image. You can work with as many snapshots as you want, all with different histories. You can save a snapshot before a major set of changes in case you'd like to back up to it, branch off and make multiple versions of the same image from a particular point in your process, and even paint parts of an earlier stage of an image you took a snapshot of onto a later stage of the image.

The Delete Current State button deletes snapshots and stages of the History stack. If you select a step in the History stack and click the Delete Current State button, that step and all the steps that followed it will be deleted from the stack unless you have Allow Non-Linear History checked in the History palette options, described below.

As usual, the options for the History palette drop down from the circled arrow in the upper-right of the palette. You can specify the maximum number of commands to include in the History palette and set other options that customize the way you work with the palette. Use Automatically Create First Snapshot to create a snapshot of the initial state of the image when you open up the document. Select Automatically Create New Snapshot When Saving to generate a snapshot every time you save.

Check Allow Non-Linear History to make changes to a selected state layer in the History palette without deleting the steps that come after. By default, if you select a history state more than one step back and then make a change, all the steps that were after the step you jumped back to get hosed.

Put a check in the box for Show New Snapshot Dialog by Default to force Photoshop to prompt you for snapshot names even when using the buttons on the palette.

I use the History palette every day to backtrack when I'm not satisfied with my choices. The ability to change your mind is an awesome freedom because it lets you experiment and take risks as much as you want. Eventually, as you get to know Photoshop better and your skills increase, you will use this palette less and less.

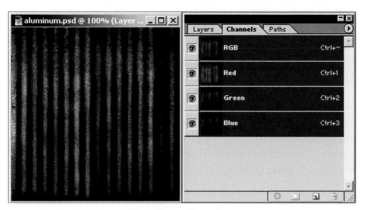

The Channels palette

CHANNELS

I use the Channels palette most often for creating Alpha channels, which are the transparent parts of an image They are often used to make sprites, which is a texture applied to a flat plane. An example of a sprite would be a clump of tall flowers. The Alpha channel embedded in the flower texture makes the plane the flower texture is applied to disappear, but leaves the flowers, creating the illusion of a flower patch growing out of the ground all by itself. Sprites like this are also used for particle effects.

A channel is a grayscale image that stores different types of information. Channels store color information, transparency information, and spot color information for printing. The Channels palette contains the color channels that comprise an image. Usually, if the image is RGB color, there is a channel for red, blue, green, and also an RGB pseudo-channel that is a combination of the three. If the image is grayscale, only one channel will be displayed in the Channels stack.

ALPHA CHANNELS

Many RGB image types can also have a fourth channel, or Alpha channel. Instead of representing color, the grayscale values in an Alpha channel represent transparency: black is transparent, white is opaque, and gray is semi-transparent (more or less transparent depending on how dark or light the gray is).

An Alpha channel is created by drawing a selection around something and then saving that selection using the Save Selection command located at the bottom of the Layer drop-down menu.

Look in the Channels palette if you think you have created an Alpha channel but can't tell. If you did create one, it will be included in the layer stack of the Channels palette. Turn the eyeballs on and off (click to toggle) to either see or not see the channels in your image, just as in the Layers palette. Right-click on the channels to duplicate or delete them.

To load a channel as a selection, select a channel in the Channel palette, click on the Load Channel as a Selection button, and the image in that channel will be selected with a flashing marquee. Now all of the options available for selection marquees can be applied to this selected channel. Since the selection will remain active if you switch to a layer, you can also use additional channels to store complex selections for repeated use.

When you click the Save Selection as Channel button, a new channel will be created with white information in the shape of whatever is currently selected. This is a fast way to create Alpha channels.

The Add a New Channel button adds a new channel to the stack. The channel that is created will be black (empty). Use the Photoshop tools to add information to new channels.

The Delete Channel button erases channels. You can either highlight a channel and press the Delete Channel button, or drag a channel down to it like a trash can.

The Channels palette options can be located by clicking on the round arrow icon at the top-right of the palette. Check it out and do a little experimenting. You can dock this palette to the palette well, add and delete new channels, and configure the palette thumbnail sizes.

Use this palette to keeps tabs on your color mode, preview hues, create and preview Alpha channels, and add bump maps with the Lighting Effects filter. This palette is important for creating bump maps for textures that need three-dimensional, highly tactile surfaces, as well as stand-alone components separated from the background.

The Paths palette

PATHS PALETTE

Being able to make complex selections as you work is very important. So important, in fact, that Photoshop has an entire palette devoted to the management and manipulation of paths. The reason for this is that complex selections need a place to be stored and referred to fast. If the paths drawn were always present in the image, they would be in the way.

The Paths palette is located in the bottom-right of the Photoshop interface under the Layers and the Channels palettes. To access the Paths palette, click the Paths tab. Notice that the Paths palette is empty. This is because no path has been drawn. Once you select and begin to draw with a pen, a new layer will be generated that contains the work path. As is the case with all layer-based palettes, you can click on each path layer listed in the stack to activate it.

WHY PATHS ARE IMPORTANT

Paths are needed because they provide the best way to draw non-straight lines, create complex shapes and selections, and make curves. Take the time to practice and experiment with these tools so that you can understand how they work and integrate their functions into your projects.

USING THE PATHS PALETTE

If you have not created and saved any paths (most likely with the Pen(P) tool), then you will see no layers listed in the stack. You must create a new path to see one here. The Paths palette lists the name and a thumbnail image of each saved path, the current work path, and the current layer clipping path. Decreasing the size of thumbnails or turning them off lets you list more paths in the palette, and turning thumbnails off can improve performance. To view a path, you must first select it in the Paths palette.

Create a path with the Pen(P) tool, highlight it in the Paths palette, and click on the Fill Path with Foreground Color button located on the bottom-left of the palette to fill the inside of the path with the color currently selected in the foreground color swatch.

Paths palette button shortcuts

When you have a path selected and click the Stroke Path with Foreground Color button, an outline is drawn in the shape of the path and the color selected in the Foreground color swatch. The width of the stroke along the path is determined by the brush size you have selected for the Brush(B) or Pencil(B) tools.

Select a path in the Paths palette and then click on the Load Path as Selection button to turn that path into a selection marquee. Once the path is converted to a selection, you can save that selection and then fill, pattern, clone, or paint; whatever you had had in mind.

The Make Work Path from Selection button is the opposite of the Load Path as Selection button. First, create a new selection with any of the selection tools: Marquee(M), Lasso(L), and Wand(W). Then click on the Make Work Path from Selection button and the selection marquee becomes a workable path. This means you can now save the path, add and delete anchor points to the path, convert those points, and create pretty much any kind of shape you can come up with.

The Create New Path button adds an empty layer to the paths layer stack that's all nice and ready for a new path.

Click on the Delete Current Path button and the selected path will be on its way to the garbage can. Either select the path layer and click the button, or click and drag the layer onto the trashcan icon.

GETTING DETAILS WITH THE INFO PALETTE

You will often need to know certain things about the images you are working with. You will need to know the dimensions of the image, the dimensions of a selection or crop, or the color profile of the image. The Info palette provides all of this with just a glance.

I also use it for reading color hex values in case I need them to give to someone else so we are all painting with the same hue. The best part about the Info palette is that it's a fast and readily available reference.

The Info palette gives you feedback on tools you use and changes you make. Depending on the tool, there will be different types of information displayed, such as the X- and Y-coordinates of the cursor, the width and height of a shape you draw, the color you're about to sample, and more.

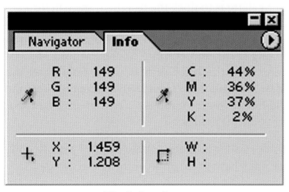

The Info palette

Use the Info palette for keeping tabs on your image information: RGB values, opacity, and the image size (do a quick Select All with Ctrl/⌘ + A to get the image dimensions in the Info palette). It is much faster to check out the dimensions of an image with the Info palette than it is to access Image Size in the top drop-down menu, or to right-click on the top bar of the image dialog. You will need to know your image's size when it comes time to offset tileable textures and when you need to resize images so that they work with the texture editor of your 3D program.

Changing the palette options is different for the Info palette. Access the Palette options command through the circled arrow, and a dialog box will come up that provides three drop-down menus that control how the information in the Info palette is displayed. There are two boxes for color feedback, so you could (for instance) have the Info palette display both RGB and CMYK values. The third drop-down sets the unit of measurement. Pixels are the most relevant for 3D artists; the others are more useful for print.

MANAGING FILES AND TOOLS

For artists on the career fastrack, knowing how to manage your array of tools is crucial to successfully negotiating a complex project. Working with other artists, I have to take into consideration how well my organizational skills work. Do I name files, tools, and presets in ways everyone can understand? Do I organize my files in such a way that others can find them without having to ask me? Do I store my palettes and custom brushes where everyone can get them on the shared server? For me, the answer is yes and this is because Photoshop makes it easy to do.

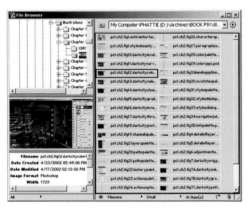

The File Browser palette

FILE BROWSER

The File Browser palette is a cool new feature, located at the top-right of the interface in the palette well, by default. Click on the File Browser tab to preview image files directly from a directory tree displayed on the left of the palette. You can click and drag the listed files into the interface to open them, select a file to view a larger thumbnail, and read the details of each file. At the bottom of the palette, there are icons for configuring the palette, choose from sorting options within the palette, options for preview size, a rotation key for rotating thumbnails, and the trusty trashcan for fast deletes. If your system is fast enough to make use of this tool, then it's a great option. If not, it may take you longer to wait for the thumbnail preview to show up than it would to just open the file the old-fashioned way.

The options for the File Browser palette can be accessed by clicking on the black arrow to the left of File Browser. Click on the tab to see the options arrow indicator, or, if the File Browser is not docked, click on the round arrow button at the top-left corner of the box.

The first option for the File Browser palette is to dock the palette in the palette well, or to show the palette in a separate window. The purpose of these commands is to make customization of the interface easy. You can use the File Browser for common operations like opening files, renaming them, and creating folders, as well as more complicated operations like renaming an entire batch of files. You can also set the size of the thumbnail previews, and even rotate them (which won't actually affect the image until the file is opened). The File Browser's options make it an excellent tool for quickly and efficiently accessing your image files.

I use the File Browser every day to open files fast, check on what I've already done and still need to do, and whether or not I have saved a file in the correct folder.

TOOL PRESETS PALETTE

The Tool Presets palette is located under the History and Actions Palette, right below the Styles palette. Click on the tab that says Tool Presets to activate this palette.

Note that if you have not saved any customized combinations of options for the currently selected tool, and the tool does not have any default presets, nothing will show in the palette stack.

There are all sorts of amazing brush effects, marquee shapes, and more that you can come up with, set up, use, and then promptly forget to save. Result: lost tool. But no longer! You can save those wild concoctions with the Tool Preset palette. Click on the Create a New Preset icon at the bottom of the Tool Presets palette and type in a name, and an icon for the currently selected tool, plus its configuration, will conveniently appear at the top of the list.

Tool Presets also stores all of the tool settings that come with the shipped program. For example, the Brush(B) tool comes with a long list of preset options you can select from the list in the Tool Presets palette as you work. What's especially cool is that you can tweak the options of the presets, too, giving you yet another level of customization.

Click on the round icon at the top-right of the Tool Presets palette to access the options for the palette. The options for this palette are similar to the other palettes: create new, reset, load, save, and replace presets.

CONCLUSION

Palettes are a step above the basics, enabling you to do more complex work. In addition to understanding key concepts such as layers, blending modes, the painting engine, how to automate tasks, and how to manage your files and tools well, knowing the options of each palette is an enormous help for saving everything you invent as you work.

QUIZ

1) A BLENDING MODE IS:

    a) An option accessible via the Styles palette

    b) A method of blending a layer with those beneath it

    c) An effect you can use to create a Bevel & Emboss

2) THE FAST WAY TO POSITION A DROP SHADOW LAYER EFFECT IS TO:

    a) Click on the Angle dial located on the Layer Style dialog box

    b) Click and drag on the image while in Layer Style dialog box mode

    c) Use the arrow keys to nudge the Drop Shadow into place

3) AN ADJUSTMENT LAYER FOR BRIGHTNESS/CONTRAST IS BEST USED WHEN:

    a) You wish to protect and retain the original brightness and contrast of the image

    b) The background layer is invisible

    c) The red parts of an image needs to be changed to green

4) BLENDING OPTIONS ARE FOR:

    a) Blending two layers together

    b) Loading, saving, resetting, or deleting blends

    c) Adding special effects to a layer

5) WHERE ARE THE COLORS TO BE USED IN AN IMAGE KEPT, LIKE A PAINTER'S PALETTE?

    a) The Swatches palette

    b) The Color palette

    c) The Info palette

6) THE PATHS PALETTE IS USED IN CONJUNCTION WITH WHICH TOOLS?

    a) The Brush(B) tools

    b) The Vector Shapes(U) tools

    c) The Pen(P) tools

7) THE LAYER STYLES DIALOG BOX CAN BE ACCESSED BY:

    a) The effects button on the Layers Palette

    b) Double-clicking on an effects icon already present on a layer

    c) Both A and B

8) WHAT IS THE FASTEST SOLUTION FOR ACCOMPLISHING REPETITIVE TASKS?

    a) Record an Action

    b) Manually, baby! I'm a purist

    c) Get someone else to do it

9) WHICH PALETTE CAN SAVE MULTIPLE VERSIONS OF ONE DOCUMENT WITHIN THE SAME FILE?

    a) The Actions palette

    b) The History palette

    c) The Layers palette

10) THE THUMBNAIL PREVIEWS CAN BE CHANGED ON EACH PALETTE BY:

    a) Editing the general preferences

    b) Right-clicking on them

    c) Accessing the palette options via the round black arrow button

IN THIS CHAPTER YOU WILL LEARN ABOUT:

- Using the File menu to open, save, and print documents
- Using the Edit menu to move and transform elements
- Making color and lighting changes to your files
- Manipulating layers with the Layer menu
- Tailoring perfect selections
- Applying special effects with the Filters menu
- Using Zoom and Guides with the View menu
- Arranging the interface using the Window menu

INTRODUCTION

The drop-down menus serve a lot of purposes and cover a wide scope of functions you can apply to your work. The File menu, located in the top-left corner of the Photoshop interface, deals with the practical commands needed to create new files, open files, save files for a variety of purposes, and printing them.

The Edit menu is next on the list and is home to commands like unlimited Undo, the Spell Checker, copying and pasting commands, and is where to find Transform mode. The purpose of these commands is to let you move around and manipulate the bits and pieces of your work that need rearranging. As with the File menu, many of the commands housed in the Edit menu can be quickly executed by a shortcut command. My advice is to memorize these shortcuts and begin using them right away.

Some of the most important decisions you make as you work will have to do with the Image menu. Similar to the Edit menu, the Image menu is where to find the commands that have to do with moving around the hues, saturation levels, and lighting levels of your texture work. Between the Edit and Image menus, just about any sort of positioning and colorization idea can be realized.

Another key concept is how to manipulate layers, taken to a higher level with the Layer drop-down menu. This menu has the commands that create new layers, background layers, and layer sets. It has the sub-menu for the Layer styles, the easily accessible Type and Rasterize sub-menus, and the set of commands that let you merge and flatten layers when needed. Flatten Layers is especially important because you will use it to help tile seamless textures.

Selections play a major role in maneuvering work into a place that fits your designs. The Select menu contains the commands needed to get the selection you draw to perfectly match what you are working to isolate. Here, it's possible to expand and decrease a marquee, as well as create special selections such as feathers and borders. The most important command of this menu is the Save Selection command which is what you will use to add and save Alpha channels into your textures. You will use the Select menu commands again and again as you work.

Special effects are the most fun feature of Photoshop and retain a major role in creating texture art. Everyone has different tastes where the famous Filters of Photoshop are concerned, but I use them often (albeit subtly) to achieve a variety of effects. The filters listed in this chapter are examples of some of those I use a lot. With filters, you can simulate painterly effects, create patterns, blur, sharpen, and distort, plus create cool surfaces. Here too lives the Offset filter, critical to removing seams in textures meant to be tiled.

The View and Window drop-down menus have the commands that determine how you will look at your documents. View is where to find the zooming features, rulers, and Guides. Window is where to choose how to display your open files, and how to save a workspace or arranged palettes. Window is also the place to go if you want to show or hide the floating palettes, a great option for streamlining your work area.

Visit the Help menu to find out more about the program and its features. Though not highly detailed, the online Photoshop menu provides users with a decent reference for how to operate the tools. I often use the Help manual to refresh my memory on the function of a tool or option.

Not every single command is listed below. The purposes of some of them are obvious and several others are simply not that relevant. These are the ones I find most useful.

OPENING, SAVING, AND PRINTING DOCUMENTS

Since it's pretty tough to work with Photoshop without an open document, getting one on the screen is the first order of business. There are several ways to open image files. You can drag and drop a file onto the Photoshop program icon, you can drag and drop a file from a directory, and you can drag and drop from the File Browser. Once you have something to work with, you'll want to save it. Not only can you do a straight save, but you can save the file you have open into a variety of file formats.

GETTING AN IMAGE TO WORK WITH

The New command is the first on the list in the File menu, and creates a brand new document. When the New dialog comes up, you can to specify a title, set dimensions, and choose a document resolution. The image mode can also be set, as well as the preferred background of the new document. To Create a new document really fast, and avoid the drop-down menu, do a Ctrl/⌘ + N to take you right to the New dialog box.

The Open command, located right underneath New, loads an existing document. This command opens file types that are compatible with Photoshop, and are saved in an accessible location. Usually, to open a file in Photoshop, I do a Ctrl/⌘ + O, the fastest way to open a file.

The Browse command opens up the File Browser palette that is located at the top-right of the interface in the palette docking well, by default. Browse will show the File Browser if the palette is hidden, and will also open it up from the docking well. I often open files from the File Browser because it provides me with a visual reference in the form of a large thumbnail, so I can see exactly what I'm getting.

Open Recent is a very handy command for opening files you've been working on. I use this option more than any other opening method because it means I don't have to do any directory digging. The coolest thing about this option is that if you visit the Edit➔Preferences➔File Handling dialog, you can set how many files you want Photoshop to remember. This is an extremely efficient preference to set, but keep in mind that the more remembered files there are, the more memory the program uses, and the slower the performance will be.

File➔Import brings in images from other sources, such as a scanner or digital camera. Use Import to access the software for your peripheral device.

Use the File➔Close command to deactivate and shut any files that are open. The Close command comes in most handy when only one or two files need be closed at a time.

The File➔Exit command (Quit on a Mac) closes Photoshop. First, however, the program makes sure that all documents have been saved. If not, a prompt will appear asking whether or not any unsaved open documents need be saved.

SAVING YOUR WORK

As you work, it's a good idea to be able to keep your stuff, right? Right. The following commands are the various ways Photoshop accommodates the need to save files quickly and in several different formats.

Use the Save command to record image files permanently on your hard disk, in the location you specify. This command saves the document as the same type of document it currently is; for example, if you open and work on a PSD file, the Save command will save over the original, and the file will still be a PSD. To save quickly, it's always best to do a Ctrl/⌘ + S. This shortcut cancels out the need to travel to the drop-down menu and scroll down to find Save.

You will use the Save As command all the time. You'll need to save Targa files from Photoshop documents (or whatever file format your shop uses with its 3D application). You'll also need to save JPEGs and others for smaller menu screen and HUD files. The shortcut to this command is Ctrl/⌘ + Shift + S. If you don't memorize any other shortcut, memorize this one. It will save you a good fifteen minutes a day.

Save for Web sounds like it might not be helpful to a 3D person, but it is. This command launches a special dialog box and lets you save an image file into a compressed file format. This means you can take large Photoshop files and save them as JPEGs or GIFs: much smaller files. The level of control of this tool is the best part, and it's possible to get a file downsized to the byte. Now your file sizes can stay in budget. This is of great help to artists compiling online portfolios. I use it for this purpose all the time, and I also use it to compress files destined for contests and online galleries that specify strict size limits. The Shortcut combo for this command is Alt + Ctrl/⌘ + Shift + S.

The Revert command can bail you out of big trouble. Executing Revert takes you back to the last version of the document that was saved, basically Undoing everything you've done since you last saved the file.

PRINTING A HARD COPY

Most of the work I do is done on computers, never making it to hard copy. Even files that go to producers or clients usually travel digitally. Sometimes, however, it helps to have a hard copy of an image, even if it's just to use as a reference hanging on your office wall. I print files for this reason, and also to help with the research and development of a new project, and to make them portable and easy to show to my teammates without sending paths to here and there on the complicated network server.

Photoshop has a pretty good printing engine. It covers all the bases and makes it easy to get something to the printer without a lot of problems. The printing commands are located at the bottom of the File drop-down menu.

Print with Preview is where to find the options that determine what orientation your image will be printed (portrait or landscape). Here you can also specify where the image will appear on the page, how it will be scaled, and the height and width dimensions on the page. Usually, I just pick the right orientation, make sure the image fits on the paper, and hit the Print button.

Do a Ctrl/⌘ + P to print your work when you know that your file is already oriented correctly and ready to go. The print command sends your art to any printer you have hooked up to your system. Print it out and see how it looks.

THE EDIT MENU

The Edit drop-down menu houses the next set of commands you'll need when working with your files: basic editing tools. The Undo command is here, as well as the commands to cut, copy, and paste, access spell-checking, and create new tools for your work, such as new brushes, patterns, and shapes. This is also the menu where the all-important Transformation tools are located: the commands that scale, skew, rotate, and flip the elements of your work.

UNLIMITED UNDO

Undo revokes the last command you executed. Otherwise known as Ctrl/⌘ + Z, this is the one command that everyone uses. Undo only goes back one step: if the last thing you did was Undo, the menu option changes to Redo (so does the hotkey). Redo goes forward one step, changing back to Undo, and at this point you may as well think of it as toggling the last step on and off.

I use this command all the time, via the shortcut for it. The same thing can be accomplished by going to the History palette and clicking back in the stack, but using the shortcut is much faster. The need for speed never ends.

Step Backward is basically unlimited Undo. At least, it is as unlimited as your Preferences are set to. (See the Edit→Preferences→History States field to set the allowable number of Undo steps.) Memorize this shortcut, it'll serve you well: Ctrl/⌘ + Alt + Z.

Step Forward is basically unlimited Redo. Just remember you have to have executed a command, and subsequently undone it, to redo it.

BLENDING FILTERS

The Fade command is important because it has to do with making paint and filtered effects blend into the image. You can use Fade after every brush stroke or painterly action to alter the opacity of the strokes, or to apply a blending mode to the strokes. This is a neat feature because it allows for a level of detail and fine tuning that you just can't achieve by applying opacity and blending mode changes to entire layers.

When you paint or filter and then go to use Fade, you'll notice that the menu command changes. If you paint with a brush, Fade will say "Fade Brush Tool". If you apply a filter, the Fade command will add the name of the filter such as "Fade Reticulation".

I use this tool every once in awhile to create atmospheric effects. I've found you can layer paint with a progressively increasing opacity to get a nice atmospheric perspective effect. However, this technique takes time, and really only works on an image that is larger so that the detail shows.

COPYING AND PASTING

I copy and paste dozens of times a week as my ideas flow and I experiment with different compositional arrangements and elements. As with so many of the drop-down menu commands, the best way to copy, cut, and paste is to use the shortcuts for them.

The Cut (Ctrl/⌘ + X) command removes a selection from the composition and sends it to the clipboard. Once recorded in the clipboard, the information is ready to be relocated, or pasted, back into an image document (the same one it was cut out from, or a different one). This command can also be used to delete elements of your work.

The Copy (Ctrl/⌘ + C) command is like Cut except it doesn't delete the selection, it just adds it to the clipboard, to be pasted elsewhere in the current document or into a different document.

The Paste command takes whatever is in the clipboard and adds it into the currently active document in Photoshop. Used in conjunction with Cut and Copy, Paste makes changing elements of your work around speedy and efficient.

Clear erases the current selection, like Cut, except it doesn't go to the clipboard.

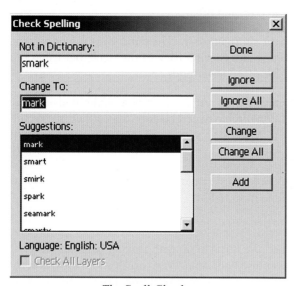

The Spell Checker

EDITING TEXT

Finally! Can't ever remember the "i before e" rule? Me niether. Now I don't need to because Check Spelling is here! Use this command to check your text work for words that are typed incorrectly or misspelled. To use this command, text or a text layer must be selected. This is no different to the spell checkers of word processing programs and is a wonderful new tool to have. I recommend getting into the habit of using spell checker for every thing you write with Photoshop. After looking at the same menu screen for hours on end, you'd be amazed at how easy it is to not notice a missing letter. It wouldn't be too funny if your load screen said "Nw Game" instead of "New Game" and no one noticed until it was too late.

Find and Replace Text finds all the instances of a string of text you specify, and replaces all those instances with something else.

ADDING AND SUBTRACTING FROM SELECTIONS

Fill is the Edit command to execute when a selection has been made within an image file and now needs a solid color or pattern applied to the entire volume of the selected area. In the Fill dialog, you can choose which color to fill with: the foreground color, background color, a pattern, a History state, or percentages of grayscale values. A blending mode and the overall opacity of the fill can be specified, as well.

Stroke is kind of like Fill, but surrounds a selection with a color border, based on the current foreground color. Click on the Foreground swatch to change hues. Type in a numeric value for the width of the line border stroke to be applied. The Stroke dialog also allows you to choose a blending option and opacity.

I use both of these commands often for covering large areas with a preset pattern, a solid color, or a pattern type. Stroke comes in handy for making lines that look evenly painted and is very helpful used in partnership with the pen. One of my favorite techniques is drawing paths and then applying a stroke to them. I can get any length or shape of line I want.

APPLYING TRANSFORMATIONS

Transform mode is important because it allows sections of your work to be interactively altered in their scale, rotation, distortion, perspective, and skew. You can enter Transform mode with a fast Ctrl/⌘ + T, and whatever is in the currently selected layer will be surrounded by a bounding box that you can manipulate. Use the Shift, Ctrl, and Alt keys to scale, rotate, distort, align to perspective, and skew. I use Transform mode a lot, to get parts of my work to fit correct perspective lines, to reduce the size of things fast, and to rotate them.

DEFINING NEW BRUSHES, PATTERNS, AND SHAPES

The Edit→Define Brush command is fun because you can use it to create new brush tip shapes of your own. Select an area with one of the selection tools and choose Edit→Define Brush from the top menu bar, and you get a dialog that gives a preview of what will become the new brush, and a place to name the new brush. If you don't have an active selection, Define Brush uses the contents of the layer that is currently selected.

Define a brush

The Define Pattern command is similar to the Define Brush command, except it turns the active selection or layer into a pattern that you can use for fills, bump maps, or lighting textures. Make your own patterns like clouds, cloth, bark, carpets, woods, walls, concrete, hair... whatever you need.

Use the Pen(P) tool to create a path, and then choose the Define Custom Shape command to turn the path into a new shape. A dialog box for the new shape will appear with a preview of the new shape, just like with the Define Brush command. Assign a title to it and Enter to finalize or Esc to cancel. A new layer will appear in the Paths palette that represents your custom shape. Choose the Custom Shape(U) tool, and in the tool options bar at the top, open the Shape drop-down. Your new shape has been added to the list, on the bottom row.

PRESETS AND PREFERENCES

Photoshop can be customized down to the tiniest detail. Taking the time to set preferences may seem like a pain at first, but it saves time and aggravation in the end.

The Edit→Presets Manager command opens a dialog that lets you administrate all the default presets and any preset files you may have created, such as brushes, styles, and patterns.

The Preferences sub-menu contains dozens of settings to customize how Photoshop looks, works, deals with files and color, and more. You can determine things like how many history states get recorded, what you want your cursor to look like, and what units of measurement you want to work with. Flip through the several dialog menus and take a look at what's available to customize.

The Purge sub-menu houses the commands that let you delete tool presets, tool settings, preferences, History states, and the clipboard. All of these features can fill up your memory, slowing down your computer's performance, and sometimes it's useful to clear them out of the cache. Purge➔Undo deletes the record of Undos and Redos. Purge➔Clipboard empties the clipboard of anything you've Copied or Cut. Purge➔Histories clears all your History states, although it leaves snapshots intact. Purge➔All is a combination of the other three commands. Careful! None of the Purge commands can be undone.

IMAGE AND COLOR ADJUSTMENT

The Image menu lists the commands you will need to perform color management, color correction, and image editing. It's where you'll go to set the resolution and color mode of the document you're working on, and it contains powerful lighting and contrast adjustment tools.

These advanced image manipulation commands can produce both subtle and dramatic effects. With the tools lodged in the Image drop-down menu, you can do just about whatever you want to the overall look of an image.

COLOR MODE

Image➔Mode is a sub-menu containing all the different ways of defining the color in an image, also referred to as a color mode.

Many image file formats define colors by combining channels of color information, and usually those channels are Red, Green, and Blue (RGB). Most monitors and TVs also display colors by mixing red, green, and blue; art meant to be displayed on them is almost always best prepared as RGB.

Not to be confused with the file type of the same name (BMP is the extension for Bitmap images, which can be quite colorful), the color mode Bitmap in Photoshop is always only two colors: black and white. You can only enter Bitmap mode from Grayscale (which discards the color information).

Grayscale looks like RGB except it only has one channel: a black and white (and gray) image, capable of having detail but not color.

CMYK (Cyan/Magenta/Yellow/blacK) is another channel-based method of defining color. In this case, the channels represent the colors of ink commonly used for professional printing. When printed, images prepared as CMYK will more closely approximate how they looked on the monitor than RGB would.

Images that use Indexed color basically have their own internal palette of color. The most common kind of Indexed image is a GIF, which has of 256 (8 bits) possible colors in each image (although it could, for instance, consist of 256 different shades of red).

If you're working in one color mode and try to save the file as an image file type that doesn't support that color mode (for example, if you're working in RGB mode and choose GIF in the Save dialog), Photoshop will save it as a copy with the color converted to the appropriate mode.

COLOR AND LIGHTING ADJUSTMENTS

Perhaps one of the most frequently used and most powerful sub-menus of Photoshop, the Adjustments are the technical commands used for working with color, color correction, tone, value, lighting, and contrast associated with digital imagery.

Auto Levels, Auto Contrast, and Auto Color perform different types of automated color correction. They are best used to treat images that have slight overall color casts. I use them every once in a while to even out the values of a good quality source image, for example. Be aware that anything automated takes away from your ability to be original. Use these tools with care.

With the Color Balance command, it's possible increase or reduce the percentage of Cyan, Red, Magenta, Green, Yellow, or Blue in an image. Drop the cyan of a bad photograph, or up the red in a blood-red sky. This tool is simple to use and very handy for quick but subtle color shifts.

The Brightness/Contrast command makes basic changes to the value scale of an image, applying the same adjustment evenly to the entire image or selection. Brightness/Contrast is sort of a general approach to lightening or darkening an image. Since it affects the entire image, it has a tendency to gray out detail if it's used to make dramatic changes of value. Use Brightness/Contrast if you just need to brighten or darken your imagery slightly, or if you are working with a small file, 64x64 or below. This is my favorite tool for upping the contrast level of a small texture file fast. Photoshop has other options for more complex value changing; check out Curves and Levels.

Use the Hue/Saturation command to adjust the hue, saturation, and lightness within images, such as the red, yellow, or blue channels. Adjusting the hue, or color, can be likened to moving along the spectrum. This is another great tool for fast fixes that I use often. For texture art, it's often perfectly acceptable to make major color shifts within the basic spectrum. This command is great for shifting, for example, a bright, strong blue over to a bright, strong green. I also use it for taking a color out of a texture that has too much. For example, I might take down the yellow of a sand texture if it's too saturated.

The Desaturate command removes all of the color information in an image, resulting in a grayscale image.

The Replace Color command takes a hue from an image (selected in advance) and then replaces the chosen color with a new color. For example, an image has a lot of orange in it, and you wanted to change the orange to red, this would be the tool to use. Manipulate the hue, saturation, and lightness of the new hue, just as with the Hue/Saturation command.

The Invert command flips the color values in an image, making what looks like a photographic negative. For example, this command will switch a black document with a white line drawing to a white document with a black line drawing. I use Invert to switch the black and white values of UV maps, when the UV border color is important.

SIZING COMMANDS

Because it is often necessary to change the size of an image or the size of the image canvas, Photoshop has added easy sizing commands to its Image drop-down menu.

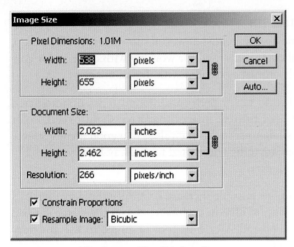

The Image Size Dialog Box

The Duplicate command creates an exact replica of the active layer. The layer, when duplicated, will become the active layer, and appear directly above the originally selected layer.

You will use Image→Image Size often. In the dialog for this command you can specify which unit of measurement you want for the document, the dimensions and resolution you require, and check or uncheck the all-important Constrain Proportions box. Constrain Proportions, when checked, will prevent the image from being distorted when you change one of its dimensions. You'll know when you have not constrained proportions because after you hit enter to finalize the image resize, the document will be badly distorted. If you forget, just do a Ctrl/⌘ + Z.

The Canvas Size command expands or contracts the dimensions of your Photoshop canvas. There are several units of measurement to choose from, and it is also possible to select which side (or the center) you would like the canvas to be added along.

Here's a super fast tip for increasing canvas size with the Crop(C) tool: if the crop area is larger than the image instead of smaller, it adds to the size of the image just like the Canvas Size command.

You can rotate your entire image 180 degrees, 90 degrees clockwise, 90 degrees counter-clockwise, and arbitrarily using the Rotate Canvas command.

MANIPULATING LAYERS

The Layer menu contains all of the commands specific to the layers of Photoshop. Create new layers, duplicate them, add styles, delete, arrange, merge, and flatten with the Layer drop-down menu. It's a good idea to go through this menu thoroughly, because it does have several commands not available anywhere else in the application.

NEW LAYER SUB-MENU

The New sub-menu contains several commands for creating new layers in a variety of ways. The New→Layer command creates a new layer in the layer stack directly above the last layer selected. The layer will be named numerically by Photoshop in the order in which it was created. A new layer can also be added to the stack using this shortcut: Shift + Ctrl/⌘ + N. Always name your layers!

It is important to distinguish between a New Layer and a Background Layer. A Background layer is the first layer in an image: the layer created when you first added or imported content to the image. By default, the Background layer is locked and can't be manipulated. Use the Layer From Background command if you want to change a Background layer into a workable one.

LAYER STYLES SUB-MENU

The Layer Style command opens up the Layer Style dialog box. This dialog is the tool used to set drop shadows, bevels, overlays, and the like to layers in the layer stack. Combinations of these effects are referred to as Styles. This command can be quickly accessed by either right-clicking on a layer in the Layers palette or by clicking on the effects "f" icon along the bottom of the Layers palette.

TYPE SUB-MENU

The Type sub-menu houses several controls for manipulating text. It's grayed out unless you've got a text layer selected. Create Work Path and Convert to Shape convert a text layer to paths or shapes, like those created with the Pen(P) tools, and give you all the advantages vector paths afford.

Warping text is pretty fun. Type some text, and do a Layer→Type→Warp Text to access the tool. Then choose a style from the drop-down, a linear orientation, and set the sliders to your specifications. I use Warp text for menu screens. For smaller texture sizes, it doesn't work too well because the text becomes too hard to read, and any effects applied to the warped text become less resolved and harder to see. Definitely save this tool for larger works with room for detail.

Some commands and tools, such as filter effects and painting tools, are not available for type layers, because text is rendered from letter shapes instead of a bitmap of pixels. Rasterizing converts a text layer to a normal layer, which will let you use those filters and painting tools, but makes its contents uneditable as text. A warning message appears if you choose a command or tool that requires a rasterized layer.

One thing I do to avoid a permanent rasterization is to duplicate the original, unrasterized text layer, slap a lock on it, then make it invisible. This way, if my experiments with the rasterized version don't work out, I can always scrap it and go back to the original.

COMBINING LAYERS

Merging layers comes up often. I always add new layers whenever creating new elements for a texture. After the work progresses to a certain point, however, it's often obvious that it's easier to consolidate one or two layers into a single layer. There's no specific formula for knowing when to do this, but don't do it if you think there's a chance you'll want the layers separate any time in the future.

Merging layers means that you are compiling two separate layers into one layer. To Merge Down means that the layer that is currently selected will become one with the layer directly below it.

The Merge Linked command will combine all layers with the chain-link icon, which signifies that they are linked together, into one layer. You can see the chain icon in the box on the layer directly to the right of the eyeball. Note that Merge Linked will only appear in the Layer drop-down menu if there are, in fact, linked layers in the stack. When this is the case, Merge Linked will appear instead of Merge Down.

Merging the visible layers will combine all of those with an eyeball icon next to them into one layer, titled with the title of the layer that was selected at the time of the Merge Visible command. If there are any invisible layers in the stack, they will remain independent.

There will come a time when all of those layers painstakingly stacked in your document are no longer necessary. Perhaps you need to save a file format that doesn't support multiple layers, to add a web version of the image to your web site, or put a texture map into a game engine. This is when flattening the image comes in: all the layers get squashed into one thin pancake. Never ever flatten an original document. The original PSD should always be saved in your archives in case you need to change something later, work on it some more, or show someone what you did to get the piece to work. Make a duplicate or save a copy of your original, saving it as a later version, and then (and only then) will it be safe to flatten. Flattening is undoable, but once you save, close, and then reopen after a flatten, that's all she wrote if you suddenly decide you need those layers back.

TAILORING SELECTIONS

Selections are another key component to working in Photoshop. Selections include or exclude areas of an image in the series of commands executed upon them. The Select menu is a collection of commands that have to do with specifying how an image will be changed and altered. Use this menu to carefully tailor selections to fit your work.

BASIC SELECTIONS

Select➔All selects everything contained in the selected layer. It is very helpful for getting info on the dimensions of your image or, followed by a Delete, simply erasing everything all at once.

Deselect deactivates any active selection.

Change your mind after that Deselect? Use the Reselect command to return to your last selection. Beware, however, that if you use the Layer via Copy or Layer via Cut command, this command will no longer be available.

Select➔Inverse selects everything that wasn't selected, and deselects everything that was.

SELECT BY COLOR

Select➔Color Range works much the same as Replace Color. Use this command to select certain colors within an image. You can also specify a range of colors to select. Choose a color from the image, or select a range from the drop-down menu, and then use the Fuzziness slider to specify how much of that hue you wish to select. In this manner, you are able to select certain colors and then alter them however you like. I love this tool because I can select painted strokes based on color, then use the selection to make new layers to flip, filter, or whatever.

CREATE A SOFT SELECTION

Feather softens the borders of a selection. This feature of the Select menu is used for text effects a lot, but is also a perfect tool for using creatively. One thing I like to do with it is make paint look like soft light, or neon light. I create a selection on a new layer adjacent to the light source of the image, apply a Feather of 5 to 10 pixels depending on the level of edge diffusion desired, then do a solid fill with the right swatch of paint. With a little further tweaking of opacity and blending mode, I can get a lovely, gentle lighting effect.

Feather works in pixels, but keep in mind that you cannot apply a 100 pixel Feather to a selection that is only 25 pixels: the Feather would round and soften the selection right out of existence!

MODIFYING SELECTIONS

Selection marquees can also be edited in these four ways: Border, Smooth, Expand, and Contract. Border adds an additional selection as a border around the active selection. Smooth will clean up any extra pixels left over from a color-based selection. It also smoothes corners. Expand and Contract are just like they sound, and push a selection out with a number for the Expand command, or suck it in with a number for the Contract command.

Choose Select→Grow to include all adjacent pixels falling within the tolerance range specified in the Magic Wand Options .

Choose Select→Similar to include pixels throughout the image, not just adjacent ones, falling within the tolerance range of the active selection

TRANSFORMING SELECTIONS

The Transform Selection command is another way to get into Transform mode. Transform mode is the mode that allows a selection to be scaled, rotated, skewed, or distorted. It works in the exact same way as it does when applied to layer contents, only it responds to an active selection marquee. Ctrl/⌘ + T is the shortcut to enter Transform mode.

SAVING AND LOADING SELECTIONS

Save Selection is the command used for creating Alpha channels within documents, accessible via the Channels palette. Once a selection is saved as a channel, it can also be reloaded as a selection using the Select→Load Selection command and picking the name of the new channel from the drop-down.

Note that selections saved as channels can also be filtered using the Lighting Effects filter, one way to create bump maps explored later in this book. For this reason, it's a good idea to always assign a name to everything you add. Name new channel layers just as you would name all other layers.

SPECIAL EFFECTS

Filters are commands that will alter the overall appearance of a layer or a selection within a layer. For example, executing the Watercolor filter command will make an image look like a watercolor painting.

With the filters, you can simulate painterly effects, create patterns, blur, sharpen, distort, and generate interesting surfaces. The Filter drop-down menu also contains the Offset Filter, which you will need every time you make a tileable texture. Using these commands is a lot of fun; play around with this menu.

The Extract Dialog Box

Liquefy

PAINTING WITH FILTERS

Filter→Extract is an easy way to get an object out of a background. Execute the filter, and in the new dialog, paint a border around the edge of the object to be selected, then fill the area you want to retain, and then the painted border is used as a reference to remove the unmasked portion of the image.

Liquefy is a very powerful filter and you can do some pretty cool painting with it. It brings up a painting dialog with tools and effects that treat your image like it's made of thick liquid

The Filter→Artistic sub-menu contains filters that mimic fine art media, such as making your image look like it was made with colored pencils, or pastels. There are other clever uses for these filters, such as using Plastic Wrap to make a flying saucer look metallic and shiny.

Similar in concept to the Artistic filters, Brush Stroke filters make an image appear as if it was made using a particular paint brush technique. Crosshatch is great for creating cloth patterns.

MAKING PATTERNS WITH FILTERS

The Pattern Maker is a new way to make quick and dirty patterns. It takes a selection and automatically generates a pattern based on the image in the selection. You can import from the clipboard, specify exact dimensions for the pattern tile, and even offset the tile. You can keep clicking Generate until you get a pattern you like.

The Pixelate filters break up the pixels of an image to achieve effects like turning an image into a mosaic of larger pixels, or making an image faceted or crystallized.

BLUR, DISTORT, AND SHARPEN

Blurs are useful for adding softness to an image, or fuzzing out something that's too sharp. They can also be used for to simulate effects such as depth of field or motion. The Gaussian blur style produces a high-quality, smooth blur. Motion Blur blurs in a specific direction at an adjustable intensity, whereas Radial Blur blurs as if the image is spinning like a pinwheel or zooming toward the viewer.

The Distort and Displace filters twirl, ripple, pinch, spherize, and more. If you need to displace a surface for effects like water, glass, interference, or tornadoes, these are the filters to use. Some of them are very detailed, and yield some pretty cool results.

Always use Unsharp Mask, rather than Sharpen or Sharpen More, for sharpening images. It does the best job. This filter is based on a traditional film compositing technique used to sharpen edges in an image.

CREATING SURFACES WITH FILTERS

Noise is a random pattern of pixels for adding grit to industrial surfaces like concrete or rust, for organic textures like leaves and bark, and for human textures like skin or leather clothing. Noise can also be used as a way to get patterning that other filters will work from, because some filters cannot be applied to flat, solid colors. I apply a Noise filter for just about everything. It is a wonderful way to create fast variation on smaller textures, and a great way to add grittiness to surfaces

The Render sub-menu contains some the most powerful filters of the lot. Clouds, Difference Clouds, and Lighting Effects are all important to experiment with and learn because they can add that extra third dimension to your 2D work. Difference Clouds are created from a mix of the foreground and background colors, and it's a cool filter to use for rocks and other natural elements that require subtle color variation. Lighting Effects can be used to add the illusion of lighting in the form of various types of lights: spot, omni, parallel, and colored lights.

Sketch filters simulate a wide variety of effects, including charcoal, chalk, photocopies, and stamps. The Chrome filter creates the illusion that the image is a shiny metal surface. I use Halftone Pattern quite a bit for a variety of purposes, but mainly to get a pattern of horizontal, perfectly straight lines. These lines are great for simulating the look of a TV or computer screen, for stripes on cloth, bump maps, and ridges. The Reticulation filter is good for creating textures and bump maps that require clumpy, grainy surfaces like drywall or Styrofoam.

The Stylize filters produce more abstract effects on a selection by displacing pixels and upping contrast. Emboss takes a surface and indents it, as if you had a very powerful stamp and used it to plant a detailed pattern on the wall. Extrude imitates 3D effects. Wind drags pixels in a specified direction to make them look blown by the elements, similar to Motion Blur but without blurring the pixels as much. Wind can also be used to create drips and streaks and stripes by rotating the layer with the wind filter applied to a vertical, instead of horizontal, orientation.

Use the filters in the Filter→Texture sub-menu to give an image the appearance of depth, or to add an organic look. Grain is a lot like Noise, but better: it's configurable and can yield much more specific effects than just a chaotic pattern of pixels. Patchwork is great for creating dimensional-looking tiled surfaces. You can mess with the square size and relief to create the right depth and pattern for your designs.

The Texturizer is another important filter for achieving the look of 3D with Photoshop. This filter loads a PSD into whatever document you are working with as a bump map, kind of like Emboss with a different image source. You can specify the scale and relief values for the texture, whether or not to invert it, and then which direction the light comes from. This filter is excellent for building depth and adding life to textures.

THE OFFSET FILTER

Hidden away in the Filter→Other sub-menu is the Offset filter, an important filter you will get to know very well. Offset is used to create tileable textures, which is covered thoroughly later in the book.

To practice with it, first find out the height and width of the active image. Divide those numbers in half. Now run the filter and enter those halved numbers into the Horizontal (width) and Vertical (height) offset fields. You will see two lines appear in the image, crossed in the center. These are the edges of the document that are now meeting in the middle of the image. Hit Enter to finalize the filter and now you can set about getting rid of those edges. This is where the healing and cloning tools come in. See if you can remove those edges without messing up the texture.

THIRD-PARTY FILTERS

There are many filters made by other companies that you can plug into Photoshop. Kai's Power Tools are excellent for fractal patterns, motion blurs, vector effects, thick paint, spherical surfaces, buttons, dimensional plastic, fur and fibers, and noise.

I use the Xenofex filter package for a variety of purposes, though not necessarily what they're designed to do. For example, the Impressionistic setting for the Origami filter gives a very beautiful surface that I have used to create colorful silk fabrics for my characters. Baked Earth comes in handy not just for earth, but rock walls and scales.

Eye Candy 4000 filters have been around a while and are well-known companions to Photoshop. Eye Candy has wonderful chrome and fabric weave simulators, and also comes with glass, fur, fire, and water drops.

Filter➜Brush Strokes➜Spatter

Filter➜Brush Strokes➜Sumi-e

Filter➜Brush Strokes➜Ink Outlines

Filter➜Brush Strokes➜Sprayed Strokes

Filter➜Brush Strokes➜Crosshatch

Filter➜Brush Strokes➜Accented Edges

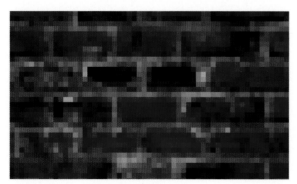

Filter➜Pixelate➜Mosaic

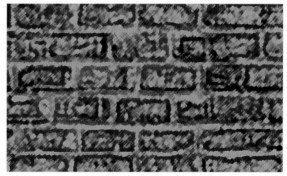

Filter➜Artistic➜Colored Pencil

Filter➔Artistic➔Watercolor

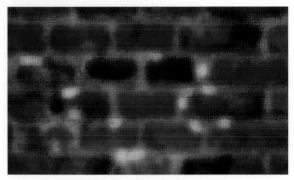

Filter➔Artistic➔Underpainting

Filter➔Artistic➔Sponge

Filter➔Artistic➔Rough Pastels

Filter➔Artistic➔Plastic Wrap

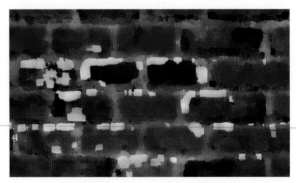

Filter➔Artistic➔Palette Knife

Filter➔Artistic➔Neon Glow

Filter➔Artistic➔Fresco

Filter➜Texture➜Texturizer

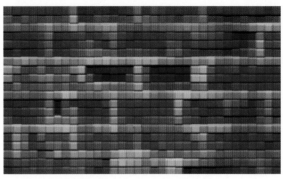

Filter➜Texture➜Patchwork

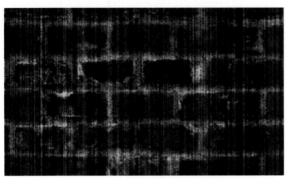

Filter➜Texture➜Grain

Filter➜Render➜Lighting Effects

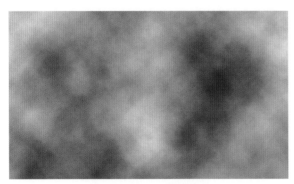

Filter➜Render➜Clouds

Filter➜Render➜Difference Clouds

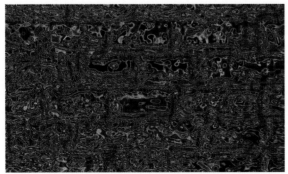

Filter➜Sketch➜Chrome

Filter➜Sketch➜Bas Relief

Filter➔Sketch➔Plaster

Filter➔Sketch➔Halftone

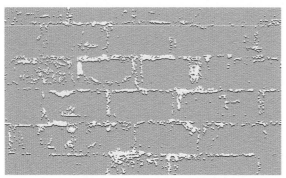

Filter➔Sketch➔Note Paper

Filter➔Stylize➔Wind

Filter➔Stylize➔Emboss

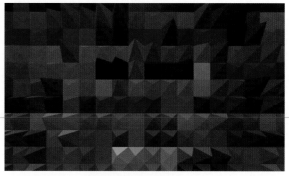

Filter➔Stylize➔Extrude

Filter➔Noise➔Add Noise

Filter➔Sharpen➔Unsharp Mask

Filter→Distort→Ripple

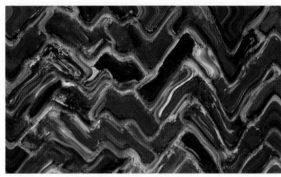

Filter→Distort→Wave

Filter→Distort→Shear

Filter→Distort→Zig-Zag

Filter→Distort→Pinch

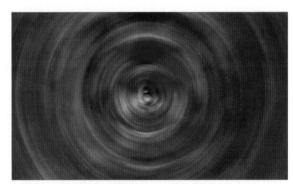

Filter→Blur→Radial Blur

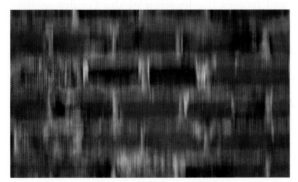

Filter→Blur→Motion Blur

Filter→Blur→Gaussian Blur

CUSTOMIZING THE DISPLAY

The View drop-down menu deals with how images are viewed, as opposed to how the Photoshop interface is set up. View commands allow you to work zoomed in, zoomed out, with new views, with or without measurement tools, and how the image dialog fits into the interface: actual size, print view, and a percentage.

ZOOM IN AND OUT

The best way to see an up close or far away view of an image is to do a Ctrl/⌘ + (plus sign) to move in, or a Ctrl/⌘ + (minus sign) to move out. If you have yet to learn and memorize these commands, however, the View drop-down menu is where to go to find the commands that let you magnify or demagnify an image.

THREE WAYS TO VIEW FILES

Fit on Screen puts the active image file into a floating dialog box that matches the dimensions of the available workspace. Using this view, you can check your composition or make the most of the work area. This view does not represent the actual dimensions of the screen unless they are less than those of the work area.

Actual Pixels is handy to use when you need to see exactly how large the image will be on a computer screen. I use this often to decide how large or small an image needs to be to look right on a computer monitor.

Print Size is the view to use when you want to know precisely how large your printed image will turn out. It is always a smart idea to check this view before you print, just in case.

USING RULERS AND GUIDES

If you Show Rulers, rulers appear along the top and left side of the image dialog. They are great for taking a quick look at the dimensions of an image. I use rulers all the time for making gridded textures and as a way to measure elements of my work.

Guides are thin straight lines that you can drag from rulers along an image's borders to use as a reference for lining things up. Use Guides to do precision work, in conjunction with the Rulers. The View→New Guide command creates a new horizontal or vertical line for you to use as a reference point while working. You can set the orientation with the dialog box, and even choose an exact location for the guide to appear. They can be moved by mousing over them and dragging the slider icon that appears.

The View→Lock Guides command freezes the location of the Guides so they can't be moved.

The fast way to get rid of Guides is to flick them off the screen with the Clear Guides command.

ARRANGING THE INTERFACE

The Window drop-down menu contains all the commands that control what is visible and available in the interface. You can selectively show or hide palettes and specify how Photoshop should display your work.

DOCUMENTS SUB-MENU

The Documents sub-menu contains the commands to rearrange and organize the image windows. Window→Documents→Cascade will tidily display all open image documents in a slightly offset, diagonal pattern across the screen. Documents→Tile results in all of the open files being reorganized in a patchwork pattern. This arrangement mode comes in handy when you have a series of images you need to look at all at once.

At the bottom of the Documents sub-menu is a list of the names of all the files currently open. This function can come in especially handy when you've got images minimized along the bottom of the screen, and need to find a specific one quickly. Select the name of the file from this list, and it will be restored to viewing mode.

WORKSPACE SUB-MENU

The Window→Workspace sub-menu controls the arrangement of all of the palettes and interface elements of the active screen. Workspace→Save Workspace stores the current configuration of floating palettes for later use. Delete Workspace deletes a saved workspace arrangement.

Window→Workspace→Reset Palette Locations returns your palettes, shown or hidden, to their default state: lined up nicely on the right of the interface with the Tools palette on the left.

I use the option to save workspaces all the time. It's great because I work with a set of files of a specific dimension consistently. I can set up a separate workspace for my 640x480 screens, my 512x512 actor textures, my 256x256 tileable terrain textures, and so forth. Another use for this option is to save a view with all of the palettes docked to the palette well along the top bar of the interface. Arranged this way, the palettes are still accessible, but are out of the way, represented by a row of nice neat tabs I simply have to click on.

SHOWING AND HIDING PALETTES

Not all of the palettes have to be visible all the time. Most of the time, you probably won't need the Navigator palette, for instance. Since there's no point in cluttering up your work area with it, you can hide it away by unchecking it in the Window drop-menu. Subsequently, if you need it, or any other currently hidden palettes, you can show them again, by visiting this menu and clicking on the palette name you want to show. A checkmark will appear next to the palette name, denoting its visibility.

CONCLUSION

Although most commands can (and should!) be executed using hotkeys and shortcuts, the drop-down menus have them all, and some functions, such as filters, are only accessed via the drop-downs. You can also see the shortcut next to the command name in the drop-menu, so you can add new shortcuts to your Photoshop vocabulary as you learn and find yourself using particular drop-menu commands frequently.

Remember that the idea is to get into a flow as you work. I know from experience that sorting through the drop-down menus every time I need to make a basic change is a major concentration-breaker because they are hard to read and there's just a lot listed in them.

QUIZ

1) WHICH IS BEST FOR CREATING NEW AND ORIGINAL PAINTING TOOLS?

    a) The Define Pattern tool

    b) The Brush tool

    c) The Define Brush tool

2) RGB STANDS FOR _____, AND IS THE DEFAULT COLOR MODE.

    a) Red, Grey, Black

    b) Red, Green, Black

    c) Red, Green, Blue

3) WHAT IS THE FASTEST WAY TO ADD MORE WORKING SPACE TO AN IMAGE?

    a) Image→Canvas Size

    b) Use the Crop Tool to enlarge the canvas

    c) Image→Image Size

4) WHAT DOES THE VIEW DROP-DOWN MENU CONTROL?

    a) Workspace arrangements

    b) Zooming in and out

    c) Tiling images

5) WHAT COMMAND MUST BE PERFORMED TO MAKE A TEXT LAYER AVAILABLE FOR USE WITH CERTAIN FILTERS, BLENDING MODES, AND OPTIONS?

    a) Anti-aliasing

    b) Rasterize

    c) Create an active selection

6) WHICH SELECT DROP-DOWN MENU COMMAND IS USED TO CREATE APHA CHANNELS?

    a) Select All

    b) Select Inverse

    c) Save Selection

7) LIGHTING EFFECTS ARE LOCATED UNDER WHICH FILTERS MENU?

    a) Render

    b) Artistic

    c) Distort

8) WHICH FILTER IS USED FOR CREATING TILEABLE TEXTURES?

    a) Tiles

    b) Mosaic

    c) Offset

9) WINDOW→DOCUMENTS→CASCADE WILL:

    a) Frame an image within its floating dialog

    b) Sort the open images in a slightly offset, diagonal pattern

    c) Zoom into an image

10) SPECIAL EFFECTS CAN BE TONED DOWN OR BLENDED BY USING:

    a) The Fade command

    b) The Feather command

    c) The Fill slider

KEVIN KILSTROM

ART LEAD

MONOLITH PRODUCTIONS

What is your job?

I am an Art Lead for Monolith Productions in Kirkland, WA. What that entails is making sure that the art gets done. Right now I work with four world artists every day, and three character/animation artists.

Each team has an Art Director and an Art Lead. The Art Director is in charge of how the game looks, and the Art Lead is too, but I'm more responsible for making sure everything gets done on schedule. I also work with the engineers who create new tools for us, and then train the artists to work with the new tools.

I've been with Monolith since 1996 and it's a really great place to work.

How did you get started in the game industry?

One of my hobbies through high school and college was making animatronic puppets and latex masks. I wanted to make horror movies. So, I went to Washington State University and got a Bachelor of Arts in Sculpture and Screenprinting. I then saw an ad in the paper for a person who could paint and do stop motion animation – stuff I'd been doing for years, just for fun. So I called the guy, went over to his house, and he hired me. We started off making a video game in the rec room of his house. We did that for 2 years and then one day, my boss called me and said, "Now we're going to be working for Monolith". That started in 1994, and I've been here ever since. I was just really lucky.

Which 3D packages do you work with?

The first four years, we used Softimage, but we've recently switched over to Maya.

How did you learn the tools you use?

I'm self-taught. When I started, we made everything with 2D Sprites, which means I was doing a lot of stop motion stuff with blue screens. Then I was given a copy of True Space 2.0 and started using that to create simple props. I found that if you know how to sculpt in real life, like with clay, then it's an easy step to adapt that to working with a 3D tool. At Monolith, we have a system for learning Maya. We started off with a couple of Maya gurus, then rotate the other teams onto Maya where they can learn from the tutorials but also learn from the people who already know it. It's a good system. We have a very open atmosphere here at Monolith. Everyone gets along really well between the teams and people get to use each other as resources.

How do you use Photoshop?

We use it for creating skins and textures. Some people start from scratch, then a lot of people have digital cameras so they can go out and take pictures to paint on. Basically, every way you can think of is used to make our textures.

How long have your worked in the industry?

Since June of 1994, so eight years.

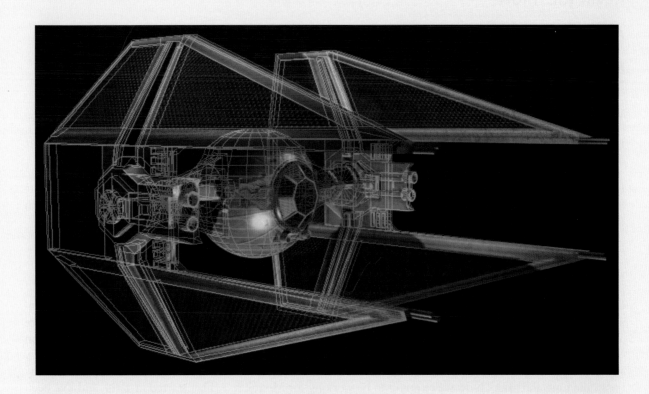

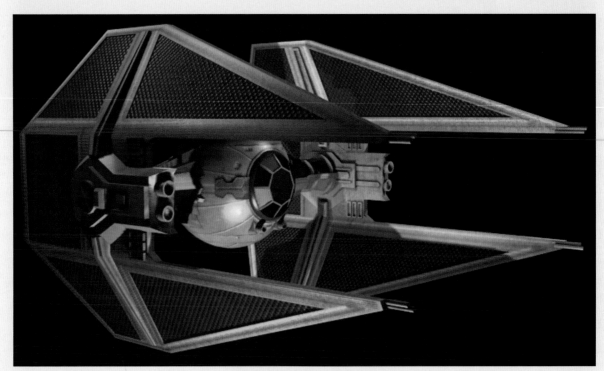

Artwork by Kevin Kilstrom

KEVIN KILSTROM 2001

How early do you have to get up? How late do you have to stay?

I work eight hours a day and then I go home. Around crunch time, I may work longer a few days a week. Some people do work 12 hours a day, but it depends on what they do when they get here. The only requirement is that the work gets done. It's all up to self-discipline.

What are your interests outside the job?

I have my own hobbies, like making masks and remote-controlled puppets. I also like to work on my house, and spend time out of doors. Playing with my two sons is fun, and gives me exercise. I try to be active, too, and work out at least once or twice a week.

What games do you play?

Recently, I got a Playstation 2 at home. We played The Simpsons Roadrage and that was fun. I like driving games. I also love Starcraft and I play that on my PC at home.

Where do you find inspiration for your work?

The kind of stuff that inspires me are movies like Spiderman, full of cool effects and animation

Do you have an ultimate goal for your career?

Right now, I'm really comfortable with my job and my family. But I would like to get back into making short movies. A goal of mine is to spend more time working on my own stuff, like building robots again, and making latex masks.

What's the best advice you could give to new artists entering the industry?

Don't be afraid to use your creativity. Lots of times I see really good artists who are afraid to give their work that little extra push to make it really cool. Let your own creativity come through. That's what really impresses other people.

IN THIS CHAPTER YOU WILL LEARN ABOUT:

- Hotkeys and shortcuts
- How to organize files
- Efficient workflow tactics
- Naming conventions
- Tips about Layers
- Working with original documents

INTRODUCTION

Computers can accommodate a lot of different individuals using them in different ways. Just as everyone has different patterns of behavior and thinking, so too do they have different patterns of working. There isn't a right or wrong way to use the software, but some ways are more productive than others.

The order that you perform tasks in (known as "workflow") combined with shortcuts and hotkeys will dramatically influence your speed and efficiency, and ultimately improve the quality of your work. We'll start with hotkeys and move on through naming conventions, organizational issues, and finally management of your layers and files.

HOTKEYS

Hotkeys and shortcuts are the key combinations used to perform functions more quickly than having to navigate the interface with the mouse. For example, instead of mousing up to File→Save, you could use Ctrl/⌘ + S to save the file with your left hand while continuing to work with your mouse hand.

Rather than just attempting to memorize hotkeys from a list, let's use them in practice by going through the following tutorial to make a simple logo that will be incorporated into later projects.

SHORTCUTS AND HOTKEYS TUTORIAL: AT A GLANCE

TOPICS COVERED

This tutorial is all about how to begin working quickly with Photoshop. The end result will be added to the final scene in a following chapter.

YOU LL LEARN HOW TO:

- Use hotkeys
- Use shortcuts

TUTORIAL: SHORTCUTS AND HOTKEYS

In this tutorial you'll create a simple logo, using as few menu commands as possible. At first it may take you longer to remember which hotkey is right for a particular command than it would for you to go select it from a drop-down or the Tool bar, but use the hotkey anyway. Once you've gotten used to using the hotkey or shortcut, your hands will thank you for saving you so much dragging and clicking!

STEP 1: CREATE A NEW DOCUMENT

First, create a new, blank file to work on. Ctrl/⌘ + N is the shortcut for File→New. Set the background to Transparent, dimensions to 512x512 pixels (not inches!), and color mode to RGB in the New Document dialog.

STEP 2: CREATE TWO NEW LAYERS

Do a Shift + Ctrl/⌘ + N to create a new layer, the equivalent of choosing Layer→New→Layer from the top menu bar. Then hit D on the keyboard to restore the foreground and background swatches to their default (black and white, respectively), and then hit X to switch the foreground and background swatch colors.

Select the new layer and hit G for the Paint Bucket(G) Tool. Click on the layer to fill it with white. Right-click (Control-click on a Mac) on the layer, choose Layer Properties from the drop-down, and rename the layer "White". Create a third layer with Ctrl/⌘ + N and name it "Happy Face Logo".

STEP 3: PAINT BY FILLING A SELECTION

Select the Happy Face Logo layer in the Layers palette and hit M for the Elliptical Marquee(M) tool. Alt + Click on the Marquee(M) tool in the Tool bar to access the Ellipse if it's not up. Click and drag a circle onto the center of the canvas.

Next, hit L on the keyboard for the Polygonal Lasso(L) tool. (Again, Alt + Click on the icon in the Tool bar to scroll through to the Polygonal Lasso if it isn't already selected.) While holding down the Alt key, use the Lasso to subtract a pie-shaped wedge from the elliptical selection, for the mouth.

Hit G on the keyboard to access the Paint Bucket(B) tool. Next, click on the foreground swatch on the Tool bar to access the color picker. I chose bright yellow, but you can choose whatever color you like. Click inside the selection to fill in the face.

Step 3

Step 4

STEP 4: SELECT AND FILL A SUNBURST

Do another Shift + Ctrl/⌘ + N for a new layer, and name it "Blast". Hit L on the keyboard again to get the Polygonal Lasso(L) tool and draw a sunburst shape around the logo, making sure you are working on the new layer (it should be highlighted in the Layers palette). Once you have what you like, choose another color from the color picker. Hit G again on the keyboard for the Paint Bucket(G) tool and click to fill in the blast with the color. I chose a nice bright green.

STEP 5: CREATE A BORDER

Next we're going to create a border around the logo by duplicating the layer, changing its color, putting it behind the original layer, and making it bigger.

Here's a couple really awesome shortcuts for duplicating a layer and selecting the contents of a layer: click on the Happy Face Logo layer in the Layers palette and drag it onto the Create a New Layer icon on the bottom of the palette to duplicate the layer. Right-click and rename the layer "Outline". Do a Ctrl/⌘ + click on the Outline layer to select the contents of the layer. Pick another color (I chose a dark green) and hit G on the keyboard for the Paint Bucket(G) tool. Click inside the selected area on the Outline layer to fill it.

Now we are going to alter the scale of the Outline with the Transform tool. Make sure the Outline layer is selected and do a Ctrl/⌘ + T to access Free Transform mode. Hold Shift (to keep constrained), then click and drag on a corner point of the bounding box to increase the scale of the Outline. The idea is to get a green border around the yellow. Mouse around the corner points to rotate the Outline, or hold down Ctrl/⌘ while you click and drag to skew it, to make it slightly warped.

In the Layers palette, drag the Outline layer underneath the Happy Face Logo layer by clicking and dragging it down in the layer stack. Next, cut a quick eye hole: select the Happy Face Logo layer and hit M on the keyboard for the Elliptical Marquee(M) tool. Draw two circular selections for the face's eyeballs, then Ctrl/⌘ + X to cut out the hole.

Do a Ctrl/⌘ + S to save the document. Locate the correct directory (wherever you'd like to save it), and hit Enter.

Step 6

STEP 6: ADD SOME INTEREST TO THE SUNBURST

Let's add a border to the sunburst as well, starting in a way similar to Step 5 but then cutting out parts of the shape with the Polygonal Lasso(L) tool. In the Layers palette, duplicate the Blast layer by clicking and dragging it to the Create a New Layer icon at the bottom of the palette, then select its contents by holding Ctrl/⌘ and clicking on the layer, also in the Layers palette. Choose a new color (the same color you used for the Outline, if you like) and fill the selection with the Paint Bucket(G) tool. Name the new layer "Blast Bolts".

Use the Free Transform tool (Ctrl/⌘ + T) to make the Blast Bolts larger and slightly skewed, as you did for the Outline in Step 5. This time, though, let's put the Blast Bolts on top of the Blast layer and cut some holes in it. Drag the Blast Bolts layer down in the layer stack in the Layers palette, so it's above Blast but below the Outline.

Hit L on the keyboard to select the Polygonal Lasso(L) tool and draw in some shapes to cut out of the Blast Bolts to make an outline, roughly in the shape of the Blast but leaving some irregularity. While the selection for each shape is active, hit Ctrl/⌘ + X to cut it out.

STEP 7: CREATE A FLATTENED VERSION OF THE IMAGE WITHIN THE SAME DOCUMENT

Next you'll create a merged (or "flattened") version of the image so you can make changes to all the layers at once, and copy the whole thing to paste it onto another document. However, instead of just flattening the image and losing all the flexibility of having separate layers, you're going to create a merged layer within the original document, leaving the separate layer information intact.

Choose Layer→New→Layer Set from the top menu bar. (Sorry, no hotkey, unless you're using Windows, in which case you can press Alt + L to access the Layer menu, but it's not much faster than just clicking on it in the top menu bar.) Name the new set "Merged". Duplicate all your layers, and then drag each duplicate onto the Merged layer set. Make sure you arrange the copied layers in the same stack order within the Merged layer set folder as they were in the overall layer stack. Highlight the Merged layer set in the Layers palette, and do a Ctrl/⌘ + E to merge the layers in the set. You'll now have a flattened Happy Face Logo in a single layer named Merged. Click on the eyeball icons next to the original layers (Happy Face Logo, Outline, Burst, etc.) to turn them invisible, for now.

Do a Ctrl/⌘ + S to save.

STEP 8: ADD SOME EFFECTS AND PAINT TO THE MERGED LAYER

Add some noise to the Merged layer by choosing Filter→Noise→Add Noise from the top menu bar. This will give the surface of the image a little more grit.

Next, paint in some detail on the eye. Hit W on the keyboard for the Wand(W) tool and click inside the eyehole to create a selection that only allows you to paint within the eye, protecting the outside of the selection. Hit I on the keyboard for the Eyedropper(I) tool and click on the outline to select that color.

Next, choose the Brush(B) tool. Use the [ ] keys to scale your brush diameter up or down. To soften the brush, hold down Shift + [. To harden the brush, hold down Shift +]. To change brushes, use the period (.) key to scroll forward through the brushes, and the comma (,) key to scroll backwards. Once you've chosen the right brush, paint inside the selection to create an eye. Have fun with it; make him crazy or something.

STEP 9: HOW TO COPY THE HAPPY FACE LOGO TO ANOTHER IMAGE

Now you've got one document with a conveniently flattened version of the logo, but the original layers have also been retained in case you want to change them, or use them for something else. The logo is now ready to travel to another document, in my case a city wall where it will be graffiti. To use the image, hit W on the board for the wand and click in the white area. Do a Shift + Ctrl/⌘ + I to invert the selection and then do a Ctrl/⌘ + C to copy it to the clipboard. Next, open the destination document, select the layer you want to add it to, and do a Ctrl/⌘ + V to paste. Go back to the man document and do a Ctrl/⌘ + D to deselect.

CONCLUSION

Remember that saving often is a very good idea. Computers crash, and if yours goes down and you have not saved the last 350 steps of your work, there's only one word to say... and I can't say it here. Train your hand to hit Ctrl/⌘ + S every few minutes without your brain having to tell it to.

Once you are finished working with a document, do a Ctrl/⌘ + W to close it. To exit Photoshop, do a Ctrl/⌘ + Q to quit.

For a comprehensive list of Photoshop hotkeys and shortcuts, refer to the guide located in the front of the book. This tutorial covered the most frequently used shortcuts that everyone should know, plus a few more. Since there is a shortcut for almost any command in Photoshop, there are many obscure key combinations that you may not need now, but that can be incorporated into your workflow as you get more proficient.

The end product

NAMING CONVENTIONS

When you have a certain formula for determining the name of a file in a project, that's called the "naming convention". Naming conventions are useful for keeping yourself organized, and being able to tell what is in an image file (or set of image files) without actually having to open it. In a production environment where there will be hundreds – if not thousands – of separate files comprising a project, you will almost certainly be given a naming system to follow. Using a set-in-stone guideline for naming all files generated on a project makes them easy to save and easy to find.

For yourself, create a naming convention that makes sense to you. For a group of folks working on a single project, it's a good idea to stick to file names and categorizations that are logical and obvious. Here's an example of a naming convention: category_objecttype_description_artist_version.extension. With this naming convention, if you had a file called environment_tree_pine_jaimy_1.ma, you'd immediately know by the name of the file that it is a Maya scene file that contains a model of a pine tree that's grouped with the environment objects. With the larger categories coming first, the file list on your computer's operating system might group similar files in alphabetical or numerical order, like this:

```
characters_NPC_clown_anthony_1.ma

characters_NPC_lumberjack_anthony_1.ma

environment_rocks_boulder_jaimy_1.ma

environment_tree_pine_jaimy_1.ma

environment_tree_birch_rick_1.ma

environment_tree_birch_rick_2.ma
```

Further organization can be achieved with a file folder system (in fact, the above example could have two separate folders called Characters and Environment, and strike the first part of the file naming convention, shortening the file names). The rest of the information for a file, such as the date and time it was last revised, can be provided by the operating system. When naming files, always use an underscore between words, and never spaces; some operating systems, such as Unix variants and most game engines, don't like file names to contain spaces.

NAMING ELEMENTS WITHIN A FILE

Not to be confused with naming conventions, assigning a name or title to the elements of your work is a very important facet of managing your Photoshop files. You can assign an identifying tag to just about everything you create: layers, selections, new brushes, patterns, custom shapes, alpha channels, color channels, new styles, new swatches, History states, and Actions, to name a few. Naming all of these creations is vitally important to keeping track of your work. Get into the habit of typing in a name for your new creations, and you will notice how much it helps your efficiency, and relieves anxiety. Anxiety arises from the little voice in the back of your head that's yelping about how your poor brain is supposed to keep track of all this unlabeled information. Such anxiety will totally violate all of the efficient workflow tactics.

Here's an example: neglecting to assign titles to 17 separate layers of small details (details that are invisible in the small Layers palette thumbnails) within a complex Photoshop document will cause problems. Photoshop simply assigns the title of Layer 1, Layer 2, Layer 3, etc. to each new layer it creates for you. Without the clue of a layer title specifying what that layer contains, you'll be spending a lot of time peering at thumbnail previews and clicking the invisibility eyeball on and off in an effort to determine what is what and what is where.. In short, wasting time. Name everything.

KEEP ORIGINALS INTACT

Never flatten an original document. To flatten an image means to collapse all of the layers that contain all of the separated image details into one, and only one, layer. Documents are often flattened to minimize file size, to convert a PSD into another file type that doesn't support multiple layers (almost all of them), or for ease of editing multiple layers at once.

However, flattening an original, multi-layer image is a terrible idea for several reasons. The first is that you can no longer make any changes to the layers individually. Another is that you have no reference about how you got your results, making reproducing a particular effect potentially difficult. A third is that you will no longer be able to use layers from one document in another document; a wonderful freedom you don't want to lose.

If you need to flatten an image, and you will, the simple answer is to duplicate it and flatten the duplicate, leaving your original multi-layer PSD file intact. You can use your computer's operating system to duplicate the file, or use File→Save As to save a copy of the document. Keep your priceless originals intact.

BACKING UP

Always make back-up copies of your work. This is true of anything you create with a computer, but bears mentioning here. There are a lot of external storage devices out there, a CD burner being the most effective for the money these days. Save all your files externally; that way, if anything happens to the Precious... I mean your hard drive, you've got back-ups.

This may sound extreme, but you might even want to keep your back-up disks in a different location than the computer the originals are stored on. My backup disks are locked up in the bank; if the house burns down, at least I have one less thing to worry about.

CONCLUSION

Using hotkeys and key-combination shortcuts will vastly improve your speed and efficiency. Master the common shortcuts you learned in this chapter, and add more to your virtual vocabulary as you practice. Naming all the elements of your PSD files and using a consistent naming convention for a particular project will keep you organized, and making regular back-ups will ensure all your beautiful, well-organized artwork will survive when your computer doesn't.

QUIZ

1) WHAT DO CTRL/⌘ + C AND CTRL/⌘ + V STAND FOR?
   a) Copy and Move
   b) Copy and Paste
   c) Cut and Paste

2) WHAT IS THE FASTEST WAY TO SAVE A DOCUMENT AS ANOTHER, DIFFERENT DOCUMENT?
   a) Ctrl/⌘ + Shift + S
   b) Ctrl/⌘ + S
   c) Alt + Ctrl/⌘ + Shift + S

3) WHAT IS THE HOTKEY FOR THE BRUSH TOOL?
   a) S
   b) B
   c) R

4) WHAT SHORTCUT LETS YOU ROTATE, SKEW, AND TRANSFORM?
   a) Ctrl/⌘ + T
   b) Ctrl/⌘ + Alt + T
   c) Alt + T

5) THE ORDER AND METHOD BY WHICH YOU PERFORM TASKS IS CALLED:
   a) Workflow
   b) Pipeline
   c) Haphazard

6) YOU CAN DUPLICATE A LAYER IN THE LAYERS PALETTE BY CLICKING AND DRAGGING IT TO THE CREATE A NEW LAYER BUTTON AT THE BOTTOM OF THE PALETTE.
   a) True
   b) False
   c) N/A

7) HOLDING CTRL/⌘ AND CLICKING ON A LAYER IN THE LAYERS PALETTE IS A SHORTCUT TO:
   a) Delete Layer
   b) Load Selection
   c) Add a Layer Style

8) WHY SHOULD LAYERS BE GIVEN NAMES?
   a) So you can tell what's on them
   b) So they stay separated
   c) So they are invisible

9) WHY SHOULDN'T ORIGINAL MULTI-LAYER DOCUMENTS BE FLATTENED?
   a) Because it's harder to change individual elements of the image.
   b) Because you lose the ability to retrace your steps for future work.
   c) Both A and B

10) WHERE SHOULD BACK-UP FILES BE STORED?
   a) On your hard drive
   b) On an external storage device
   c) What's a back-up?

IN THIS CHAPTER YOU WILL LEARN ABOUT:

- What source art is used for
- Where to find source art
- Tips on making source art yourself
- Recommended equipment for digital artists

INTRODUCTION

Texturing is the art of creating visual imagery and applying it to models built with 3D applications such as Maya, Softimage, and 3d studio max. Textures – sometimes called "skins" – add color, surface, depth, and details too fine to include in the geometry of the model.

Source art is the reference material taken from real life, given to you from other artists on your team, or created yourself, and is used to gain inspiration and information for your work, and sometimes even to build the work itself. Source art is key to making great 3D work for three big reasons.

SOURCE ART AS REFERENCE

The first reason to use source art is to remember detail. Having a picture to reference is always the best way to go because the human mind will not remember all the elements of a given scene. This is especially true when dealing with high levels of detail in your work. There is no shame in letting a drawing or a camera be your memory, and your work will flourish with sound reference material behind it.

SOURCE ART AS INSPIRATION

The second reason to use source art is to get ideas. There have been a whole lot of humans on this planet since we came down from the trees. It's a good bet someone will have thought up something that works for you and your project concept. Do some research: get a book on the subject, or hop on the internet and search for sites and images in the same vein as what you're working on.

If you're working on a team, chances are you will be given a lot of concept art created in the early stages of production, not just for reference when building specific models or textures, but to put up on the walls for inspiration.

SOURCE ART AS A STARTING POINT

The third reason to use source art is to actually incorporate it into the work you are making. Creating a brick texture tile? Go outside and take a digital picture of a brick wall, load it in Photoshop, and start from there. Having a hard time recreating the texture design your concept artist gave you? Scan the artwork and build on it like a painter might use a sketch on canvas.

It is important to note that, as always, you can't use other peoples work without their permission. If the source art you're using actually appears in the final artwork (as opposed to simply being used as reference or inspiration), make sure it's something you made yourself, something someone made for you to use, or that you've gotten permission from the original artist. Using clip-art or something in the public domain is technically OK, but generally frowned-upon, especially if you're getting paid for the work.

MAKING SOURCE ART YOURSELF

There are all kinds of reasons for making your own source art, whether you're working alone or on a team. Not only is it useful for creating the art, in the case of actually incorporating photographs or paintings in your Photoshop images, but also for the planning process. It's much easier to make changes to an idea when all you've got is a pencil sketch than it is to change an idea when you've got a 30-layer Photoshop file you've been working on for days.

DRAWING AND PAINTING

In a production environment, drawn or painted source art will most likely be provided for you. If so, it is important to reproduce these source images as closely as possible, in the correct format (such as an unwrapped UV map, discussed later in the book). If the design is up to you, however, drawing may be a great place to start in order to understand the work you will make for 3D.

Painting (or using colored pencils, or whatever your preference is) is the next step of working with hand made source art. Sometimes a grayscale drawing is simply not detailed enough, and a color representation is necessary.

Drawing is a great way to figure out how to describe the important concepts of dimensionality on a 2D plane. Many 3D artists draw, and draw well. Having the ability to translate what is in your mind's eye with your hand onto a surface where others can see what you mean is a glorious power and asset. Some people can render things with minute detail directly from their memories and imagination.

SCANNERS

Scanning is the most widely used option for turning images from real life into images you can edit on a computer. It's cheap, it's easy, and it's very versatile. Scanners come in all sorts of shapes, sizes, and quality levels, though these days even the most inexpensive scanners have extraordinarily high resolution. Use them to get your drawings into Photoshop and your traditional photographs digitized. In fact, scan anything that's flat: why scan a photograph of a leaf when you can just scan the leaf?

PHOTOGRAPHY

Perhaps the most accurate and interesting method of acquiring and making use of source art is taking pictures of real people, places, and things with a camera. Photography is an art form in its own right, and bears further study if you want to take full advantage of the medium to augment your digital art. Photography can be used for getting subject-specific reference files, taking shots for direct conversion into textures, and as a way to document your projects.

A conventional, manual 35mm Single Lens Reflex (SLR) film camera is an amazingly versatile tool that every texture artist should have. These cameras use mirrors to reflect what's in the lens to the eye of the photographer, so you know exactly what the camera is seeing. They allow you to manually set the camera's features to adjust for any sort of conditions that may arise while shooting. In addition, most new cameras come with a mode that will automatically detect light, focus, and set shutter speed.

Tip: When you go out to take pictures, take notes on whatever you do, as you do it. Later, instead of wondering how you managed to get such a great shot when all the others were not so hot, you'll have a record you can use to reproduce those conditions in the future.

DIGITAL CAMERAS

Digital cameras provide an excellent option for recording reference images and shooting subjects to be added into the work. Pictures taken with a digital camera have the advantage of being able to be transferred directly to your computer from the camera, skipping development and scanning. You also immediately know whether you've got a good picture or not, without having to wait for the film to be developed.

Picture quality depends on several factors, such as the optical quality of the lens, the quality of the image-capture chip (the camera's processor), and the type of compression used to store captured images. Digital camera resolution can range from the standard 640x480 pixels, all the way up to a remarkable 2048x1536 pixels, and even beyond.

Some digital cameras store files in a proprietary format that can only be used with software provided by the camera manufacturer, but more often, digital images are stored in JPEG or TIFF format.

TABLETS

Not specifically a tool for creating source art, but worth mentioning while we're on the subject of digital art gear, drawing tablets are input devices that take the place of a mouse, and consist of a flat "workpad" that you draw on with a pen-like "stylus". Many digital artists swear by drawing tablets. Some Photoshop tools take advantage of the pressure sensitivity of a tablet. For example, a stroke with the Paint Brush(B) tool might be thick or thin depending on how hard you're pressing with the stylus, allowing for a much more painterly approach to creating digital art.

ACQUIRING SOURCE ART

Sometimes the best reference and inspiration can be found in images other people have created or captured, and there are plenty of resources to find what you're looking for. Here are some tips to help you in your search.

FINE ART

Fine Art is an excellent source of inspiration. Looking at examples of Fine Art can show you all sorts of fascinating things about mixing color, composition, how brush strokes are used, building volume, creating depth and dimension, and how to organize space. It also provides a nearly limitless variety of concepts, themes, and images from which to draw ideas.

THE INTERNET

The Internet is a vast landscape of photographs, art galleries, portfolios, and written information. A big advantage is that it's free. A disadvantage to the Internet, however, is that often the image quality is poor. Plenty of folks out there have no idea how to optimize imagery for web sites, leaving obvious artifacts, distortions, and blurriness in posted images. Be mindful of this as you surf, especially if the goal is to use appropriated images as additions to your own work. Also keep in mind that copyright laws apply to a lot of the images out there. Use your judgement when working with Internet images, and it's always best to err on the side of caution.

BOOKS AND MAGAZINES

Books and magazines are another fast and easy source of research materials. A great advantage to these is that they can be purchased in large quantities, inexpensively. They can also be ordered from distant and exotic lands, chock full of new ideas. Another great advantage is that many books and magazines are topical: if you need a lot of pictures of tattoos, there are tons of tattoo-only books and magazines. Yet another advantage is that, unlike the Internet, image quality is often great. Finally, books and magazines are highly portable, and can go along with you just about anyplace.

STOCK FOOTAGE AND DIGITAL PHOTOGRAPHS

There are many companies that specialize in selling royalty-free images to professionals for money. Usually, the purchaser has a choice of quality and dimension. Some images can be acquired for a flat fee, while other images are sold with limited usage (how often the image can be used, and what the image can be used for) or license agreements. This option can be very expensive, especially if the intent is to merely look at the image, instead of use it as an addition. Examples of businesses that sell digital photographs are Corbis (www.corbis.com) and Getty Images (www.getty-images.com).

USING SOURCE ART

After the photos have been taken and the drawings drawn, and been digitized, it's time to get them ready to use as textures. This process is largely subjective: you can infuse quite a bit of unique style into these basic operations.

Once you have a digital photo or image on the screen, first decide how you will use it. Will it be a seamless tile, or added to a map as an Overlay? Then, decide what it is that is best about the image. What is the most interesting characteristic? Is there a peculiar stain? Or a series of deep scratches? Is it perfect for tiling with no distinguishing marks? Then, decide what needs fixing. Does it need to be rotated? Does it need a color correction to add or remove a certain cast of color? Do you need to crop out just a small section? All these issues will be addressed in the next chapter, Textures and Tiling.

Lastly, remember that (for various reasons, sometimes practical and sometimes for the sake of tradition) textures need to be at a resolution that corresponds to a number of bits (128x128, 256x256, 512x512, etc). If you're working on textures that will go into a game engine, you'll probably be given the correct specifications for file type and resolution. If you're making textures for yourself, file size is a consideration: for example, if you need a nice little rust texture for a garbage can or pipe that's going to take up a small portion of the image, don't make the texture 1024x1024. That level of detail will be unnecessary and the image file will be enormous.

Photograph before Auto Color

Photograph after Auto Color

SOURCE ART GALLERY

Evil Rabbit

Dragon

This music shop has a colorful, interesting facade

Architecture source material

Jaimy McCann character art

Red devils

Patterns

Great for reference or as a background

Gunslinger Girl character art

Great source for something creepy

A great big head

Rick McCann character art

Detail shot of a small shop

CONCLUSION

In this chapter, you have learned what texturing is all about and how using source art adds to your work. It can be used for research and reference, inspiration, and even as the groundwork for the textures themselves. You learned about some of the tools of the trade, some of the better places to look for art created by other people, and got an introduction to some of the concerns you'll have to think about as you move forward creating textures.

QUIZ

1) TEXTURES GO ON 3D MODELS...
>   a) To make them rough.
>   b) To add detail.
>   c) Textures don't go on 3D models.

2) THE INTERNET IS A GREAT SOURCE OF FREE, HIGH-QUALITY IMAGERY.
>   a) True
>   b) False
>   c) N/A

3) WHY IS A DIGITAL CAMERA AN IDEAL CHOICE FOR CAPTURING PHOTOGRAPHIC IMAGES?
>   a) Because it's easy
>   b) Because it's fast
>   c) Both

4) MANUAL CAMERAS ARE EXCELLENT CHOICES FOR EVERY REASON, HOWEVER...
>   a) The image quality is poor.
>   b) You don't have much control over the camera's settings.
>   c) You have to know what you are doing to get the best results.

5) DRAWING IS AN ARCHAIC PRACTICE THAT HAS NO PLACE IN THE DIGITAL AGE.
>   a) True
>   b) False
>   c) N/A

6) WHEN TAKING PHOTOGRAPHS, WHAT IS A GOOD EXERCISE TO KEEP TRACK OF HOW YOU ARRIVED AT AN END PRODUCT?
>   a) Take notes
>   b) Commit the process to memory
>   c) Sit-ups

7) THE MOST COMMON METHOD OF DIGITIZING DRAWN AND PRINTED IMAGES IS...
>   a) Painstakingly recreating the image from scratch in Photoshop.
>   b) Using a scanner.
>   c) Using a digital camera to photograph the picture.

8) REPRESENTING SOMEONE ELSE'S ART AS YOUR OWN WITHOUT THEIR PERMISSION IS...
>   a) OK, as long as it isn't really that recognizable.
>   b) A time-honored and noble tradition.
>   c) Plagiarism.

9) LOOKING AT SOMEONE ELSE'S ART FOR INSPIRATION IS...
>   a) Not OK; all art must be 100% original.
>   b) A time-honored and noble tradition.
>   c) Plagiarism.

10) WHAT IS THE GOAL OF USING PHOTOGRAPHY FOR TEXTURE AND REFERENCE WORK?
>   a) High quality, high detail, and accurate depiction of form
>   b) Convenience
>   c) To look cool

TEXTURES AND TILING

IN THIS CHAPTER YOU WILL LEARN ABOUT:

- Painting textures using source art
- Painting textures from scratch
- Making textures from a photograph
- Making textures using layer styles
- Making seamless, repeating texture tiles
- How to use the Pattern Maker

1

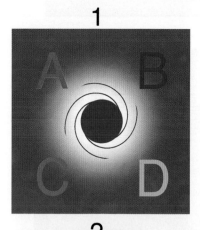

2

3

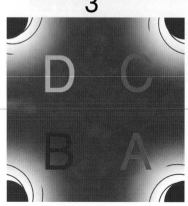

A texture tile before Offset (1), after Offset (2), and with the seams repaired (3), so it can tile seamlessly

INTRODUCTION

Texture tiles are precise squares of imagery that can be repeated without a seam, potentially carrying on infinitely. Tiles are used to create repeating surface textures, such as brick walls, asphalt grounds, tree bark, rock walls, clouds, and water. Tiles are very handy because it only takes one, or one set, to texture a surface of any size, saving you a lot of time and – particularly important in the case of video game textures – disk space.

This chapter covers various methods of tiling your textures, almost exclusively by hands-on tutorials. First, you will learn how to begin making useful textures and how to tile them. You will create a bark texture, a concrete texture, a brick texture from a photograph, and a brick texture using Photoshop Layer Styles. After the tutorials is a discussion of a few other options to use in your texturing efforts.

BARK TEXTURE TILE: AT A GLANCE

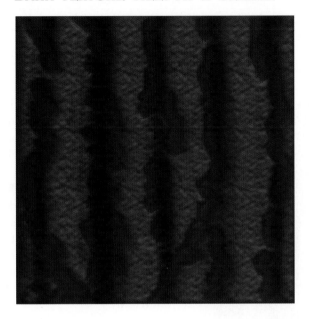

TOPICS COVERED

Paint a natural bark texture with the features of Photoshop in this tutorial.

YOU LL LEARN HOW TO:

- Paint a texture by hand using Blending effects
- Prepare to make a seamless tile by Offsetting
- Edit out seams using the Cloning(S) and Healing(J) tools

MATERIALS REQUIRED

PineBarkSource.psd for reference; search for Courseware in the File Bank at www.mesmer.com to download the work files for this book.

TUTORIAL: BARK TEXTURE TILE

The purpose of this tutorial is to paint a tree bark texture for a pine forest scene. Bark textures are useful because they are common. Remember that looking at a source is the best plan: tree bark has a great deal of detail, and is very patterned. Nature tiles itself.

Example of photographic source image: bark

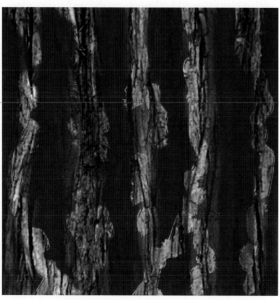

Use the Brush Tool to paint on the bark strips

STEP 1: CREATE A NEW FILE

Press Ctrl/⌘ + N for a new document, name it "Pine Bark", and give it a resolution of 512x512 with RGB color mode and a transparent background.

STEP 2: LOAD A REFERENCE IN THE BACKGROUND

Open PineBarkSource.psd and copy it to your new document, either by using Select All, Copy, and Paste (Ctrl/⌘ + A, Ctrl/⌘ + C, Ctrl/⌘ + V); or with both windows open, activate the Move(V) tool and drag the source image onto the new document. Once it's loaded into the layer stack, right-click on the layer and name it "Source Art".

Do a Ctrl/⌘ + A (select all) and then a Ctrl/⌘ + T (free transform) to scale the image so it's the same size as the new document. Hold Shift to maintain its proportions while you scale, but don't worry about it being blurry: the source picture won't appear in the final art in this case, it's just there as a guide.

Click on the Source layer in the Layers palette, drag it below Layer 1 to make it the background, and hit Lock All so the Source can't be accidentally edited. Now you can paint on the layers on top of the Source background, and simply turn it off when you are finished.

STEP 3: MAKE A BLACK BACKGROUND

Right-click on Layer 1 and call it "Black". Hit D on the keyboard to restore the foreground/background defaults. Then hit G on the keyboard to get the Paint Bucket(G) tool. Click to fill the Black layer with…yep…black. This will be the actual background for the texture, but for now click off the eyeball to make the layer invisible so you can see the Source.

STEP 4: START PAINTING STRIPS OF BARK

Now do a Shift + Ctrl/⌘ + N to create a new layer. Call it "Strips". This is the layer the bark strips will be painted on. Make sure it is the layer selected in the Layers palette.

The bark tutorial layer stack

To paint on the strips for the bark, choose a brownish hue. Select a large brush, around 80-100 pixels. Click on Wet edges and paint with 100% Opacity. Don't make the strips too straight. Bark is not perfectly linear. Paint on 4 strips in the center of the image and a half a strip on each side.

Tip: When painting anything – be it textures, master works in oil, or the walls in your house – always start with a large brush and work your way down to a smaller brush. Not only is this very efficient, but it makes sense: what could you possibly want with a detail brush, when the background hasn't been done yet?

Save the document. Call it "Pine_Bark.psd".

Next, choose a smaller brush, say around 40-50 pixels, and paint some smaller strips over the first set. Downsize the current brush with the [hotkey. Paint inside the wider stripes to thicken them up a bit. Repeat this process until you're satisfied. I used a Natural Brush (click the right-facing arrow at the top of the Brushes palette to access the drop-down for loading different brush presets) to jag up the edges of the bark strips a bit. Scroll forward and backward through the brushes with the . (period) and , (comma) keys.

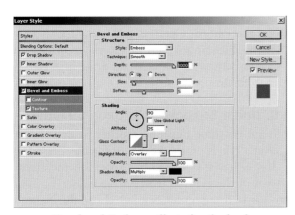

Bevel and Emboss effects for the bark

STEP 5: MAKE A BROWN FILL LAYER

Make another layer with Shift + Ctrl/⌘ + N and name it "Brown Fill". Drag it underneath the Strips layer. Hit G on the keyboard and fill this layer with the same brown used to paint the strips. Next, click and drag the Strips layer onto the Create New Layer Icon on the bottom of the Layers palette to duplicate the layer.

There are now five layers in the layer stack: one Source image, one Black layer, one Brown Fill layer, and two versions of the Strips layer. Right-click on the second version of the Strips layer and call it "Strips II". Click on the Strips II eyeball to make the layer invisible. We'll turn it back on later.

STEP 6: ADD AN EMBOSS EFFECT TO THE STRIPS

Now click back on Strips in the Layers palette. Right-click on it, choose Blending Options, and check Bevel and Emboss. Click to highlight Bevel and Emboss to access its settings. Set the Layer Style to Style: Emboss, Technique: Smooth, Depth: -1000, Size: 8, and Soften: 5.

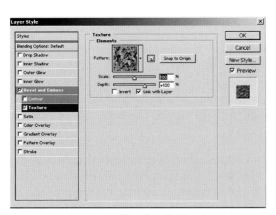

Pattern effect for the bark

Then change the light direction. In an effort to get as versatile a light direction as possible, uncheck Use Global Light, try a few different Angle settings (I chose 90 degrees), and enter 25 in the Altitude field to get fairly high relief. Finally, change the blending of the Highlight Mode to Overlay and 100% Opacity, and change the Shadow Mode blending to 100% Opacity, leaving it on Multiply.

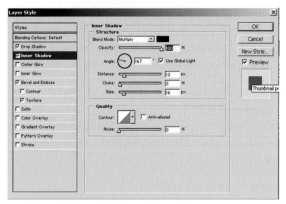

Inner Shadow effect for the bark

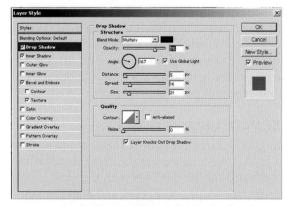

Drop Shadow effects for the bark

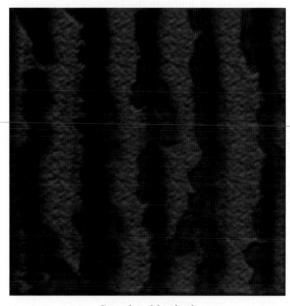

Completed bark tile

Next check the Texture box beneath Bevel and Emboss, and click on the word Texture to access its settings. Set the Pattern to Wrinkles with a Scale of 80% and a Depth of 15. Click OK. Note: if all you see when you click the pattern drop-down are thumbnails, click the right-facing arrow in the pattern drop-down and select Small or Large List to see the names of the patterns in addition to their thumbnails.

STEP 7: ADD BEVEL AND EMBOSS AND PATTERN OVERLAY EFFECTS TO THE BROWN FILL LAYER

Click on the Brown Fill layer to activate it, right-click, and choose Blending Options. Select Bevel and Emboss. Set Size to 90 and Soften to 0. Uncheck Use Global Light Source and type in a value of 90 degrees for Angle. Change the Highlight Mode to Overlay and crank it up to 100%. Bump up the Shadow Mode to 100% also. Next, click on Texture, select Clouds from the Patterns, set Scale to 150, and Depth to 20. Last, click the Invert button.

Now select the Pattern Overlay style and click to activate. Set the Blending Mode to Overlay, Opacity to 100%, set the Pattern to Clouds, and Scale it at 100%. Hit Enter to finalize.

STEP 8: INNER SHADOW, AND DROP SHADOW

Time to put on some finishing touches. Click on the Strips layer. Hit E on the keyboard for the Eraser(E) Tool. If you haven't done so yet, click on the arrow drop-down of the brushes icon on the Eraser(E) Tool Options bar to bring up the brushes. Load the Natural Brushes and Faux Finish brushes. Choose one that's jagged like pine bark and erase along the edges of the strips. Add some depth with this tool and break up the strong linear style of it here and there.

Once these strokes are completed, access the Blending Options for the Strips layer and give it an Inner Shadow to darken the edges of the brush strokes. Set the Inner Shadow 's Blending Mode to Multiply, Opacity to 100%, Angle to 167 degrees, Distance to 13, Choke to 3, and Size to 6.

Next add a Drop Shadow to accentuate the affect of the Bevel and Emboss. Click on Drop Shadow and experiment with the settings. I set the Blending Mode to Multiply, Opacity to 75%, Angle to 167 degrees, Distance to 5, Spread to 16, and Size to 21.

Hit OK when you are satisfied.

STEP 9: LIGHTEN THE IMAGE USING THE STRIPS II LAYER

Drag the Strips II layer to the top of the stack (if it isn't there already) and click the small blank square to summon the eyeball icon, indicating the layer is visible again. Use this layer to lighten the effect of the heavily embossed Strips layer by making it less opaque (50% opacity is what I used), and taking a few runs through it with the Eraser(E) tool as you did for the Strips layer. You might also experiment with the Image→Adjustments→Hue/Saturation command on the Strips II layer to tweak its effect on the rest of the image.

STEP 10: FINISHING TOUCHES

I added a Filter→Blur→Gaussian Blur of 1 to blur out some of edges that were too sharp, then added a Filter→Sharpen→Unsharp Mask to redistribute the focus. Just be sure to keep the original PSD intact with all of the layers unflattened so you can go back and tweak some more, depending on the final results you are striving for.

STEP 11: PREPARE TO MAKE THE BARK TEXTURE A SEAMLESS TILE

Now it's time to get this baby seamless so your tree doesn't look like it's been sliced up, then stacked. The secret is to offset the image so the middle (which fits together seamlessly already) is the outer edge, and the outer edge is in the middle, ready for you to repair the seam.

In order for the Offset filter to work on the whole image, the whole image needs to be on one layer, but you don't want to flatten your original. So, save the original Pine_Bark.psd file as Pine_Bark_Flat.psd using File→Save As, then choose Layer→Flatten Image from the top menu bar to compress your new copy into one layer (discarding the hidden Source layer, as prompted).

STEP 12: OFFSET THE FLATTENED IMAGE

With Pine_Bark_Flat.psd selected, do a Filter→Other→Offset. With Preview and Wrap Around checked, enter a few different values into the Horizontal and Vertical fields to see the effect.

Bark tile offset for eliminating seams

Since the pixel dimensions of this file are 512x512, enter 256 and 256 so the tile is divided into 4 equal sections. Hit Enter to finalize the filter.

STEP 13: CLONE CLEAN PARTS OVER THE SEAMS

Hit S on the keyboard for the Clone Stamp(S) tool. This part is tricky so look alive. What you want to do is get rid of the seams: you can see where it does not match up along the cross-section in the center of the tile. You can see the dark areas along the edges caused by the bevel. Formerly, this process would have been accomplished with careful cloning, but Photoshop 7.0 has introduced a new tool: the Healing(J) Tool, which will be used in partnership with the Clone Stamp(S) tool to clean up this tile.

Start with a medium-sized cloning brush. With this brush, the goal is to first rough out the main problem areas. Alt + click to specify the source point and then clone away the seams. You can use a cloning brush at full Opacity, and Maximum hardness (to retain high detail), while not worrying about the hard edges of your brush being visible. The Healing(J) tool will fix that.

STEP 14: COLOR-CORRECT THE EDGES OF THE CLONE STROKES

Once you have roughly cloned out the seams, hit J on the keyboard to select the Healing(J) Tool. Choose a medium brush of 40 pixels or so, set the Blending Mode to Normal, and check Source. Now, as with the Clone(S) tool, Alt + click to specify a source point and slick around the areas where the brush edges are obvious. The Healing(J) tool will match the color and light of the source point to make its repairs. Everything will wind up matching perfectly, edits indistinguishable to even the keenest eye.

This technique is far superior to previous techniques for removing seams. It is fast, efficient, and the results are really great. No more worrying about loss of detail, or agonizing hours fine-tuning everything. Alright!

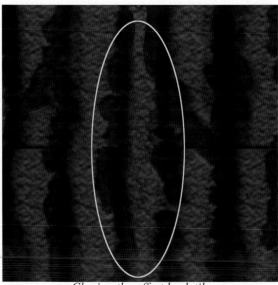
Cloning the offset bark tile

Tip: Use Ctrl/⌘ + Z to undo one step and Ctrl/⌘ + Alt + Z for multiple undo. Remember not use a soft brush, otherwise the textures will lose detail and you'll get fuzzy spots. Also try not to have any features that are too distinguishable from the overall texture. A large knot, for instance, will repeat over and over in a very regular way that will look silly.

When you can Offset the image any amount without seeing a seam, your tile is done. Try out your tile by making a new document that is 1024x1024 and paste four copies of the tile into it, arranging them so they fill the space. If you have immediate access to a 3D application and already know how to set a texture to repeat over a model (such as setting the model's material to be the texture you just created), test this texture out. You may have to save the file as a different type, like TIF or BMP, depending on the 3D application.

These methods work for just about any sort of surface tile you might want to make: concrete, wood, metal, grass...

CONCRETE TEXTURE: AT A GLANCE

TOPICS COVERED

In this tutorial you'll create a concrete texture out of a few brush strokes and a whole lot of Layer Effects. Instead of a small texture that tiles seamlessly, it will be a large texture that doesn't repeat at all.

YOU LL LEARN HOW TO:

- Create a texture with Layer Effects
- Quickly and efficiently make a large texture out of a smaller one

Concrete step 1

Concrete step 2

Concrete step 3

TUTORIAL: CONCRETE TEXTURE

The concrete created here will become the wall surface of a building in the city scene that is one of the objectives of this book. It will be a different style of texture than the bark tile, created using mostly Layer Effects in the layer Blending Options.

STEP 1: CREATE A NEW DOCUMENT

Ctrl/⌘ + N (the equivalent of File→New) to create a new document. Name it "Concrete", set it to 512x512 resolution, RGB color mode, and Transparent background.

STEP 2: CREATE A BASE SURFACE COLOR AND ADD NOISE TO IT

Do a Shift + Ctrl/⌘ + N to create a new layer. Name it "Main Surface". Next, click on the Foreground swatch and choose a gray in the middle range, using the Paint Bucket(G) tool to fill the Main Surface layer with gray. Choose Filter > Noise→Add Noise from the top menu bar. Check Gaussian and Monochromatic, and hit Enter to apply the Noise filter.

STEP 3: ADD ANOTHER LAYER WITH A STONE PATTERN

Do another Shift + Ctrl/⌘ + N to create a new layer and name it "Surface 2". Change the Blending Mode of the entire layer to Color Dodge (either in the Create New Layer dialog, or afterwards in the Layers palette); the stone pattern you're about to create will blend with the noisy Main Surface layer.

Fill this new layer with a lighter gray value. Right-click on Surface 2 in the Layers palette, choose Blending Options, and give it a Pattern Overlay. Set the Pattern Overlay Layer Style to Multiply with 75% Opacity. Open up the list of patterns, and click on the right-facing arrow to load the Rock Patterns presets. Choose the Stone pattern, and set its scale to 715.

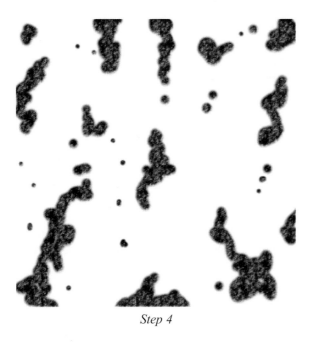

Step 4

STEP 4: ADD SOME WEAR AND TEAR

Do another Shift + Ctrl/⌘ + N to create... yes, another layer. Call it "Erosion Bevel", the purpose of the style and which style is associated with the layer. Hit B on the keyboard for the Brush(B) Tool and set the brush Options to something like Diameter 100, Hardness 0%, with 100% Opacity and Normal blending mode.

Paint some marks on the layer to represent variations in height on an uneven concrete surface. Don't overdo it, we're adding more details soon.

Do a Ctrl/⌘ + S to save the file.

After you're happy, set the Erosion Bevel Layer mode to Overlay. Right-click, access the Blending Options dialog, and click Bevel and Emboss. Make the Emboss effect deep, but smooth and soft. I chose Emboss style with Smooth technique and a Depth of 75%, Size 8, Soften 1, Gloss Countour Gaussian, and Soft and Hard Light for Highlight and Shadow Mode, respectively.

Then, click on the texture box. Select the Clouds Pattern at a Scale of 200 and a Depth of 100. Click the foreground swatch to set the paint color. Choose a very dark (but not black) gray.

STEP 5: ADD ANOTHER LEVEL OF DETAIL

Time for another new layer. Hopefully, you know the shortcut by now, but I'll help you out: Shift + Ctrl/⌘ + N. Name it "Erosion Clouds", and set its Blending Mode to Overlay. Get out the Brush(B) tool and set it to something like Diameter 40, Hardness 35.

Concrete step 5

Now paint on some more strokes. I chose to follow the contours of some of the raised strokes from the last layer. The idea is to add more depth and dimension to the texture. Add a Bevel and Emboss Layer Effect (right-click on the Erosion Clouds layer in the Layers palette, then Blending Options). Set the style to Inner Bevel, which will make these divots and craters look recessed. The technique should be Smooth, with a medium Depth and Size; I chose 31 and 5, but at this point you probably have a good enough idea of the effects of these settings to set it to whatever you like. Setting the Gloss Contour to Ring (again, hit the right-arrow drop-down and choose Large or Small List if you can't see the names of the presets next to the thumbnails) will make the bevel bumpier. Finally, set Highlights and Shadows to Overlay, and decrease the Shadow Opacity to 65% so it's not quite so harsh.

Next, click on the Texture box of the Bevel and Emboss style. Set the Pattern to Clouds with a Scale of 47 and Depth of 63, and Invert the pattern. That adds a cloud pattern to the Bevel effect; add another to the whole layer: check Pattern Overlay and set it to Blend Mode Soft Light, choose the Clouds pattern, Scale 99%, and Invert it as well.

Do a Ctrl/⌘ + S to save.

Completed concrete tile

STEP 6: YET ANOTHER LEVEL OF DETAIL

Next add some smaller holes and pits. Create a new layer named "Pits". Hit D on the

keyboard for the default (black/white) foreground/background swatches. Next, hit B for a brush and set the brush to about Diameter and Hardness 50.

Now paint on some asymmetrical, rounded organic shapes that are meant to represent chunks of concrete that have actually left the building. Make it gritty. Make it old. Make it belong to the bad part of town.

Make the holes look recessed with an Inner Shadow layer effect. I used Multiply Blending Mode, 75% Opacity, Distance 8, Choke 2, Size 2, and Cone Contour.

Add some more effects to the Pits layer: Bevel and Emboss, and a Clouds Texture to break up the uniformity.

Click OK to finalize, and there you have it: a very interesting concrete texture ready

for some old apartment walls. You can open up ConcreteComplete.psd from the book file directory to see my results and deconstruct it to see how I got them.

STEP 7: MAKE A LARGE, UNIQUE TEXTURE FROM THE TILE

Unlike the previous tutorial, this concrete is not designed specifically for tiling seamlessly with copies of itself. A way to make great map art fast is to create tiles that can be easily replicated with the duplication option of the Move(V) tool, flattened together, and then edited with the Clone Stamp(S) tool to remove repetitive characteristics. Creating a small section of texture then making variations of it to create a larger, unique texture is a great method. It's also a great way to get away from the more repetitive tileable versions of similar textures, though it's more appropriate for video or effects work where you can afford to have enormous textures that are unique throughout. I call it "Texture Templating".

Create a dupe of the concrete tile you have just made, name it concreteflat.psd, and flatten it with a Layer→Flatten Image. Choose Image→Canvas Size from the top menu bar, and set the pixel dimensions to 1536x1536, tripling the size of the image. Using the Move(V) tool + Alt, click and drag on the tile to duplicate it. Keep Shift held down to align the tiles. Create a 3x3 grid of the tiles, select the top texture layer, and Ctrl + E to flatten then down.

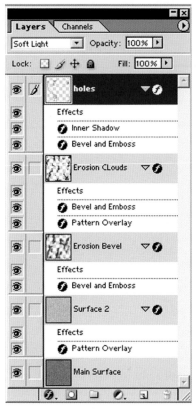

Layer stack for the concrete

Now you will see a pattern that has too many outstanding and obvious repeating features. Bust out the Cloning(S) and Healing(J) tools to even out the pattern so that it is not so monotonous. Use your own sense of aesthetics and balance to decide on the look you want. The finished product is a new texture created from a single tile that was done very quickly and efficiently.

Example 1 of concrete tile

Example 2 of concrete tile

TILE FROM A PHOTOGRAPH: AT A GLANCE

TOPICS COVERED

In this tutorial you'll create a tileable brick texture out of a photograph of a brick wall. The questions posed at the end of the Source Art chapter will be addressed, and you'll pick up some handy tips and tricks along the way.

YOU LL LEARN HOW TO:

- Look at a photograph for tiling
- Use transform mode to fix perspective
- Crop the tile
- Create a texture from a photograph

MATERIALS REQUIRED

The image file "bricksimageediting.psd" located in the courseware folder for this book, which you can download from the File Bank at www.mesmer.com.

TUTORIAL: TILE FROM A PHOTOGRAPH

Creating textures from photographs is a big part of texturing work. The upcoming tutorial will show you how to convert a digitized photograph into a tileable brick texture.

STEP 1: LOOK AT THE PHOTOGRAPH

Open the bricksimageediting.psd. This shot will become a seamlessly tiled brick texture for an urban alley scene. First, double-click on the layer that says Background to make it an active layer and enter a name for the layer, like "Original". Examine the picture. Apparently the photographer didn't have a tripod and was listing slightly to the right, and was not precisely perpendicular to the wall. The image is tilted and warped, which is not acceptable for a tile.

STEP 2: USE FREE TRANSFORM MODE TO FIX THE TILT AND WARP

Do a Ctrl/⌘ + A to select the entire image and then a Ctrl/⌘ + T to get into Free Transform mode. (Note: If you're in Standard Screen Mode and the window for the image is not maximized, you may need to stretch the window by clicking and dragging on the lower-right corner, so that you can see the points on the bounding box.)

Original photo of a brick wall

Holding down the Ctrl/⌘ key while manipulating the anchor points of the box will activate Skew mode in Free Transform. Carefully experiment with manipulating the anchor points of the box. Take care here: it is not a good idea to go nuts with the transform Tool; the results will be blurry, overstretched surfaces that are obviously poorly handled. Remember that every Crop and Transform you make resamples the image, leaving less and less detail each time.

If you want to be precise, create a new layer and use the Line(U) tool to draw several straight (hold Shift) horizontal lines across the new layer, lined up with the mortar on the left side. Then, activate Free Transform on the Original layer and Skew the points on the right side so the mortar lines up with the other ends of your straight lines. Hit Enter to finalize the Transform, and delete the new layer with the lines drawn on it.

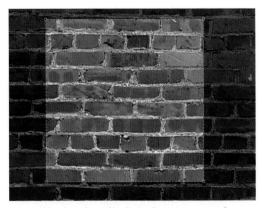

The brick wall photo being cropped

STEP 3: GET INFO BEFORE YOU CROP

With the selection still active (Ctrl/⌘ + A to Select All if you lost it), check out the Info palette to determine its exact pixel dimensions. In this example, the picture was taken with a digital camera set to an unfortunately low resolution: 640 x 480. Since the image is not large enough to accommodate a 512x512 crop, which is on the large side anyway, then 256x256 is the next best thing. (If the tile absolutely needed to be 512x512, the best thing to do would be to take another picture at higher resolution, because scaling it up would make it blurry.) An even smaller bit-sized dimension would be 128x128, another oft-used width and height. Do a Ctrl/⌘ + D to Deselect.

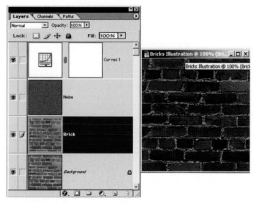

Layer stack for the bricks

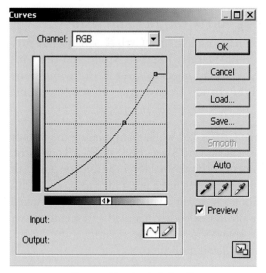

Curves for the bricks tile

STEP 4: CROP THE IMAGE INTO A 256x256 SQUARE

Go up to the Options bar for the Crop(C) tool and type 256 into the width and height fields (make sure the unit of measurement is set to Pixels in Edit→Preferences→Units & Rulers). The crop box you draw will be constrained to a square, and the area within it will be scaled to 256x256 when the Crop operation is complete. Make sure the crop area you draw is greater than or equal to 256x256; if it's less it will be scaled up, causing blurriness.

Draw a crop area and manipulate its location and scale before completing the operation. Try to frame the texture with the crop marquee in such a way that when it comes time to tile the swatch the process will go easier: try to visualize the texture as a wraparound. The sides of the crop area should divide the bricks at the edges horizontally in half. The top and bottom of the crop area can either divide bricks vertically in half, or be aligned to the horizontal strips of mortar. That way, when it comes time to clone those bricks, they will be more evenly balanced. Once you have the marquee placed where you want it, hit Enter to complete the crop. Now you've got a perfectly sized texture tile to begin working with.

STEP 5: PREPARE THE BRICKS FOR EDITING

The photograph is a great starting point but don't be constrained by it: you can make it a wall of gold bricks, or shade it like a cartoon, or whatever you need. In this case, this texture is for a dilapidated building on the wrong side of the tracks, but these bricks are fairly clean. Let's rough them up a bit.

Leave the Background layer and make sure it's locked up, so you have an untouched original left in the PSD file. Duplicate the Background layer and name it "Brick"; this will be the brick base that actually gets edited.

STEP 6: ADD A RED-GRAY OVERLAY LAYER WITH NOISE

Create another new layer with a Shift + Ctrl/⌘ + N (or click the icon o the bottom of the layers palette). Name it "Noise", set its Blending Mode to Overlay, and lower its Opacity to around 70%. Hit G on the keyboard for the Paint Bucket(G) tool and, with a red-tinged medium gray selected as the foreground color, click to fill the layer. Next do a Filter→Noise→Add Noise and set the Filter to Amount 7, Gaussian, Monochromatic.

STEP 7: MAKE A COLOR CURVE ADJUSTMENT LAYER TO DARKEN THE IMAGE

Click on the Create New Fill or Adjustment Layer icon at the bottom of the Layers palette, and choosing Curves. Double-click on the new Adjustment Layer in the Layers palette to access its controls. Add a point to the curve near the middle and pull it down a bit on the graph. The effect is similar to lowering the Gamma: the image is darkened overall but the darkest and lightest points are changed least, preserving the contrast.

STEP 8: ADD GRIME TO THE MORTAR

The mortar between the bricks is way too pristine for a seedy urban street. Try a manual approach: use the Burn(O) tool to darken those bright whites. Bear in mind that too drastic of a darkening will not look natural and any features that stand out too much will make the tiling obvious when it's repeated over a surface. In the Burn(O) tool Options, lower the exposure to around 10% and set the Range to Highlights so the strokes don't affect the dark parts of the image as much.

STEP 9: SAVE THE ORIGINAL, THEN FLATTEN AND OFFSET

As always, make sure you retain the original Photoshop document complete with your layers intact. Save the original (if you haven't already) named bricks_original.psd, and make a copy using Save As and name it bricks_flat.psd. In the bricks_flat.psd, do a Layer→Flatten Image.

Do a Filter→Other→Offset and enter in 128 (half the actual resolution) for both axes. Make sure Wrap Around is checked, and hit Enter. Hit Z on the keyboard and click in the image to zoom in.

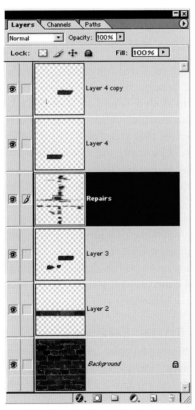

The Sneaky Patch Technique

STEP 10: BEGIN REPAIRING THE SEAMS

This time, make the seam repairs on a separate layer instead of right on the original. Create a new layer and call it "Repairs". Hit S on the keyboard for the Clone Stamp(S) tool and check Use All Layers in the Options bar. In this case a totally soft brush will not be good because it will have the effect of blurring out the fine details of the texture, so set your brush's Hardness to around 50. With the Repairs layer selected, set to work cloning out the seams of the texture. Change the brush settings to whatever you need to do the best possible job.

STEP 11: SNEAKY PATCH JOB TECHNIQUE

Here's a quick and dirty way to deal with realistic textures that are fairly complicated. I call it the Sneaky Patch Job Technique. Look carefully at the center of the texture where the top and bottoms of the original swatch meet after offsetting. Unless you were way more careful than I was when you cropped the image back in Step 4, there may be too much brick and not enough grout. To fix this fast, find a section of the swatch that is already seamless. Take the Rectangular Marquee(M) tool and surround a brick, including half of the mortar above and below. Making sure the Background layer is selected, do a Ctrl/⌘ + C to copy and then a Ctrl/⌘ + V to paste. Hit V to switch to the Move(V) tool and drag the new layer of bricks up to the bad area. You can see this helps a lot but will take some painting to make it perfect.

In mine, there's also a light colored brick in there that really sticks out. I used basically the same technique as in the previous paragraph to steal a less obvious brick from elsewhere in the image, this time using the Freehand Lasso(L) tool. Repeat the copy and paste maneuver.

STEP 12: FINAL TOUCHES WITH THE CLONE(S) AND HEALING(J) TOOLS

Click back on the Repairs layer and resume cloning and healing. Repair the rest of the seams in the image, periodically using Offset in various amounts to make sure you're not creating new seams at the edges. Remove any features that stand out too much: the bricks shouldn't all be identical, but anything that's too distinct will make the tile repetition obvious, which looks bad.

Pattern defined for use with the Pattern Maker

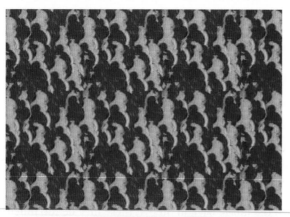

Resulting pattern tile

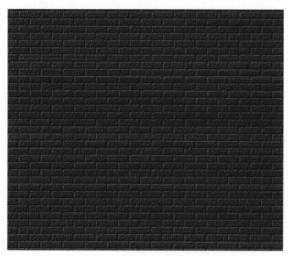

The Photoshop bricks layer style

OTHER TILING TECHNIQUES

There are other ways to tile patterns with Photoshop, such as Layer Styles, the new Pattern Maker tool, and Four Sections tiling, which comes in very handy for seamlessly tiling simple patters quickly.

THE PATTERN MAKER

The Pattern Maker tool is located under the Filter drop-down menu, and is new to Photoshop 7.0. It's a little engine designed to take a swatch of pattern and turn it into a larger, seamless pattern that can then be used as a source for cloning, or as an image all its own, destined to be mapped to a 3D model.

The Pattern Maker can get workable results from the smallest of interesting details. Say you have an image that has an area within it that would be a cool background, or wall, or hat texture. Use the rectangular Marquee(M) Tool to select that area you like, then do a Filter→Pattern Maker. The entire image is included in the Pattern Maker dialog, leaving the selection active. Set the dimensions you want your tile to be and click on the Generate button. The selection chosen from the original image will be made into a new pattern right before your very eyes. Keep clicking until you have one you like. The tile samples will be stored in the Pattern Maker's history at the bottom of the dialog, which has forward and backward controls to flip through the tiles you've generated. Click OK when you're happy.

PHOTOSHOP LAYER STYLES: EXERCISE

The Layer Styles in Photoshop offer many options for creating textured surfaces. Perform this short exercise to create another brick texture from scratch. Though quite obviously of Photoshop Preset origin, these bricks can always be painted on and added to if some disguise is needed.

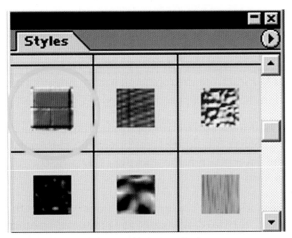

The Bricks Layer Style

A wood texture before tiling

Marquee for tiling

Create a new 512x512 document and select White for the content background. In the Styles palette, click the right-facing arrow to get the Presets drop-down, and load the Textures style set. Click the right-facing arrow again and select Small or Large list so you can see the names of the Layer Styles. Make a new layer, and with it selected, pick the Brick Wall Layer Style.

The Layer Styles are really just a set of Blending Mode option Presets: the Brick Wall style adds a Pattern Overlay, Color Overlay, and a Bevel and Emboss to make the brick pattern three-dimensional. You can edit any of these settings using the standard method: in the Layers palette, right-click on the layer and choose Blending Options, or double-click on one of the Blending Options below the layer. To edit the look of the bricks in some other way (like scaling them or painting on top of them), flatten the image.

This is quite a bit easier and faster than other methods covered above. However, these bricks are very obviously made with some kind of default pattern (and are much less realistic than the brick texture made from a photograph), which may or may not be appropriate for what you're working on.

FOUR-SECTION TILING: EXERCISE

This is a quick and dirty method to create a seamless tile, best used for textures with even edges and consistent patterning. Open FourSectionsWood.psd (a 256x256 photograph of a hardwood floor), located in the file download folder.

Choose the Selection Marquee(M) tool, and in the Options bar, and set the Style to Fixed Size with a Width and Height of 128, and click once near the lower-right corner of the image to summon a selection box that takes up a quarter of the canvas and is snugly and precisely packed in the lower-right quadrant.

Now we're going to fill the canvas with copies of the corner section, flipped around. Copy (Ctrl/⌘ + C) the selection, and Paste (Ctrl/⌘ + V) with the selection still active so the image is pasted in the same spot. A new layer (Layer 1) is created with just the lower-right quadrant of the wood picture. Rename the layer "A". You might want to turn off the visibility (click the eyeball icon) of the Background layer so you can better see what's going on in the next few steps.

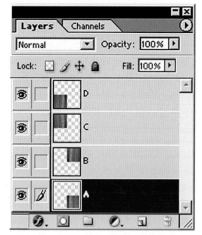

Layer stack for the wood exercise

Duplicate layer A by clicking on it in the Layers palette and dragging it down to the Create a New Layer icon (the page with a corner turned); rename the new layer A copy "B". Select layer B in the Layers palette, Select All (important!) with Ctrl/⌘ + A, and choose Edit→Transform→Flip Vertical from the top menu bar. A mirror image of the lower-right section should be flipped to the upper-right.

Repeat the process on B, using Flip Horizontal instead: duplicate layer B, rename the dupe "C", Select All, Edit→Transform→Flip Horizontal. Repeat again: duplicate layer C, rename the dupe "D", Select All, Edit→Transform→Flip Vertical.

In the center of the image, it's easy to see how the sections blend together. In the case of this wood, the two dark boards being next to each other in the middle doesn't look good. Get out the Clone Stamp(S) tool, or use the Sneaky Patch Job Technique to steal one of the other boards so there aren't two dark ones in a row. Done! Do a Save As (not Save, or you'll overwrite the original file that came with the download) and name it "foursection_original.psd", then Save As again and name it "foursection_flat.psd". Flatten the image and try different Offset values: no seams.

The results of four-section tiling aren't always as slick as the Offset/clone/heal method, but this technique is extremely fast and will work in a pinch.

Coincidentally, though, the boards being perfectly vertical and more or less the same color from top to bottom means there's hardly any seam to fix using the Offset method anyway. Try it out on the original FourSectionsWood.psd file.

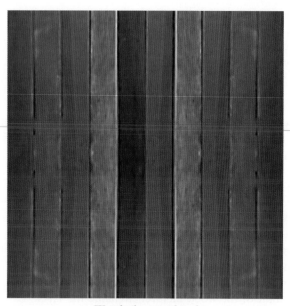

Wood tile completed

TRANSITION TILES

Sometimes, particularly when making terrain, you need to have a smooth transition between two different textures. If the two textures are repeating tiles, the transition needs to be a tile too. For example, you might have three tiles for a terrain that changes from grass to dirt: a grass tile that can be repeated to cover the grassy area, a dirt tile for the dirt area, and a transition tile that blends between the two.

To create a transition tile, first complete the final versions of the two tiles that need to be connected. Create a new document that is the same size as the two tiles, and Paste them into it as separate layers. Use the Eraser(E) tool on the top layer to get rid of one half of that layer. (This example assumes the transition tile has a vertical split.)

Create a new (third) layer, and paint, clone, and add effects as needed to get the kind of graphical transition you want, taking care not to make any changes to the left or right edges of the tile, which you know will already blend seamlessly into their corresponding texture tile. When it's time to shift the image around to repair the seam, choose only Vertical in the Offset dialog, leaving the Horizontal Offset at 0. Then, when the seam is fixed, Offset the image again in the opposite direction (enter a negative number), putting it back precisely where it was before you Offset it the first time. Otherwise, there will be a seam between the original tiles and the new transition tile when they are put side by side.

CONCLUSION

You can now make textures from scratch in a variety of different ways using Photoshop features, and you can create textures from photographs. The Mysteries of the Seamless Texture have been revealed to you: combined with the Offset filter, nothing can defy your will. You are also armed with several other methods of tiling, a few good tricks, and hopefully hotkey and shortcut use are becoming second nature.

QUIZ

1) WHAT IS A SEAMLESS, TILEABLE TEXTURE?
   a) A texture that has no visible start or finish
   b) A texture that can continue on infinitely
   c) Both

2) WHICH OF THESE RESOLUTIONS IS NOT APPROPRIATE FOR A TEXTURE MAP?
   a) 256x256
   b) 512x512
   c) 1024x768

3) WHICH FILTER IS USED FOR OFFSETTING TEXTURE TILES?
   a) Other
   b) Offset
   c) Wrap Around

4) WHAT IS A HANDY TECHNIQUE FOR CREATING REALISTIC TEXTURES?
   a) Importing a source image into the layer stack
   b) Staring out your window
   c) Drawing from your head

5) WHAT DOES IT MEAN TO CREATE A PHOTOSHOP TEXTURE "FROM SCRATCH"?
   a) That you have the recipe
   b) That you can create great textures exclusively from Photoshop's in-house features
   c) That you start from a photographed texture

6) WHAT IS THE MOST IMPORTANT TOOL FOR TEXTURE REPAIRS?
   a) The Move(V) Tool
   b) Transform Mode
   c) The Clone Stamp(S) Tool

7) WHICH TECHNIQUE BELOW OFFERS A QUICK WAY TO MAKE FAIRLY DIFFICULT REPAIRS?
   a) The Sneaky Patch Job Technique
   b) Skewing the perspective
   c) Cloning

8) WHAT IS A FAST METHOD OF TILING FOR SIMPLER TEXTURES?
   a) The Sneaky Patch Job Technique
   b) Offsetting
   c) Four-section tiling

9) LAYER STYLES CHOSEN FROM THE STYLES PALETTE ARE:
   a) Unique operations for special circumstances
   b) Preset combinations of standard Blending Modes
   c) Preset images that can Overlay a layer

10) WHAT IS A GREAT FILTER TO USE FOR ADDING GRIT AND TEXTURE TO YOUR TILES?
   a) Clouds
   b) Sumi-e
   c) Add Noise

JOHN GRONQUIST

3D ARTIST

GAS POWERED GAMES

What is your job?

I'm a 3D Artist for Gas Powered Games in Kirkland, WA - one of seven artists. As artists here, we keep things pretty versatile, mixing it up with just about everything: interface elements, characters, animation, modeling, and textures. We've just released Dungeon Siege, an action-oriented all-3D RPG.

How did you get started in the game industry?

Pure luck. I was working as a programmer at the time, and downloaded a TrueSpace demo from the Internet. I fell in love with it and started doing sci-fi stuff. So I saved up and bought Lightwave, and soon after that, I got a job doing a couple covers for the Babylon 5 role-playing game. Then I started pitching myself to game companies and hooked up with Chris Taylor (head of GPG) while he was still at Cavedog. It all happened in about 8 months. It can happen, it just boils down to losing a lot of sleep.

How did you learn the tools you use?

Totally self-taught. I just started playing around and figuring things out, and upgraded my skills from there. Books and online communities were a massive amount of help.

Art by Jon Gronquist

Art by Jon Gronquist

How do you use Photoshop?

I use Photoshop with another paint program, Painter 7.0. Both of these programs have painting tools, but Photoshop has things other painting programs don't, like filtering options and transforming tools. With two painting programs, you can really add to the quality of texture work. For Dungeon Siege we paid a lot of attention to the quality of our textures, making sure they were all even and of the same resolution. We wanted a great-looking game.

Which 3D packages do you work with?

I work with 3D Studio Max at work. We are also one of only a few game companies right now that is shipping a Gmax Pack, a free version of Studio Max gamers can use to modify game content. It's a really great way to see how games are made, and what some of the technical issues are that are involved with making games.

At home, I use Lightwave. It's a really great program for creating models fast. More of a common-sense tool. It's also great for fast and efficient vertex weighting for characters. Lightwave would be a great program to start with, and comes in a student version.

How long have your worked in the industry?

I've worked in the game industry for about 5 years, in Seattle. For graphic artists the choice of whether to stay here or go to a broader job market is always an issue. I like Seattle because it's a good community.

How early do you have to get up? How late do you have to stay?

We've been in crunch time for about 2 and a half years now. Lots of late nights and hard work. But everyone loves what they do here. And we're very happy with our game.

The hours are always an issue in the gaming industry. Conflicts with family and friends are inevitable, as well as health issues related to stress. I try to keep distractions down to a minimum at work and get as much done as possible during the day, to reduce the amount of late-night catch up. But in the end there's always more work to do that can be done, and you have to constantly balance your priorities and personal needs again and again and again.

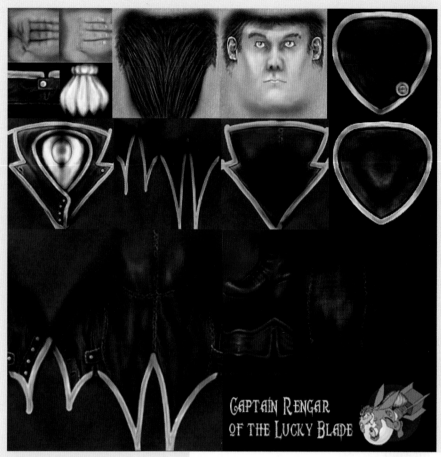

CAPTAIN RENGAR
OF THE LUCKY BLADE

It's just part of the job. Still it's less stressful than being a paramedic or something like that, so I try to keep that in mind when things get bumpy.

What are your interests outside the job?

I'm a pretty domestically oriented guy. I have a family I like to spend time with and I like to be outside working in the yard or around the house. I also have a small orchard on my property that I tend to. Relaxing stuff. And, I'm working on 3D illustrations for children's books, a hobby of mine.

Another thing I'd like to do more is get outdoors and do some painting. Traditional art skills are very important for artists working in the 3D industry. These skills help you know how to look at and evaluate your work from a greater perspective than the limits of the 3D-application tool. Art is a learning process that never ends.

Art by Jon Gronquist

What games do you play?

I like to play role-playing games, our game Dungeon Siege, Baldur's Gate, and first person shooters like Tribes 2. I also play console games like Super Monkey Ball on the GameCube, with my two sons.

Where do you find inspiration for your work?

Inspiration's always elusive. Getting outside is always good to clear the head and fill it with new ideas. And when that doesn't work there's always Google image search or Gettyone.com.

Do you have an ultimate goal for your career?

Continue to work in the local games industry until my house is paid off and then illustrate books from my basement until the cows come home.

What's the best advice you could give to new artists entering the industry?

Stay in love with it. Love every little dinky bit about it. Play with it. Don't get frustrated, or depressed, or worry about being as good as the guys at ILM. Enjoy it as much as you can. Enjoy every thing you have to learn, no matter how painful it is. Learn to observe everything as a lifestyle. Keep with it and work hard.

7   BUMP MAPS AND ALPHA CHANNELS

IN THIS CHAPTER YOU WILL LEARN ABOUT:

- How to add depth and dimension to your work with bump maps
- Using Lighting Effects and the Texturizer to add to surfaces
- Applying a Bevel and Emboss style to add height and volume
- How to create areas of transparency with Alpha channels
- How to paint Alpha masks

INTRODUCTION

There are ways to add extra dimension to textures that work differently than simply editing the texture image itself. Bump maps, and displacement maps, and Alpha channels are images and image components that affect the appearance of a surface when it is displayed by a 3D application or game engine.

Alpha channels have to do with transparency, whereas bump and displacement maps are alternate methods of adding the illusion of depth and detail to a 3D model without it being present in the actual geometry of the model.

This chapter is about how to create the illusion of three-dimensionality in texture art. Three-dimensionality is determined by how light falls upon a surface. Bump maps can be added to anything that needs dimension such as ground textures for cities, dirt, gravel, rock, concrete, cloth, skin, architectural details, any type of flooring, and any type of wall.

Similarly, Alpha channels will be a big part of your work. An Alpha channel adds transparency to a texture file. You can use it to make areas completely clear, or you can use an Alpha channel to add a transparent quality to a certain type of material. I have used Alpha channels for character hair, creature details, adding leaves to trees, making car windows appear see-through, and adding translucency to plastic, water, and crystal textures.

BUMP MAPS

A bump map is an image that is added to a texture in order to create the illusion of depth and dimension. A bump map does not actually alter the surface of a texture or a model, but the application being used to display the surface adds highlights and shadows – in the pattern of the bump map – that respond to the lights in the scene or game. The result is a dynamic illusion of bumpiness on a surface that is actually smooth.

Bump maps are useful because they are a simple, fast, and inexpensive way to simulate low-relief details too fine to warrant including in a model's geometry. (Walls in video games are a good example: one square section of wall might necessitate consisting of only two triangular polygons, since there might be hundreds of instances of that wall section on a given level. If the engine supports bump maps, adding one to the texture might take a fraction of the system resources required to render an equivalent level of geometric detail.)

A well-crafted bump map can make a model look as if it has many, many polygons, when in fact it is a much simpler model. For broadcast and film, a bump map can be a fast, quality substitute for levels of detail that would take an unrealistic amount of time to model. For video games, several systems currently support real-time bump mapping, and it will surely be a standard feature of games in the near future.

DISPLACEMENT MAPS

A displacement map is a grayscale image that is applied to geometry to alter the appearance of its surface, similar to a bump map. Unlike a bump map, however, a displacement map actually affects the geometry of a model, "displacing" the surface in the pattern of the map.

Displacement maps are useful because they can alter geometry to create detail without having to model the detail. You can use these maps to create terrain, architecture, facial features that match the texture exactly, and in place of a bump map when the illusion of depth is not good enough.

Displacement maps are not covered specifically in this chapter, since they are created the same way as bump maps, just used differently. Displacement maps are used to create terrain tile geometry for games, in pre-rendered video (such as films or cut-scenes), and any other creative uses you can come up with.

THE LIGHTING EFFECTS FILTER

Lighting Effects is a filter in Photoshop that can add a variety of lighting schemes to texture art, and can also be used to add a bumped effect to filtered images. 3D Artists seem to either like this filter or they don't like it. I like it because it's possible to use it coupled with other Photoshop features to get very unique results for any sort of texture.

The lighting options of this filter coupled with its bumping attributes are a combination that can greatly enhance the look of your work. This filter is very useful for creating a uniform, evenly lit set of textures for a scene.

THE TEXTURIZER FILTER

Lighting Effects is not the only filter that can do great things for your bump maps. My favorite bump-mapping filter is the Texturizer. I use this filter all the time to create sand, soil, denim, rock walls, painted drywall, concrete, bark, wood grain, and more.

The Texturizer Filter is located under Filter→Texture→Texturizer, and it has four built-in texture bumping options: Brick, Burlap, Canvas, and Sandstone. The fifth option is to load a texture from a separate image file saved as a PSD. This image file can be an exact copy of your original, or it can be any sort of pattern, tileable texture, or photographic image you want to use as a stamp on your texture.

Once you have loaded in a document, you can control the scale and relief of the bump texture. I have used it for creating painted walls, popcorn ceilings, roof shingles... tons of things!

Line texture for Texture filter

EXERCISE — THE TEXTURIZER

Create a new 256x256 document with a transparent background using Ctrl/⌘ + N. Name it "Lines".

Hit Shift + U on the keyboard a few times to scroll to the Line(U) tool. Go up to the Options bar for the Line(U) tool and type in 8 pixels for the Weight. Hit D on the keyboard to restore the default foreground/background swatches. Hold Shift, then click and drag with the Line(U) tool to create a pattern of horizontal lines, evenly spaced, down the canvas. Do a Ctrl/⌘ + S and save the document as a PSD file.

Create a new document of the same dimensions and specifications. Fill Layer 1 with a medium gray of 40-50%, then choose Filter➔Texture➔Texturizer from the top menu bar. Click on the Texture arrow drop-down and scroll to the bottom to select Load Texture. Browse until you locate the Lines document just created and hit OK. Now set the Scaling to 100% and the relief to 6. Hit Enter. And there you have it.

This texture was used to create an industrial type garage door. A photographic reference could also have been used to create the bump map with the Texturizer Filter, or any of the other texture tiles or samples.

BEVEL AND EMBOSS

So far, you've learned how to add the illusion of depth by hand-painting bump maps and creating bump maps with filters. Next, it's time to visit the old standby: Photoshop's Bevel and Emboss Blending Option.

Getting back to standard image editing, there are other methods of quickly adding depth and dimension to textures. Bevel and Emboss can add the illusion of relief to an image, and can be a great way to add height, volume, depth, and dimension quickly and easily. This effect can be applied to virtually any kind of image, and can be used very successfully with other Layer Style options such as Texture, Contour, Pattern Overlay, and all of the Blending Modes. Examples of this feature have already been encountered in the chapter on Tiling, and will be examined throughout this book. Experiment with this option frequently, it will come in very handy.

To apply this Blending Option, select a layer from the layer stack. Double-click in the empty area of the layer to access the Blending Options Dialog box. Next, place a checkmark in the Bevel and Emboss option. Click to highlight the Bevel and Emboss section and the options menu comes up.

Make sure that Preview is checked so you can see the effect of the Bevel and Emboss as you mess around with its settings. Go through all of the menus, experiment with the sliders, and play with the directional controls. Try different combinations of each tool to get an idea of what this versatile Blending Option can do for you.

In the Texture box below Bevel and Emboss, you can add preset patterns to the Emboss option. If you choose a Clouds pattern, for example, the pattern will appear on your layer with height and volume applied to it via Bevel and Emboss.

I use Bevel and Emboss regularly, for things like signs, rivets and nails, adding detail to character art, making windows, guns barrels, tire wheels, and pitted wall textures. I can't count how many times I turn to Bevel and Emboss to achieve the look I need and I encourage you to get to know this feature of Photoshop well.

CREATE A BUMPED LEAF: AT A GLANCE

TOPICS COVERED

In this tutorial, you will learn how to make a bumped leaf texture for a maple tree.

YOU LL LEARN HOW TO:

- Get a scan ready to work on
- Set up a new document for painting
- Paint a bump map pattern the Dodge and Burn Tools
- Add extra detail to the leaf

MATERIALS REQUIRED

Leafscan.psd

TUTORIAL: CREATE A BUMPED LEAF

This tutorial focuses on how to make a hand-painted bump map. Painting a bump gives you a high level of control that some of the more automated options for bump mapping don't have. I often paint grayscale bump maps for projects that need a fine touch and a lot of detail.

STEP 1: OPEN AND EXAMINE THE LEAF SCAN

For the leaves of the maple tree for my forest scene, I went out and collected leaves based on their color and texture, then scanned them in at a high dpi: 300. The leaf scan needed some color correcting to most closely match it to the real leaf.

Open the Leafscan.psd.

STEP 2: COLOR CORRECT THE LEAF

To color correct the leaf, I use the Hue/Saturation command to even out the yellows. Do a Ctrl + U to access this dialog box and click on the Master drop-down menu. Choose "Yellows" and play with the sliders until you see a result you like. I desaturated the yellow a tiny bit.

I also use Variations to add more yellow, which evens out the overall general hue. To access the Variations command, do an Image→Adjustments→Variations, click on "More Yellow" once, and hit OK.

STEP 3: ADJUST THE BRIGHTNESS AND CONTRAST

Next on the list is Brightness/Contrast, which I use to take down contrast a bit. Access this command by doing an Image→Adjustments→Brightness/Contrast and experiment with the sliders. This leaf needs to be bright because it will be placed in the middle background of a forest scene, the leaves will be small, and they will be reflecting firelight. In the interests of creating a night scene with a complimentary color scheme, I decide the leaves can remain a little unnaturally over-saturated.

STEP 4: FOCUS THE IMAGE WITH AN UNSHARP MASK

The last preparatory step is to do a Filter→Sharpen→Unsharp Mask. Unsharp Mask applied to the leaf scan will even out the tones and add an overall focusing to the image.

STEP 5: CREATE A NEW DOCUMENT AND BACKGROUND

Now it's time to put the leaf to work. The first step is to determine how large the leaf scan is so that those dimensions can be recreated in the new document. With the LeafScan document selected, do a Ctrl/⌘ + A to select all. Take a glance at the Info palette where you will see the dimensions of the document.

Create a new document based on these dimensions with a dpi of 300 and a transparent background. Name the PSD file "BigLeaf", or something you'll remember to be the main document for the leaf. Right-click and name Layer 1 "Black". Hit D on the keyboard to restore default colors, hit G for the paint bucket, and click to fill.

STEP 6: COPY LEAFSCAN AS A NEW LAYER IN THE NEW DOCUMENT

Go back to LeafScan, click the Leaf layer in the Layers palette, and while holding down the Shift key, drag that layer into the new document. Shift constrains the leaf to a central placement. Do a Ctrl/⌘ + W to close LeafScan.

STEP 7: MAKE THE BUMP MAP LAYER

Next, select the Black layer in the layers palette, or right-click on the image and select Black. Do a Shift + Ctrl/⌘ + N to create a new layer in the Layers palette; it should appear right above Black. Right-click on it and name it Bump or Bump Map. Fill the bump map with 50% gray by clicking on the 50% gray swatch in the Swatches palette and using the hotkey for the Paint Bucket(G) tool. (You can determine which swatch in the Swatches palette is 50% by hovering the cursor over the swatches.) Next, click on the Leaf layer. Put a check mark in the position lock at the top of the palette and then reduce the Opacity of the leaf layer to 20%. In this way, you will be able to use the leaf as a reference from which to paint the bump map. You should now have a Black bottom layer, a gray Bump map layer above that, and the Leaf layer on top.

Dodged veins

STEP 8: USE DODGE TO MAKE VEINS IN BROAD STROKES

Next it's time to draw the bump map. Select the Bump layer, and press O on the keyboard for the Dodge(O) Tool. I prefer to use the Burn and Dodge tools because of the quality of dark and light they produce. The Burn tool makes a rich, charcoal-like black, and the Dodge makes a warm, shiny highlight. Each of these works well for a bump such as this one.

Select a brush that is wider than the veins on the leaf with a little softness to the edge: Brush 18, Hardness 45. Use the [ ] and Shift + [ ] hotkeys to adjust the brush. Set the exposure of the Dodge(O) Tool to 40% and paint along the veins of the leaf, starting with the largest veins. Use the Z hotkey or Ctrl/⌘ + (plus sign) to zoom in to see your work. Use the Space bar to navigate around the image.

Note: If you cannot see your cursor against the gray, do an Edit➔Preferences and change the cursor display to Standard. Make sure Caps Lock is off, and you will be able to see the brush just fine.

STEP 9: USE DODGE TO REFINE THE VEIN DETAILS

Once the largest veins have been painted, lower the size of the brush and sharpen it a bit. This will better represent that plastic texture common to large leaf veins. Click on the Leaf layer eyeball to turn it invisible. Now begin to paint over the largest veins with the smaller brush. The goal is to add thinner and thinner highlights along the highest part of the leaf vein and to exaggerate dimensionality.

Turn the leaf visible again. Begin painting the smaller veins, as well, and continue to reduce the brush size until you have a believable map of dodged-out veins. You'll want to wind up dodging with a small 5-pixel brush, with a 100% Hardness, and have the Dodge(O) tool set to a higher exposure, like 80-100%, for the highest part of the veins. Remember that white is high. Hit Tab to get rid of the palettes and tool bars if you need to see more of the canvas.

Do a Ctrl/⌘ + S to save.

Burned veins

Dodged leaf surface

Completed bump painting

The rendered bump map

As you paint with the Dodge(O) Tool, try to follow the contours of the leaf image. And don't forget the stem! Recall that leaves like this usually have hard veins that are shiny. Because of this, the highlights of the veins will have a harder edge and won't diffuse much like a more matte material's highlights would.

STEP 10: USE BURN TO EMPHASIZE THE HEIGHT OF THE VEINS

To emphasize the height of the veins, it's time to use the Burn(O) tool. Use it to darken the areas around the veins of the leaf. Start with a larger and softer brush, just as before, and move the Burn(O) tool along the edges of the largest veins. Use your judgment as you work, deciding how dark or light you want which area. As before, start with larger brushes, and work down to smaller brushes. Do a Ctrl/⌘ + S to save.

STEP 11: DODGE AND BURN FOR DETAIL

Next start adding some other details to the leaf. Use the Dodge(O) and Burn(O) tools to paint over the highest and lowest areas of the leaf, and areas that have any marks, scratches, or discoloration. To get a variety of interesting brushes, you can load them in from Photoshop, or create your own. Drag the corner of the Brushes palette down so that you can see all of them. That way, you won't waste time scrolling up and down for that one particular brush, or use the [ ] hotkeys to scroll through the different brushes.

By the time you have completed painting on the bump map layer, there should be a nice array of various marks, and blotches on the surface of the leaf. The highest areas of the leaf should be represented with white and the lowest areas by black. Click on the leaf layer again and slide the Opacity back up to 100%. If you want to, you can go back to the bump layer and use the eraser to take out some more highlights. Ctrl/⌘ + S to save.

STEP 12: BACK UP THE DOCUMENT, THEN FLATTEN IT

You have created a bump map for the maple leaf. In the interests of keeping the original intact, I duplicated the Leaf document. With the duplicate selected, I deleted the leaf scan layer, and did a Ctrl/⌘ + E to flatten the rest of the image.

Before the Leaf image and the Leaf Bump are ready to be added to a texture in the material editor of your 3D application, you'll need to create an Alpha channel. For this leaf, the Alpha channel will make the areas around the leaf totally clear so that when the texture is added to the geometry of the tree that represents a leaf (in this case a two-poly plane), the black area around the leaf will be gone.

Creating Alpha channels is covered in a later tutorial.

STONE TEXTURE WITH LIGHTING EFFECTS: AT A GLANCE

TOPICS COVERED

In this tutorial you will be making a stone texture with the Lighting Effects Filter. Lighting Effects can import a grayscale channel and use it as a bump map.

YOU LL LEARN HOW TO:

- Configure and apply the Lighting Effects Filter
- Use a color channel as a texture for Lighting Effects

MATERIALS REQUIRED

StoneComplete.psd

TUTORIAL: STONE TEXTURE WITH LIGHTING EFFECTS

Difference clouds for a stone texture

In this tutorial you'll learn how to bend the Lighting Effects filter to your will in order to get a good result. The end product is a stone texture that has a nice amount of graininess to it. I used this texture to create a tileable surface that went on the inside of a cavern wall. You can use it as a starting point for further experiments with the Lighting Effects filter.

This technique uses a combination of filters to get the ball rolling... or in this case, the rocks rolling. This method of making a tileable texture can be used for a variety of purposes, not just for making stone.

STEP 1: CREATE A NEW DOCUMENT AND LAYER

First, create a new document and name it "Stone Texture". Set the dimensions to 256x256. Do a Shift + Ctrl/⌘ + N to create a new layer and name it "Difference Clouds". The Difference Clouds filter effect is what will give a sense of dimensionality and volume to the texture.

The red channel of the channels palette

STEP 2: FILL THE LAYER AND APPLY DIFFERENCE CLOUDS

Fill the layer with a mid-range gray and then hit D on the keyboard to restore the default foreground and background colors. Next, do a Filter➔Render➔Difference Clouds. You are shooting for a pattern of difference clouds that is about 50% white and 50% black. The only way to determine the percentage of white and black in the image is to eyeball it. With this filter, you may need to do a few Ctrl/⌘ + F's to run the filter until you get the result you want.

STEP 3: CREATE A NEW CHANNEL

Now click on the Channels palette tab and then select one of the color channels (Red, Green, or Blue). Drag the selected color channel onto the Create New Channel icon on the bottom of the Channels palette. In my case, since I copied the Red channel, the new channel was titled "Red Copy". Now you have a channel to use with the Lighting Effects filter, when it's time to add one.

STEP 4: CREATE A NEW LAYER AND APPLY A PATTERN OVERLAY

Create a new layer and call it "Stone Surface". Fill that layer with darker gray. Right-click on the stone layer and select Blending Options, or click on the circle-"f" button on the bottom of the Layers palette to access the Blending Options dialog. Checkmark and then click on the Pattern Overlay option. Scroll through the patterns and choose Stone. Set the Scale to 160 or smaller and click OK. You do not want to have a scale setting that is too large or too small, because too large won't show enough detail and too small will show way too much detail. The idea is to get an even, balanced pattern.

Red channel copy

STEP 5: CONVERT THE PATTERN OVERLAY INTO A NORMAL LAYER

Go back to the layer stack and right-click on the Pattern style applied to Stone surface. Select Create Layer from the list. Look at the pattern closely in order to see where the tutorial is going. You should be getting an idea of how the final texture will look. Now the pattern is in its own layer and can be further manipulated.

STEP 6: APPLY THE LIGHTING EFFECTS FILTER

Click off the visibility of the new Stone Pattern layer so you can see what you're doing. Click back on the stone surface layer and do a Filter→Render→Lighting Effects. Lighting Effects is a very cool Photoshop feature, but it takes a little getting used to.

STEP 7: ADJUST THE LIGHT SOURCE SO IT LOOKS AMBIENT

The first thing to adjust is the light source. Select the default light from the drop-down at the top, and click and drag the round point that represents the light into the center of the image. The goal here is to create even lighting because this is going to be a tiled texture and the light should seem ambient instead of directional.

STEP 8: EXPAND THE AREA OF THE LIGHT

Click on the black handles along the ring of the light and configure them until you have a perfect circle. Next drag the circle out, constraining proportions, until the gray is entirely lit. Keep your eye out for dark corners.

STEP 9: SET THE REST OF THE LIGHTING EFFECTS FILTER SETTINGS

The following is a list of the settings I used and an explanation for each, but you can experiment with combinations of your own.

Light Type: Spotlight. The spotlight is used because it focuses a round light straight at the texture that can be dragged to cover the entire area.

Stone texture after Lighting Effects

Intensity: 7. This setting is low because if it were high, it would cause the highlights of the texture to become too hot and contrasted, upsetting the balance. Remember the goal is an ambient light fill, nothing too strong or too faint, that covers the texture surface evenly.

Focus: 100% Wide. This Focus slider needs to be cranked up all the way so that you can be sure all of the texture is covered by the light source. A problem with this filter is that sometimes the corners are black because the light is round, not square, and the focus of the spot leaves the corners out.

Gloss: Matte, 50. Matte is ideal for this texture because it is not a shiny surface; stone is a gritty surface, pocked here and there, and dirty.

Material: 0. This is left at 0 because the texture is not going to be plastic or metal. It is going to be rock, so any sort of specular highlight is not good.

Exposure: 0. Exposure is set to 0 because otherwise it would interfere with the general ambient feel that is the goal here. Altering exposure makes the texture look like a photographic negative that has been in the light too long, or not long enough. In other words, the contrast is too high, or too low.

Ambience: 8. This is the default setting for this filter and works well as is.

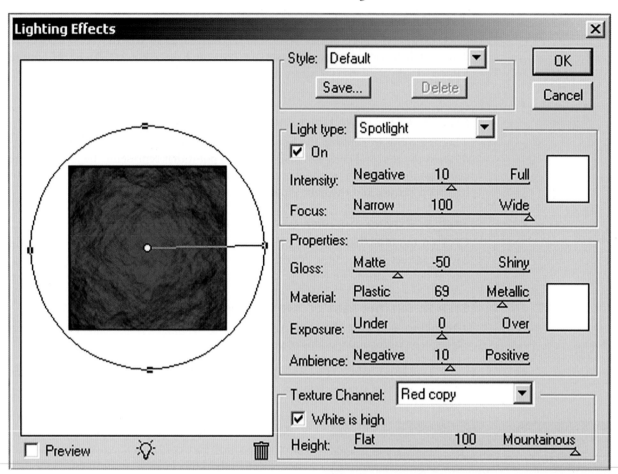

Lighting Effects Filter for the Stone Texture

STEP 10: USE THE COPIED CHANNEL AS A TEXTURE

Click on the drop-down menu for the Texture Channel. Scroll down until you find the new channel you created in step 3: Red copy, or Green copy, etc. Select it and then head to the Height slider. This texture was set very high: a 92 Mountainous, because it needs to be very craggy and eroded. Put a check in the White is High box.

STEP 11: REACTIVATE THE PATTERN STONE LAYER AND ADD FILTERS

Now click back on the Pattern Stone layer and restore its visibility. Here you can add various filters to the pattern to achieve even more depth and detail. I like Noise; a Filter→Add Noise→Noise and a low setting works well. Try setting the layer to Overlay with an Opacity of 100%. To make the Stone Texture even more interesting, set the Stone Surface layer blending mode to Overlay, as well.

Completed stone tile

There are a million different variations on this technique of using the Lighting Effects filter. It can be used to create plastic, metal, cloth surfaces... you name it. Another variation is to use a photographic image in place of the stone surface layer.

A last note on this texture is that a lot of other characteristics can be added such as moss, lichen, mushrooms – whatever is relevant to your project can be painted on as extra details to these surfaces.

Layer stack for the stone texture tutorial

ALPHA CHANNELS

Photoshop stores files as channels of information – Red, Green, and Blue – that are mixed together when displaying the image. Some file formats also support a fourth channel, known as the Alpha channel. This channel represents transparency rather than color.

Like the other channels, the Alpha can be represented as a grayscale image: white is opaque, black is transparent, and shades of gray are various gradations of semi-transparent. Refer back to the Leaf Bump map tutorial earlier in this chapter. Here is where you will revisit the leaf image, save an Alpha channel into it, and create a clear background for the leaf texture.

ALPHA CHANNELS IN ACTION

Leaves are a good example of a great use for an Alpha channel in a texture. You could make a detailed maple leaf model that consists of dozens of polygons, and duplicate that leaf hundreds of times to fill the boughs of a tree, resulting in thousands (if not millions) of polygons in a single tree. That may render too slowly for production deadlines, and be simply out of the question for use in a video game.

On the other hand, each leaf could consist of a single polygon whose texture map contains an Alpha channel that makes a cut-out in the shape of a leaf, reducing your million-polygon tree to mere hundreds. If you're making trees that only appear in the distant background, an entire tree could be a single-polygon plane - like the fake facade sets in spaghetti Westerns.

IMAGE FILE FORMATS

TIFF (TIF), Targa (TGA), Portable Network Graphics (PNG), and Photoshop (PSD) are common file types that support RGBA. JPEG (JPG), Bitmap (BMP), and GIF are common file types that are either RGB-only or do not store image information as channels at all. (While the GIF image format does not technically contain an Alpha channel, one color in a GIF image's palette can be designated transparent; however, semi-transparency is not possible.)

Although not always useful for output (few other software applications or game engines can read PSD files, with some notable exceptions discussed in this book), Photoshop files allow you to create multiple additional channels. These channels can be loaded as selections or masks at any time, which can be very useful when you're working on an image.

Note that Photoshop 7.0 was initially released with a bug that prevented the addition of the Alpha channel to a Targa file; an unfortunate bug, since the Targa format is used by many game engines. This has since been fixed, and anyone who needs to remedy the problem can go to the Adobe website (www.adobe.com) and visit their support/downloads page to get the Targa plug-in for Windows file.

USING ANOTHER IMAGE AS ALPHA INPUT

If you are forced to use a file type that does not support a fourth channel, many engines and 3D applications allow you to use a separate image as the Alpha channel of the primary image. All you need to do is create a black and white image that represents what the Alpha selection would be, and plug it in as the Alpha by whatever method the application uses.

EXERCISE — CREATE AN ALPHA CHANNEL

Re-open the Leaf file you worked with for the bump map tutorial from wherever it lives on your hard drive. You are going to use the Pen to draw a series of points around the edge of the tree and will then turn the points into a selection. That selection will then be saved as an Alpha channel.

Select the Leaf layer, hit P on the keyboard to get out the Pen(P) Tool, and click to place anchor points around the edge of the leaf. Make sure your points are leaving at least one pixel to the inside of the leaf edge.

Drawing with the Pen creates a work path around the leaf. Create the work path by clicking to place control/anchor points around the border of the leaf. You can move them by depressing the Alt key and holding down the mouse button while you drag the point into place.

Once the path is complete, right-click along the edge of the path and select Make Selection from the context-sensitive dialog box. The path will now turn into a marquee.

Choose Select→Save Selection from the top menu bar. Type in a name for the selection and hit Enter. Congratulations! You have created an Alpha channel.

To finish, do a Ctrl/⌘ + D to deselect. To make sure the channel now exists, click on the Channels palette tab. At the bottom of the stack you will see a new layer that is black and white. Remember the black area is the clear part, the white area is the solid part, and gray areas are partially transparent parts.

Once the Photoshop file is complete, you can save it into the file format compatible with your 3D application. Do a Shift + Ctrl + S to perform a Save As. When the box comes up, click on the file extension drop-down menu, scroll down, and click on Targa. Make sure to remove the word "copy" from the file name. Choose where you want to save it, and hit Enter.

The Targa Options box will pop up, giving you three choices. Each choice saves the file with a different amount of information. 16 bit has the lowest amount of color information, 24 bit is the standard (and default) amount of color information, and 32 bit is the option that allows an Alpha channel to be stored in the file.

PAINTING ALPHA MASKS: AT A GLANCE

TOPICS COVERED

Many images and textures need to be transparent in certain areas. The Alpha channel defines the transparency. Using Quick Mask mode, Alpha channels can be created quickly and accurately.

YOU'LL LEARN HOW TO:

- Use Quick Mask mode
- Make a basic shape
- Hand-paint an Alpha channel
- Save a selection

MATERIALS REQUIRED

rabbit.psd

TUTORIAL: PAINTING ALPHA MASKS

Another way to create an Alpha channel is to paint one using the Quick Mask feature. This method for adding transparent areas to textures is really great for two reasons. The first is that you can paint with any shade of gray, resulting in any percentage of transparency. The second reason is that you can simply paint along the border of the image quickly and efficiently to select it, rather than taking the time to use the Lasso(L) or the Pen(P).

STEP 1: OPEN RABBIT.PSD

Open the rabbit.psd file from the PS4Animators folder. This image needs an Alpha channel so only the rabbit shows up in the game or video, and not the square black background.

STEP 2: CHOOSE A VALUE

Choose a value based on what percentage of transparency there is supposed to be in the texture file. You can choose any gray value: the darker the gray, the closer to totally transparent the mask will be; the closer to white, the less transparent the painted area will be.

For this tutorial, you will use black to create a totally see-through background for this rabbit shape.

STEP 3: SETTING THE BRUSH

You will want to paint with a hard brush, for this exercise. This will ensure that the rabbit looks solid along the edges of the shape instead of blurry.

Hit B for the paintbrush and then click on the Brushes palette tab. Choose the Hard Round 19 Brush. Now click on Brush Tip Shape and mouse over to the Hardness slider; click and drag to set it at a full 100%. Lastly, make sure the Opacity of the paintbrush is set to 100% as well.

Now you are ready to begin painting the mask.

STEP 4: ENTER QUICK MASK MODE

Hit D on the keyboard to ensure the Foreground and Background swatches are set to their default white and black, then X to flip the black swatch to the top. Now hit Q. Q is the shortcut to enter into Quick Mask mode. Another way to enter into this mode is to click the Edit in Quick Mask Mode button directly beneath the swatches on the tool bar.

STEP 5: PAINT THE MASK

Begin painting inside the rabbit shape. It will appear as if you are painting with red paint even though black is the foreground swatch on the tool bar. This simply tells you that you're in Quick Mask mode.

As you paint, stay within one or two pixels to the inside of the border and fill in the shape. Look carefully to make sure you are applying the paint thickly over the area. If you miss spots with the brush, there will be holes in the final rabbit texture.

STEP 6: EXIT QUICK MASK MODE AND INVERT THE SELECTION

Once the shape is solidly painted in, and you have inspected your work for holes, hit Q again to exit Quick Mask Mode. A selection marquee will appear that surrounds the painted area.

However, the marquee needs to be inverted so that it borders the shape of the rabbit instead of the shape of the canvas. Do a Ctrl/⌘ + Shift + I to invert the selection. Now you can save the selection and make the background disappear.

STEP 7: SAVE THE SELECTION

To save the selection as an Alpha channel choose Select→Save Selection from the top menu bar. Hit Enter to finalize, and there it is! To make certain you have created an Alpha channel, check the Channels palette. There should be a tiny white rabbit in the bottom layer of the stack.

STEP 8: CREATE AN ALPHA WITHOUT QUICK MASK MODE

If you need to create an Alpha channel to cut out the subject in an image that has other elements like a background, or detailed edges that need to be defined by hand, painting using Quick Mask mode is the best method. However, in this case there's a faster way, since there's nothing but the rabbit in the image, and its edges are smooth.

Re-open the original rabbit.psd file (or File→Revert if you haven't saved). Choose the Magic Wand(W) tool, set the Tolerance to 0, make sure Anti-Aliased is checked, and click in the black background area to select it. Ctrl/⌘ + Shift + I to invert the selection, and choose Select→Save Selection from the top menu bar to convert the selection to an Alpha channel. Done!

Also keep in mind you can select the contents of a layer by holding Ctrl/⌘ and clicking on it in the Layers palette. This can be a useful shortcut when making an Alpha channelin an original, unflattened PSD.

CONCLUSION

The whole point of texture mapping is adding detail to a model that isn't actually present in the geometry; bump maps, Alpha channels, and filters like Lighting Effects and Bevel and Emboss give you even more power to add those details. Choose between your own painting skill, powerful filters, or comprehensive Blending Options to build your cities, towns, space vehicles, alien forests, and character art.

I use all of these concepts and techniques on a daily basis. As always, practice makes perfect. Push ahead of the tutorials and make your own innovations so that you can figure out what works best for you.

QUIZ

1) AN ALPHA CHANNEL DEFINES THE _____ AREAS IN AN IMAGE.

    a) Effects
    b) Transparency
    c) Green

2) AN ALPHA CHANNEL CAN BE VIEWED IN THE:

    a) Channels palette
    b) Layers palette
    c) Paths palette

3) YOU CAN MAKE AN ALPHA CHANNEL OUT OF A SELECTION BY DOING A:

    a) Ctrl/⌘ + S, then choosing Save Selection
    b) Ctrl/⌘ + Shift + S
    c) Select→Save Selection

4) THE DIFFERENCE BETWEEN A BUMP MAP AND A DISPLACEMENT MAP IS THAT:

    a) A bump map actually moves the geometry of a model b) A displacement map actually moves the geometry of a model
    c) None of the above

5) WHICH FILTER IMPORTS OTHER PSD FILES TO USE AS BUMP MAPS?

    a) The Displace Filter
    b) The Lighting Effect Filter
    c) The Texturizer Filter

6) THE PURPOSE OF A BUMP MAP IS TO:

    a) Add gray areas to a texture
    b) Create the illusion of depth on a 2D surface
    c) Add a light source to an image

7) A BUMP MAP CAN BY CREATED BY:

    a) Hand painting
    b) Using the Texturizer Filter
    c) Both A and B

8) A WORK PATH CAN BE USED TO:

    a) Define a custom shape
    b) Create a selection for a new channel
    c) Provide a border for Quick Masking

9) QUICK MASK MODE IS USED FOR:

    a) Painting selections for saving Alpha channels
    b) Painting holes into solid areas
    c) Adding solid areas to a texture

10) A WAY TO ADD SIMPLE DIMENSIONALITY TO AN IMAGE IS USING THE:

    a) Quick Mask Mode
    b) Brush Tool
    c) Bevel and Emboss Blending Option

8

IN THIS CHAPTER YOU WILL LEARN ABOUT:

- Using Define Pattern and the Texurizer to build a brick wall
- Adding doors and windows with Layer Styles
- Putting up signs with Custom Shapes and Type
- Getting down and dirty with filters and paint

INTRODUCTION

This chapter is about making textures for environments. "Environments" in 3D industries are the overall settings and details of a concept all added together that make a place or an area in a game or film. Jungles, beaches, forests, and cities are all examples of specific environments. Each environment has specially designed lighting, palettes, structures, foliage, and other details that are all planned out in advance, and then built together so that they match. Environments determine the look and feel of a game and are the foundation for whatever action takes place within them.

ARCHITECTURE

Since this chapter focuses on urban environment textures, I'd like to say a word about architecture because it figures very heavily into lots of types of environments. Architecture can be houses, skyscrapers, churches, factories, temples, castles, fortresses, art museums, hobbit burrows, Atlantean bubble cities, flying citadels, or igloos to name a few. Architecture can be made out of wood, stone, brick, steel, mud, straw, concrete, paper, or snow. Architecture reflects the ideas, concepts, and purposes of its designers, illustrating such things as culture and history. Elements of decoration are another expression of human creativity and ingenuity that give architecture that extra amount of meaning and artistry that characterizes the human race. In my opinion, it's the decorative elements of environmental design and construction that are the most fun because they add so much richness to a game or film.

Architecture sets the context of a scene, game, or film. It can also be used to emphasize spatial relationships, or as a destination for a quest. Often, architecture is used simply for props. Architecture can also be used as a tool to evoke a range of emotional responses in an audience such as fear, excitement, or outrage.

WALLS

In most cases, you need walls if you're building architecture. Mud walls, wood walls, stone, ice, steel, concrete, or brick walls. So, the time has come to begin some heavy-duty work on the environmental side of painting up a texture map based on a UV snapshot or a seedy apartment building.

To get started on painting up an unwrap from such a building, it's a good idea to have an advance idea of what the textures should look like. Pay attention to the details of the environment. The most important thing to determine is how the light falls into the environment. Do buildings or trees obscure it? What color is it? Lighting is hard to do in urban environments, so you've got to pay attention to how it works.

The second thing to do as you work is decide how much detail should go into the artwork. Is this a prominent, large building or a smaller, less-central structure? Will a player see it in the background, or run right up to it? Often, you'll have a texture budget that is smaller than you'd want it to be. Whether you opt for high detail or low, keep in mind what will show up and what won't. It's pointless to spend hours on fine details that are invisible on a TV screen.

Next, is what is most important to the overall look and feel to the building? Maybe it's dark and seedy and creepy, or maybe it's a fast food restaurant with a giant, bright plastic playground in front. Whatever it is, be sure to use the right palettes and tools to convey the environment's style. The more consistent the look or the environment, the more compelling the feel of the environment.

Walls are where it all starts. Nail down the base textures and you can build upon them with more and more refined detail until you've got a great piece of work that matches the environment perfectly.

Later in this chapter, you are making a two-toned brick texture to slap up onto an apartment building wall. As always, experiment to your heart's content. If you don't like something I suggest, then do something different. Get into it and have fun!

FINISHING AND TRIM

You'll also want to add some smaller details to the city scene. The building needs doors, windows, drainage pipes, and more. This chapter addresses the second level refinements for the apartment texture. It's always the details of an image that make or break it.

Plenty of old buildings have very obvious pipes for drainage hanging off of them. Some pipes are straight and some are crooked. Some are rusty and some are brand new. Many have foul things growing in them. If you're working on a game, the chances are good you won't need to go overboard with adding each little spot of soot to a pipe or bracket that will be very small in game. In the exercises below, you use Bevel and Emboss coupled with a key drop shadow to get a slight sense of volume to the pipe, and a hint of distance from the wall. I use Layer Styles a lot because I can get interesting effects quickly, and I have a lot of fun just messing around with the settings. This is a practice I encourage everyone to do. After awhile, you'll get really good at it.

Doors are an essential addition to most architectural textures. The apartment texture you're making has two doors, an industrial-style garage door, and a side door. To make the garage door, you'll use the Texturizer Filter exercise from the previous chapter. The Texturizer has a lot of creative potential and can take care of bumping up smaller details that don't need too much attention. For the side door, you'll use a source image that has already been scaled down and set it within an alcove. Once again, the Drop Shadow and Inner Shadow features of the Layer Styles will come in handy to define a framed, interior space for the door to reside in.

Similarly, you'll use either my settings, or your own to add a support beam and rivets to the side of the building. You'll also use them to create some windows for the apartment building. The goal of these exercises to is to fully familiarize you with Layer Styles. As you learn how all the bells and whistles of the Layers Styles work, I want you to think about how you would replicate these effects by hand-painting. In my opinion, using Layer Styles is often faster and more efficient than trying to hand-paint small details. However, you may get lucky and be able to hand paint on a much larger, and more satisfying scale. If it happens, you'll want to know how to paint in detailed effects by hand because I find that Layer Styles are often less effective on a larger scale.

SIGNS

You can't have a city without signs. There's no limit to what you can say with clever (or not so clever) neon, billboards, and painted murals. You can make bright signs, old signs, dirty signs, naughty signs, peeling signs, funny signs, simple signs, and my personal favorite: highly detailed, complicated signs.

In this chapter, you're making three signs, three ways. The Text(T) tool lets you write vertically and horizontally, and lets you warp text into lots of different shapes. Usually when I make signs, I spend forever picking just the right font, then concoct a cool Layer Style that works for what I'm doing. Photoshop even comes with a set of "Text Effects" preset Layer Styles you can load in via the options menu for the Styles palette. Even if you don't like them, you can use them as a basis for your own experiments.

Another great way to make signs is to use source art. You can walk around a city for a week straight taking pictures of signs, if you feel like it. There are also books, magazines, movies, anime…all the usual suspects. I live in the middle of a city, so I can pick up plenty of inspiration just walking to work.

A third tool I use often for making signs is the Custom Shape tool. This is the vector graphics tool that will give you beautiful smooth-edged shapes in all dimensions. As with the Text Effects Styles, Photohsop comes with a menu of preset shapes you can put in your work. I sometimes use the simpler ones, but I prefer to make my own shapes and add them into the preset menu, which Photoshop allows. You'll be using Custom shapes to add shapes, erase areas of an image, and draw up your own to use.

ALL THE GORY DETAILS

Finally, you can move on to the subtler (though no less important) details. It's time to decide just how realistic your urban environment is going to be. Where would the grime and slime collect? What areas of the building are exposed to weather? How much graffiti does there need to be? Is the pavement old and cracked? How long have those garbage cans been sitting there, anyway? Think about these things as you work. Remember that using references is always helpful for adding details.

I love to add these details with tools like Burn and Dodge, the features of the Brushes palette, some of the image enhancement tools, and a healthy use of Blending Modes. This is the part where your creativity and eye for detail become really important.

DEFINE PATTERN AND THE TEXTURIZER: AT A GLANCE

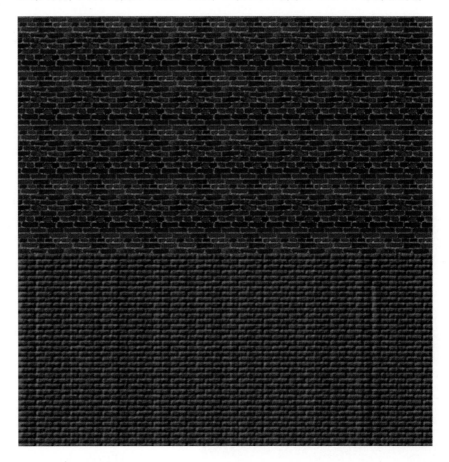

TOPICS COVERED

This tutorial helps you build and bump the base texture for an apartment building.

YOU LL LEARN HOW TO:

- Tile bricks with Define Pattern
- Bump bricks with the Texturizer Filter

MATERIALS REQUIRED

LeftSideWall.tiff
Apartment.ma
bricksimageediting.psd

TUTORIAL: DEFINE PATTERN AND THE TEXTURIZER

STEP 1: SIZE THE BRICKS

Ctrl/⌘ + O to open LeftSideWall.tif. This is a UV snapshot taken from the apartment building from the apartment.ma scene file.

Do a Ctrl/⌘ + O to open up the flattened bricks tile, bricksimageediting.psd from chapter 6. Do an Edit➔Image Size, and set it to 64 x 64, to get those bricks down to a more appropriate scale for a large buildings wall.

Now go back to LeftSideWall.tif. Leave the background layer locked. Do a Shift + Ctrl/⌘ + N to create a new layer and name it "Bricks".

The brick tile

Brick fill

STEP 2: DEFINE THE BRICKS PATTERN

Click back on the little 64 x 64 Brick tile. Do a Ctrl/⌘ + A to select all. A marquee will appear around the perimeter of the square. Do an Edit➔Define Pattern. Name it "Bricks" and hit Enter. Define Pattern allows you to create and then save any 2D patterns you make.

Now go back to the map you are working on, LeftSideWall.tif. Click on the Bricks layer in the layer stack. Next, do a Ctrl/⌘ + A to select the entire area.

Do an Edit➔Fill. Click the drop-down arrow and select Pattern. Now click the arrow for Custom Pattern and scroll all the way to the bottom. There you will find the new Bricks pattern just defined. Hit Enter and a lovely wall of seamless brick will pop up. Do a Ctrl/⌘ + D to deselect.

STEP 3: LOWER BRIGHTNESS AND SATURATION

This brick pattern is a bit too bright and too colorful, so you'll want to take it down a few notches.

To quickly lower the brightness, do an Image➔Adjust➔Variations and click on "Darker" once. Hit Enter. Then do a Ctrl/⌘ + U to access the Hue/Saturation dialog. Lower the saturation of the Master and then lower the saturation of Reds just a tiny bit to get the more grayed-out look that is needed.

Do a Ctrl/⌘ + S to save the wall as a Photoshop file. Save the small brick tile as a new document.

STEP 4: ADD GRAY BRICKS

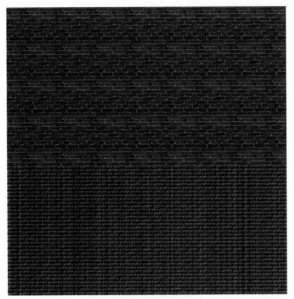

Gray bricks created with the Texturizer

Do a Shift + Ctrl/⌘ + N to create another new layer. Name this one "Gray Bricks". Now quickly select the bricks layer again and hit I for the Eyedropper(I) tool. Click anywhere except the white areas in the brick texture. A color will appear in the Foreground swatch of the Tool bar. Click on it to access the color picker, and choose a dark gray (any hue, all the way to the left so there is zero saturation).

Hit M on the keyboard for the Rectangular Marquee(M) tool and drag a selection around the bottom half of the front wall. Making sure the Gray Bricks Layer is selected hit G on the keyboard and fill the selection with the foreground gray you have chosen.

STEP5: BUMP WITH THE TEXTURIZER

Now go back to the Filter menu. Do a Filter➔Texture➔Texturizer. Select Bricks from the drop-down menu, scale the bricks at 65% with a low relief, to match the scale and lighting of the scene. Choose Top Left for the light source. Hit Enter.

Do a Ctrl/⌘ + S to save.

Do a Filter➔Noise➔Add Noise, and set it to Amount 4.5 with Gaussian and Monochromatic checked. Voila! You've got a two-toned brick texture for an apartment building, ready to use as a foundation for anything! Specifically, we're going to use it as a foundation for the next set of exercises, creating details like windows and pipes.

EXERCISE — PIPES AND BRACKETS

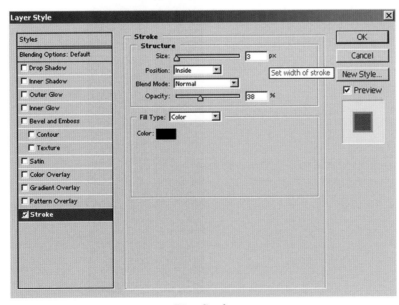

Pipe Stroke

In the LeftSideWall.tif texture from the previous tutorial, create a new Layer with Shift + Ctrl/⌘ + N. Name it Pipe. Hit U on the keyboard for the Line(U) tool, make sure the Create a Filled Region button is depressed, and set the weight to 10. Click in the Swatches palette to choose a 50% gray. Next, click and drag a vertical line along the left of the image map. Right-click on the Pipe Layer, choose Blending Options, and apply a Stroke effect by putting a check next to it. I used the settings illustrated to the left.

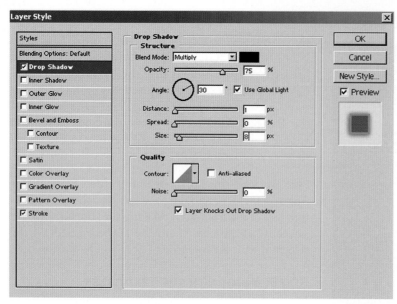

Pipe Drop Shadow

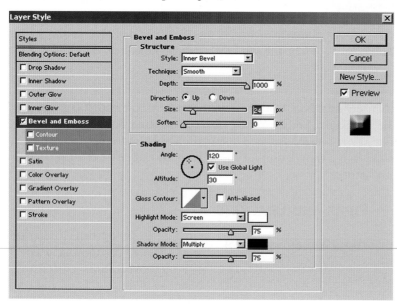

Brackets Bevel

Next add a Drop Shadow to the Blending Options.

Do a Shift + Ctrl/⌘ + N for another new layer. Call this one "Pipe Brackets". Use the Line again to click and drag four horizontal bracket shapes, using a line weight of 1 or 2. Do a right-click→Blending Options and apply a Bevel and Emboss effect.

Now you have a simple little pipe that comes away from the wall and even has a fastener.

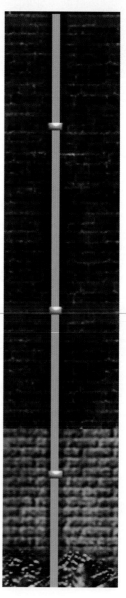

Pipe

Garage door

EXERCISE - GARAGE DOOR

Create a new layer in the LeftSideWall texture and name it "Garage door frame". Use the Line(U) tool with dark gray or black paint to draw two horizontal lines and one vertical line that represent the frame for the door; set the weight to 10 pixels. Double-click on the new layer and add Drop Shadow and Bevel Blending Options.

Now make the door. Create a new layer and name it "Garage door". Use the rectangular Marquee to select a shape that fits the frame of the door. Select a medium gray from the Swatches palette and hit G on the keyboard to fill the selection. Next, do a Filter→Texture→Texturizer. Choose Load File from the drop-down menu and open the lines_small.psd. Set the filter to Scaling 125%, Relief 15, Light Direction Top Left, with Invert checked

Another option is to create your own graphic texture, save it as a PSD file, then load it in with this filter.

This door is treated with two other Filters: Vertical Grain and some Noise because the door needs to be more gritty and grimy. I also reduced the Brightness using Image→Adjust→Brightness/Contrast by –22. The final touch is adding vertical text in another Asian font. Use your own preferences to create the details of your images.

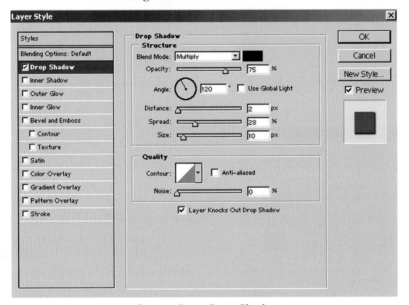

Garage Door Drop Shadow

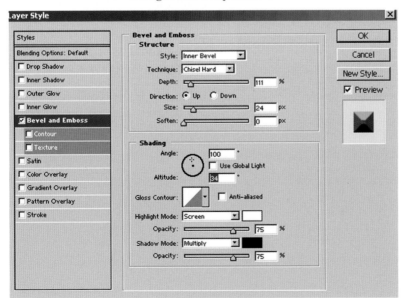

Garage Door Bevel

EXERCISE — ALCOVE AND SIDE DOOR

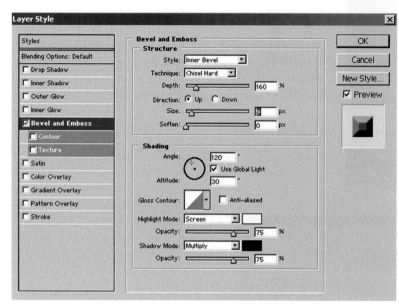

Alcove Bevel

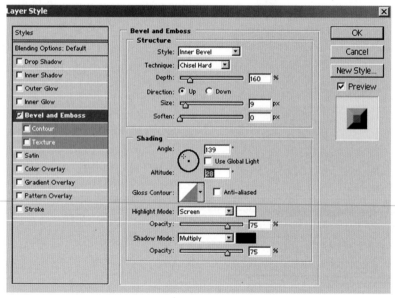

Frame Bevel

On the other side of the texture area goes a side entrance. Using your apartment wall texture, Hit M for a Rectangular Marquee and, measuring the selection against the Garage Door, click and drag to create what will be an alcove containing a side door on the side of the building. Hit D for default swatches and then fill with black. Right-click for Blending Options and apply a Bevel and Emboss.

Now create another layer to add a frame to it. With the Line(U) tool weighted at 10, click and drag to create three lines framing the alcove. Add a Bevel and Emboss to the frame.

Create another new layer for the door. Use a rectangular marquee to create the shape. Fill the layer with a medium gray.

Next, do a Filter→Texture→Texturizer and use a PSD document that resembles a material for a door. I used the wood texture from a previous tutorial (FourSectionsWood.psd). Scale it down to as low as it will go, and hit Enter. I also added another vertical grain to emphasize the texture. Right-click for Blending Options and add a Bevel, Inner Shadow, and Color Overlay.

To add a little doorknob, dab on a drop of paint and use the default settings for Bevel and Emboss to get a little dimensionality fast.

EXERCISE - BAR AND RIVETS

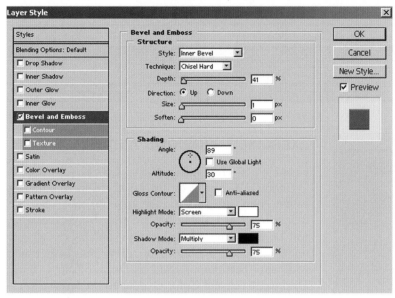

Bar Bevel

I wanted to break up the two brick textures in a way that's more attractive and less abrupt. To do this, I decided on a steel support beam.

Working with the same file, use the Rectangular Marquee(M) tool to outline a long, horizontal bar shape onto a new layer. Use G to fill the selection with a medium gray. Finish the texture up fast with a noise texture for grittiness and a vertical grain for further surface texture. Experiment with the Bevel and Emboss and Drop Shadow layer effects – try adding a percentage of noise to the Drop Shadow. (This was 57%).

Add some bolts to the center bar. Create a new layer and call it "Bolts". Do a Ctrl/⌘ + R to get the Rulers. Hit V for the Move(V) tool and click and drag from the horizontal ruler to drag a Guide down. Position this above the gray bricks. Hit B for a small, hard brush and paint some bolts evenly along the guideline. Next, right-click for the Blending Options and add a Bevel and Emboss.

Do a Ctrl/⌘ + S to save your work. Also, now might be a good time to test this map out on your model.

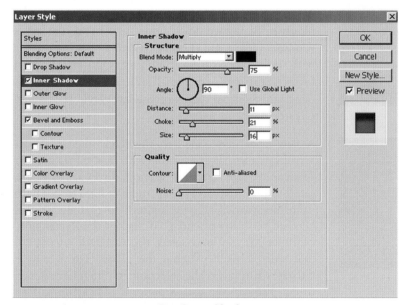

Bar Inner Shadow

Side Door

Bolts

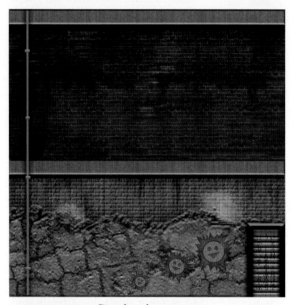

Simulated geometry

Curtains

Window Slime

EXERCISE - WINDOWS AND GLASS

Create a new layer with a Shift + Ctrl/⌘ + N. Call it "Window 1". Hit D on the keyboard for the default swatches and then U for the Line(U) tool. Set the weight to a 3 or 5, then click and drag to construct what will be the frame of the window. In this case, I just wanted something simple, so I drew on a basic frame with two partitions. Add a Drop Shadow, Inner Shadow, Bevel, and Color Overlay to the layer.

Now that you've got the frames, you'll want something behind the windows. (I transformed a shot of some blinds to fit the windows dimensions.) For the other window, make some curtains: create a new layer, fill it with light gray, do a Blending Options➔Pattern Overlay➔Streaks with a small scale appropriate for curtains, and then right-click on the layer style and choose Create Layer.

A new layer gets added to the stack filled with the Streaks pattern. However, since Streaks comes out at a 45-degree angle instead of vertical, do a Ctrl/⌘ + A to select all of the layer and then a Ctrl/⌘ + T to Transform and rotate the pattern so that the streaks become vertically oriented. Bring out the Rectangular Marquee(M) tool and select the rectangle of pattern that will be visible behind the glass. Do a Shift + Ctrl/⌘ + I to invert the selection and then Ctrl/⌘ + X to cut away all the excess pattern. Click the pattern layer and drag it beneath Window 1.

Now the streaks aren't perfect yet, so get out the Dodge(O) tool with a skinny, hard, 90-degree angle brush and dodge in additional vertical streaks.

Now for the glass, which is tricky. Pick one of the Glass Buttons Layer Styles from the Styles palette. In this case, I used Translucent Glass. However, the button style is too round and too high, so tweak the depth settings of the style until you get a better result.

Burning the bricks

Water damage

Once the glass layer is in place for the window, it's time to add some drips and more grime to them. Create a new layer and call it "Window drips". Hit B for a brush that has an interesting stroke. Choose a chalk brush to paint on some black grime at an Opacity of 60% and with Wet Edges clicked.

EXERCISE - GRIT

Go back to the left wall texture of that seedy apartment building. It's time to dirty up those pristine gray bricks.

The first thing to do is a Filter→Texture→Grain (Contrast 0, Intensity 15). Grain is excellent for adding grit that helps to kill the too-clean look of computer-generated images. Select Vertical from the drop-down menu and adjust the Intensity and Contrast to suit the scale and value range of the overall texture. Hit Enter to finalize.

Hit O on the keyboard and select a brush very like the one made in the bricks tiling tutorial: horizontal, skinny, and able to fit within a single layer of grout. Burn some soot and grime between and along the edges of the bricks. Set it between shadows and midtones with a pretty low exposure that fluctuates between 10-35%. This could take time, but it'll look cool. The smart thing to do is to duplicate the Bricks layer, lock up the original, and burn into the duplicate. That way, if it gets messed up, you can easily start over. Do a Ctrl/⌘ + (plus sign) to zoom in and get a closer look. Use Ctrl/⌘ + (minus sign) to zoom out, and repeat the burning of the gray bricks. Burning and dodging between the cracks of the bricks really increases the relief and dimensionality of the texture. Once you're done, set the Opacity of the Layer itself to around 30-40%.

EXERCISE - WATER DAMAGE

Create a new layer and name it "Water Stains". Hit B on the keyboard for the Brush(B) tool. Select a brush around 20-25 pixels wide, choose Multiply Mode, set the Opacity at 60% and check Wet Edges. Now paint some water streaks on with the brush. You may need to alter the Opacity here and there or repeat strokes to darken the edges of the drips. Use the Eraser(E) tool at a lower Opacity and a Spatter brush to break up some of the heavier edges.

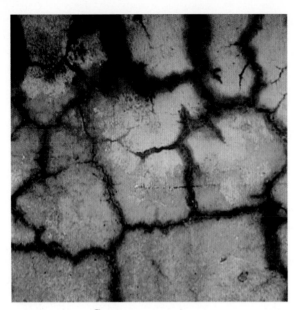

Concrete source image

Concrete created from the source image

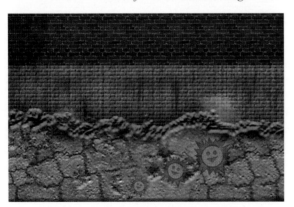

Hotkeys tutorial logo added as graffiti

EXERCISE - CRACKED CONCRETE

Next, import an image of eroding concrete: open CrackedConcrete.tif, and drag it onto LeftSideWall.psd with the Move(V) tool to create a layer out of it. Name this layer "Cracks", clone it to cover the entire area of the lower portion of the side wall, and add a Drop Shadow, Inner Shadow, and Bevel.

Set the Cracks layer to Normal with 100% Opacity, but take down the whites a little with a soft Burn brush set for Highlights at 60% exposure. To complete the layer, do a Filter➔Sharpen➔Unsharp Mask.

EXERCISE - GRAFFITI

On top of the Cracks layer, add three of the face logos from the Workflow chapter Tutorial. Open (Ctrl/⌘ + O) the file image you created for that tutorial. Make sure the image is flattened (Layer➔Flatten Image if it has multiple layers), select the one layer, and duplicate it. Use the Wand or Magic Eraser to remove the white. Then do a Ctrl/⌘ + T to transform the scale downwards, and Enter to finalize.

Now hit V for the Move(V) tool and drag the layer in to the left_side_wall document. Some further sizing might be needed to get them to fit. Then duplicate the logo twice for a total of three. Transform the second and third down even further to create a progression. Rotate them around a bit so they don't all face in the same direction. I named mine "Papa ", "Mama", and "Baby". Make sure the layers are at the top of the stack. Set each Blending Mode to Soft Light with a 60-85% Opacity.

Character sign

EXERCISE - THE KANJI SIGN

For this exercise, you'll add a single character or work to the apartment wall texture. If you don't have a Kanji font, you can go to the Internet and get one for free. I also have a Kanji dictionary that I used to make sure the character is facing the right direction and has a meaning. In my opinion, text can be used decoratively, but it is much better if it says something.

Go to the apartment wall and do a Filter➔Noise➔Add Noise to create some texture.

Now create another new layer and drag it beneath the text layer. Hit D on the keyboard for the Default swatches. Hit U again for the Line(U) tool, set the line weight to 3, and click and rage to create some dark vertical streaks that will soon become slime drips.

Once you have enough of these, do a Filters➔Blur➔Motion Blur. Set the Angle to 90 and the Distance to 65. Hit Enter. Next, do a Filter➔Blur➔Gaussian Blur. Enter in a small value like 0.7 and hit Enter. Now you have some nice slimy drips for an old and grimy sign.

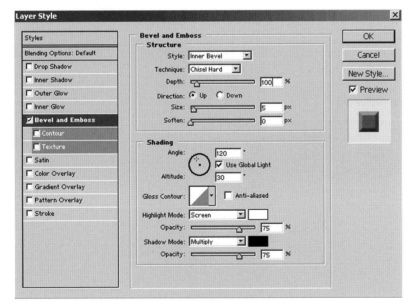

Kanji Bevel

THE GIRLIE SIGN CUSTOM SHAPES: AT A GLANCE

The final product

TOPICS COVERED

Construct a really cool billboard-type sign with custom shapes and filters. Create and use customized vector graphics by Photoshop.

YOU LL LEARN HOW TO:

- Use the Crumple Filter
- Add and subtract with Custom Shapes
- Hand Paint Light bulbs
- Configure text

TUTORIAL: THE GIRLIE SIGN CUSTOM SHAPES

STEP 1: FILL THE MAIN SHAPE

The first step is to rough out the main areas of the sign. Add a large gray fill to the top two-thirds of the map, and then a second darker gray bar to the lower third of the map: simply by selecting the area to be filled with the Rectangular Marquee(M) tool, clicking on the swatch in the swatches palette, and then using the Fill(G) tool to paint the interior of the marquee.

Grey fill

STEP 2: DRAW THE SIGN BARS

Now make the bars of the sign. This is a matter of creating a new layer, using the Line(U) tool weighted at 3, and hitting D on the board to set the default colors. Draw lines of black paint, then add a Bevel and Emboss Blending Option.

STEP 3: USE THE CRUMPLE FILTER

The Xenofex filter makes flat paint look like bunched up or folded paper or tissue. You can get a demo version of this filter pack from www.alienskin.com.

Make a new layer and fill it with light gray. Then a do a Filter→Xenofex→Crumple.

STEP 4: JAGGED EDGES

Dupilcate this layer, then lighten the brightness and contrast of the second layer. Now run the Xenofex Crumple filter set to Wrinkled Tissue on it. Name this layer "Torn" because this is the layer that would get shredded. With the Eraser(E) tool and a couple of interesting brushes remove areas along the edges and in the middle, in a jagged fashion to get a tearing effect. To give the image some depth and dimension, add a Drop Shadow and Inner Shadow style.

STEP 5: ADD THE HEART SHAPE

Now the gray heart center shape gets added. Using the source picture, get out the Lasso(L) tool, and use it to select the heart shape. To round out the heart shape, do a Select→Modify→Smooth, and smooth by 5 pixels. Then fill the layer with dark gray and run the Wrinkled Tissue filter again. Apply a Stroke Layer Style to outline the gray with a grayish pink line, then right-click on the Layer Style icon under the layer in the stack and choose Create Layer, so that the effect become its very own layer. Lastly, use the Eraser(E) tool to take out some of the edges with a splatter brush.

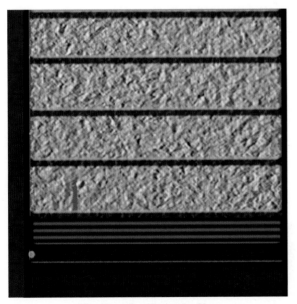

The Xenofex Crumple filter

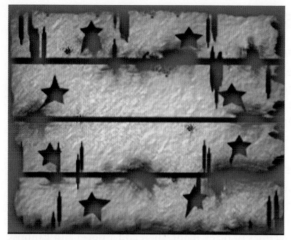

Use the Custom Shapes

Add the Heart shape

Add the Girlie's head

STEP 6: PUT THE GIRL IN

Now to add the girlie. Since the photographic source image was actually a digital version of the original, use the Lasso(L) tool to copy the girlie right off of that source image. With a Ctrl/⌘ + C to copy and a Ctrl/⌘ + V to paste, position her right in the center of the gray heart. I sharpened her up a little with Filter→Sharpen→Unsharp Mask, then set her layer mode to Overlay so that the wrinkled tissue pattern would show through.

STEP 7: CUT OUT STARS

Now, observing the source image, take note of the stars and the tears of the source sign. Using the Custom Shapes(U) tool, choose a star shape. Depress the Create a work path option and add several stars around the girl. These will appear in the Paths palette. After placing them accordingly, right-click on the path line, choose Make Selection, and with the selection active and the "Torn" layer selected, do a Ctrl/⌘ + X to cut away that paper. To alleviate their rather dull shape, I used a Lasso to cut out extra paper from some of the stars. To finish this process, use the Eraser(E) tool with a chalk brush to take out some of the edges and some lines in the center of the layer.

STEP 8: PAINT IN LIGHT BULBS

Use a soft brush to place dollops of light yellow paint along the bottom of the girlie sign. Think a little further and use an even smaller eraser to create the illusion of broken off or shattered bulbs.

STEP 9: ADD TYPE

The last bit is to add the type. I choose to use an Asian style font and a Layer Style with a hue to match the pink of the sign above. Below the sign, add a new layer, add a default Bevel and Emboss Layer Style, and then use a round brush to paint on some yellow bulbs.

Paint on lightbulbs

MARTINI NEON WITH CUSTOM SHAPES: AT A GLANCE

The finished product

TOPICS COVERED

Create and use customized vector graphics.

You'll learn how to:

• Make a Neon Martini Sign with Custom Shapes

Custom shape path

TUTORIAL: MARTINI NEON WITH CUSTOM SHAPES

STEP 1: CREATE A NEW DOCUMENT

First, create a new document. Give yourself enough space to create a good martini glass shape with all the details. I used 300 x 300 pixels. Next, add a new layer and call it "Sketch". Hit B on the keyboard, select an appropriate brush for a quick sketch of the shape you like, and paint the shape onto the sketch layer.

STEP 2: DRAW A SHAPE WITH THE PEN

Second, with the Pen(P) tool firmly in hand, begin placing points according to the rough sketch layer. Fine-tune the points to get a nice smooth edge. Click off the visibility of the sketch layer. Once the path is complete, hit D on the keyboard for default foreground and background colors (this time we want black), then hit G (for the Paint Bucket(G) tool) to fill the inside of the path.

STEP 3: DEFINE THE CUSTOM SHAPE

Do an Edit→Define Custom Shape. Enter in a name for the new shape and hit ok. Now hit U on the keyboard to access the Custom Shape(U) tool with Options . Click on the Custom Shape Tool icon located as the last choice of shape on the Options bar. Once depressed, a Shapes menu button appears. Click on the down arrow and scroll to the bottom of the Shapes menu. There you will see the new custom shape. Click on the new shape to select and use with wild abandon.

And that's that. Don't forget to save a lot and test your progress on the model.

CONCLUSION

The texture for the other side of building is up to you. You can refer to RightFrontWall.psd and RightSideWall.psd to see how I made them. Take what you have learned so far and run with it. Have fun!

The Define Custom Shape command

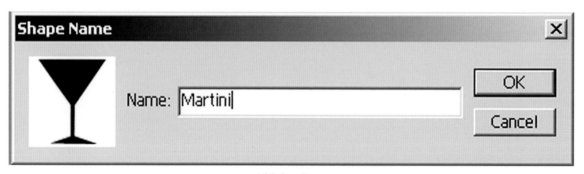

Add the shape

A peeling sign

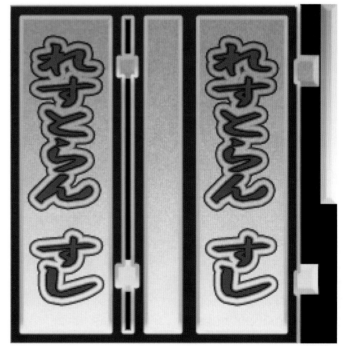

Jazz Club

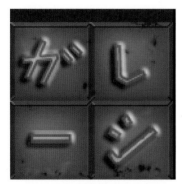

A bevelled sign

A symbol sign

Vertical sign

QUIZ

1) WHAT DO YOU NEED TO KEEP A SHARP EYE OUT FOR IN A REALISTIC SCENE?

    a) The details of the environment you are interested in creating

    b) How the light falls in the environment

    c) Both A and B

2) WHAT IS A FAST WAS OF FILLING IN LARGE AREAS WITH SMALL TILEABLE TEXTURES?

    a) By right-clicking on the tile layer and duplicating over and over

    b) Using the Move(V) tool to replicate the small tile

    c) By selecting the small tile, doing and Edit→Define Pattern, then filling in the entire area

3) WHAT IS THE FAST WAY TO REDUCE THE BRIGHTNESS OF AN ENTIRE LAYER?

    a) Reduce the layer's Opacity

    b) Change the Blending Mode to Color Burn

    c) Do an Image→Adjust→Variations

4) WHICH FILTER MAKES A BRICKS PATTERN THAT ALLOWS SCALE AND RELIEF CONFIGURATIONS?

    a) The Texturizer Filter

    b) The Emboss Filter

    c) The Extrude Filter

5) TO ADD "GRITTINESS" TO ART THAT LOOKS TOO CLEAN, USE THE:

    a) Noise Filter

    b) Grain Filter

    c) Both A and B

6) WHICH TOOL IS GREAT FOR CREATING THE LINEAR ELEMENTS OF A SCENE?

    a) The Custom Shape tool

    b) The Line tool

    c) The Pencil tool

7) WHAT IS A GOOD TOOL FOR CREATING GLASS?

    a) The Glass Button style swatches

    b) The Dodge(O) tool

    c) The Blending Options

8) CREATE A CUSTOM SHAPE WHEN:

    a) There is a need for a black shape

    b) There is a need for a simple graphic

    c) You want to make graffiti

9) BLENDING OPTIONS WORK BEST ON _____ SCALES.

    a) smaller

    b) larger

    c) fish

10) THE TEXTURIZER CAN ONLY USE _____ FILES AS INPUT.

    a) TIF

    b) PSD

    c) TGA

KAMAL SIEGEL

SURFACES AND LIGHTING LEAD

MICROSOFT

What is your job?

Surfaces and Lighting Lead for Microsoft. I've been working here for 2 years and really like it. I've gotten the opportunity to work on many interesting projects in the sports division including NFL Fever 2002 and Inside Drive 2002.

How did you get started in the game industry?

I went to the Art Institute of Seattle and at the end of the program displayed my work at their portfolio review. Well, the lady who used to be my boss saw my work there, took my card, called me for an interview, and here I am. I was really lucky.

How did you learn the tools you use?

At the Art Institute, I took one Photoshop class, but am mostly self-taught. I just practiced a lot with it, to figure things out. They also taught 3ds max at the Art Institute, so I learned that but had learned one of the earlier versions of 3D Studio on my own when growing up (back in the DOS days). When I joined Microsoft, they sent us to a 40-hour, one-week intensive training course for Maya, and that's what I work with now. I've worked with Maya for a year and a half now and it's a great tool.

How do you use Photoshop?

We mostly use Photoshop to create textures for our games from scratch and any kind of compositing, special effects that need to be done for presentations. We also use it to do color corrections and touch-ups on photographs we may use for the games. Sometimes we have photographers take shots for us, and other times one of us will take some photos. We also get reference imagery from the Internet and magazines – places like that - and use Photoshop to get the results we need.

How long have you worked in the industry?

I've worked in the game industry for 2 years and in the graphic design industry for one year. The greatest thing about my job is that it's exciting and challenging. It's exciting because the game industry is rapidly changing, engines are becoming more powerful and the liberties that artists have are becoming more and more limitless. It's challenging because a lot of times, I get a problem I have to solve without knowing anything about how to fix it. Having to go through the process of figuring it out is one of the most rewarding experiences I have at my job.

What is your favorite thing about 3D?

My favorite thing about 3D is that I don't have to draw my perspective lines and vanishing points.

How early do you have to get up? How late do you have to stay?

I sort of follow my instincts. There's not this big evil boss telling you what to do. When I interviewed, I asked my boss about the average work week, and she said between 50-60 hours. I was thinking, "wow, that's a lot", but it's not that much really. You can work on something for 12 hours and not even notice the time has passed. You work those hours because you want to. You enjoy it. And anyway, it fluctuates. Sometimes it's really busy, and sometimes it's a little slower. It just depends on what's going on.

What are your interests outside the job?

I do my own artwork and play guitar. I love to look through art books and get inspired by other artists. I like modern painters, but also the old traditionalists, like Rembrandt. I also like to watch movies. Either fun ones like Spiderman or serious ones like Good Will Hunting.

What games do you play?

I hardly ever play games any more, unless I play at work with my co-workers. Currently we play Halo and Rally Sport Challenge. Anything that's multiplayer is good.

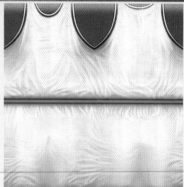

© 2001 www.kamalsiegel.com

Where do you find inspiration for your work?

For my personal work I find inspiration mostly in my own thoughts and views on life. I also constantly get inspired by seeing the great art that other talented artists in the industry do.

When it comes to 3D, there's something really magical about experiencing something you create from all angles in an interactive space like 3D. I got interested in 3D when I was a kid from a picture I saw in a computer magazine. It was a rendered image of a basketball and a sports car, but it was so realistic and cool looking. I realized then how much you could do with 3D.

Do you have an ultimate goal for your career?

What I'd like to do is combine more 2D with 3D. I'd like to experiment with matte paintings, but not matte paintings on glass, matte paintings on polygons. The mere fact that 3D packages solve the problem of perspective is an incredible advantage to a 2D artist. Combining that advantage with the 2D knowledge I have is one of the things that excites me the most and something I want to exploit.

What's the best advice you could give to new artists entering the industry?

I still remember what it was like, worrying about whether or not my work was good enough, and if I'd get hired. It was tough.

Never think you know everything. Always grow as an artist. Never stop studying, even if it means you find yourself at the zoo drawing the animals. Look at what other people are doing. That's easy to do. Don't lose faith in your work, you'll get better as long as you keep working on it.

Create a solid portfolio. Don't put anything in it that you don't feel really good about. Only the best pieces should be included.

A lot of getting into the industry is luck. Put yourself in circumstances where you can get lucky. Go to a portfolio review, set up informational interviews at companies, stuff like that. You never know…

9 MAKING TEXTURE MAPS FOR CHARACTERS

IN THIS CHAPTER YOU WILL LEARN ABOUT:

- How to make clothes for your characters
- How to make armor with filters
- Tips about how to get a good skin
- How to make a great scaly hide with layer styles
- Adding rivets with layer styles

INTRODUCTION

Characters are usually people, monsters, animals, or anything that will be animated. They can convey a perspective, or a personality, or an emotion. Characters might be old, familiar figures, or brand new creatures no one has ever seen before.

Characters are useful to 3D because they serve as the vessel that a game player or audience can transpose themselves into while playing a game or watching a film. Characters are there to heighten the suspension of disbelief and to get the audience involved. Characters are also useful as opposing forces (the enemy), background elements, or as a means to evoke strong emotions.

Character texturing is a bit different from environmental texturing. Unlike an architectural model, for example, a character model is usually far more organic in shape. Be prepared for having to spend a little more time perfecting your model's textures. There are shortcuts aplenty, but it's worth your time and effort to do it the hard way first. In the case of character texturing, the hard way is the best way.

The first thing to do with a character is decide what the costume and details of the character will be. Perhaps you will have these choices made for you already. If so, then take some time to think about how you might go about making them. This will assist your workflow.

The second step to take when working with a character model is to sort out which UVs correspond to which areas of the UV map. After you have determined this, you'll know where the seams are and how to fix them. The models in this chapter were mapped by using the doubling-up technique; what seems like only 50% of the UV information of the models, is, in fact, 100% of the UV information folded over on top of the other half.

The Babe

All of the human character tutorials in this chapter will be for the "babe" model in the file package for this book. For her, you'll paint some jeans, make a sweater, do her face and hands, her hair, and a hat texture. All of the nonhuman creature tutorials will be about the orc model. For his ugly self, you'll make his face texture, armor, a leather belt, fur hide skirt, and belt buckle.

THE HUMAN FIGURE

Artists have been depicting the human figure for as long as art has been made, and there are techniques you need to know to get your final character textures right.

The most important thing to think about when making a character is form. "Form" is a traditional term for how light falls upon the body. Light upon the human figure is what defines that body as a shape. If you're standing in a pitch black room with 50 people, they're invisible because there is no light on them showing their forms.

Lighting is a tricky business, but there is a formula. To get a decent lighting of a model, use a backlight, a fill light, and a spotlight. To get good contrast and color, add colored lights that complement your scene. This is how you will depict form on the model.

This same concept can be faked with textures on a model. Before you try to fake it though, it's a good idea to get some training on how to draw light on a body because that's exactly what you're doing. It's a good idea to figure out how core shadows and highlight work on soft thigh shapes or hard muscle shapes. Once you have command of that, you can paint a light source directly into your texture.

CLOTHES

Most characters you make will probably involve some type of clothing. True, this may be very small bits of clothing, but you'll still need to know how to get it working.

The best way to see how artists are portraying light on costumes is to just play games and see for yourself. You can also raid your own closet for examples or consult the tons and tons of catalogs and fashion magazines. The hardest part about character texturing is getting seams to match. For things like jeans, where it's really obvious where the seams are, you'll need to be vigilant about concealing them. Keep in mind that jeans on a human take up a lot of the figure.

Jeans, sweaters, jackets, hats, and every other imaginable human accouterment may easily be cloth-based. There are plenty of different ways to make woven patterns in Photoshop. There are several preset patterns you can use to get your feet wet, for example. I like to use combinations of filters to get interesting results, as well as digital photographs that I then tile. Often, the most interesting patterns I get are from simply messing around. Don't be afraid to try out new ideas.

The fun part of character texturing is adding in detail. You can add sandblasting effects, logos, tears, stains, holes, blood, bits of dinner... whatever is appropriate. As always, strong contrast is good because if your colors and details are too subtle, they'll be hard to see on screens like TVs that support much less resolved imagery than a PC monitor.

Create as much illusion of depth and realism as you can to make the character look visually intriguing and satisfying. Keep in mind is that whatever you borrow from other images needs to match. This model's jeans would look pretty awful if the separate elements used to create them were all different hues of blue. The fastest way to get your Frankenstein jeans to match up is to add the details you want to the main texture document and then use the information already present in the main document as a reference for color correcting. In this way, everything will come together easily.

SKIN

Human flesh is a pretty common element in texture maps. The thing about skin is that it's actually alive and it's tough to make it look that way. Try to avoid skin that is flat, dull, and dead looking. A traditional technique I use for game characters is to apply thin layers (called glazes in oil painting terms) of paint and build up the form of the face map that way. Glazes help give the illusion of translucency and liveliness. Obviously, not every character you get to create or work with will be a human that requires human-looking skin, but it's a good thing to be able to do well.

For this female model, let's keep things on the simple side. After examining her geometry, we can determine that the only skin that will be visible is her face, neck, shoulders, and hands. In this case, then, the UVs of her face, neck, and shoulders will all be included on the same map. Her hands, complete with red fingernails, will be mapped separately.

Adding details is another option for skin. Depending on the project, such things as scars, tattoos, bullet holes, face paint, heavy makeup, freckles, lots of wrinkles, a third eye, an eye patch, and the like are great to add. Just make sure that all of your details are well-defined, clearly visible, and distinct.

HAIR

Hair, like skin, can be as simple or as complicated as you want to make it. Some people spend a lot of time perfecting the art of hair.

Usually, there is a base texture painted to look like strands of hair and an alpha channel that goes with the hair to make it look like there is space between the hairs. However, most people don't have perfectly straight hair that ends in a blunt line suspiciously resembling the end of a geometric plane.

This chapter will keep it simple. I encourage you to experiment with hair like crazy. Choose different colors, curls, styles, mohawks, bald people with stubble – anything you want. Making hair is a really interesting way of giving your character identity.

THE NON-HUMAN CREATURE

This Orc is the second character, and a little bit more complicated than the female human. Non-human creatures are so fun to make because of all the creative leeway.

Just like humans, all other creatures are subject to formal concerns. How does the light fall on them? How is the shape best represented with painted textures? Then there may be other things to think about. Do they live in dark places or light places? What is their natural terrain? Water? Desert? The surface of Jupiter? Always take a good long look at your character concept art and think about the best ways you can make the creature come alive.

MONSTER HIDES

To begin with the Orc hide, I started with the Internet again and found myself some great pictures of lizards. Then I sewed together all the interesting bits into one source lizard that has a nice variety of patterns on the scaly hide. I made a template I could use to clone and heal from as I worked on making the texture seamless.

This works for his entire body: face, arms, legs, and hands. Use whatever source art or setup works best for you.

ARMOR AND GEAR

Armor is a common costume element and it helps to know how to make it. You can see limitless examples of it in film and video games.

Armor comes in many different designs. You can always make it up yourself, but I believe that to get it looking good, you should do a little research and development before you dive in. Decide on what looks best for you project's concept. Old and dingy or spankin' new and shiny?

A fabulous way to introduce some of the intricate patterning and metal embossing of armor is to apply layer styles to imported graphics. In the upcoming tutorial, you'll see how this is done with a black and white Celtic-style graphic. There are many such images to be had and whatever works is fair game.

FUR

Fur can be a hard to create, but there are a couple of ways to do it well. You can hand-paint it with a scattering brush set to a variety of jitters like hue and saturation jitter. Jitter simply means variation and the higher the percentage of jitter, the more your brush strokes will differ from each other in terms of color, saturation, and length.

Sometimes hand painting doesn't work well, especially if you're working on something that requires a lot of realism. In this chapter, you'll make the orc's fur with some Noise, a Motion Blur, and the Texturizer.

THE BABE'S FACE: AT A GLANCE

Source image for the face

TOPICS COVERED

Learn how to create a seamless face texture map for the babe character in this tutorial.

YOU'LL LEARN HOW TO:

Create a skin tone palette
Use a source image for the face
Paint a seamless skin texture

MATERIALS REQUIRED

thebabe.mb or thebabe.dxf
FaceMap.tif
BabeFaceSource.psd

TUTORIAL: THE BABE S FACE

STEP 1: OPEN THE UV MAP

Open FaceMap.tif. This is the UV layout of the model's face.

STEP 2: CUT OUT OLD SWATCHES

If the Swatches palette is not visible, go to the Window menu and highlight Swatches. Next, click on the Swatches palette tab to activate it. Now mouse over the swatches while holding down the Ctrl/⌘ key. A pair of scissors will appear. Still holding down Ctrl/⌘, click with the mouse over the swatches in the palette. Click until all of them have been cut out. You want a fresh, new palette for the skin tones you are about to add.

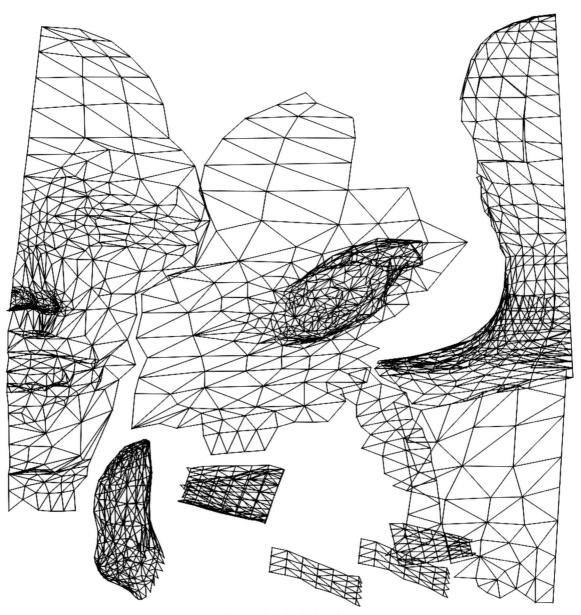

UV map for the babes face

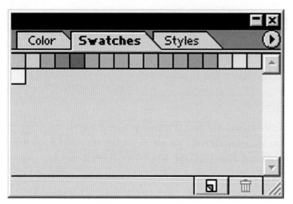

Skin tone swatches

New Swatch...

Reset Swatches...
Load Swatches...
Save Swatches...
Replace Swatches...

✓ Small Thumbnail
Small List

ANPA Colors.aco
DIC Colors.aco
FOCOLTONE Colors.aco
Pantone Colors (Coated).aco
Pantone Colors (Process).aco
Pantone Colors (ProSim).aco
Pantone Colors (Uncoated).aco
TOYO Colors.aco
TRUMATCH Colors.aco
Hair.aco
Illustrations.aco
Lizard Orc.aco
Mac OS.aco
Skins.aco
VisiBone.aco
VisiBone2.aco
Web Hues.aco
Web Safe Colors.aco
Web Spectrum.aco
Windows.aco

Save Swatches command

STEP 3: FIND SOURCE MATERIAL

Find some source images: pictures of people with the same flesh tone that you're making the texture. If you like you can just grab a few from the Internet real quick. If you can't find a good one, or would like to skip the search, you can use BabeFaceSource.PSD from this book's file package.

For this model I chose a fair Caucasian tone, but you'll be able to follow along if you pick something else. Load the images in Photoshop and hit I on the keyboard for the Eyedropper(I) tool. Zoom into the image to be sampled and click on an area that looks promising for a believable skin tone. Note that this will change the foreground color to the new hue you have just sampled. Click on the Options arrow at the top-right corner of the Swatches palette. Select New Swatch. Type in a name for the swatch when prompted and hit Enter. The new swatch has been added to the palette. Repeat until you have a nice selection of tones from various sources. Now click the round Options arrow on the Swatches palette again and select Save Swatches. Enter a name, like "skins", and hit Enter to save. Now you can load in these skin tones whenever you want. If you wish to add to them, simply save over the original once the additions have been made.

STEP 4: FILTER THE SKIN FILL LAYER

Create a new layer with a Shift + Ctrl/⌘ + N and name it "Skin Fill". Click on a Skin Swatch from the Swatches palette and then hit G on the keyboard for the Fill(G) tool. Fill the new layer with the skin tone you have selected. Do a Filter→Noise→Add Noise with a very low setting, checking Gaussian and Monochromatic.

STEP 5: SCALE THE FACE IMAGE

Next, using the selection tool of your choice, draw a selection marquee around the right half of the source image's face. Do a Select→Save Selection, and name it "face" – do this in case you mess up and need to start again. Do a Ctrl/⌘ + C to copy, then click and drag the selection into the Face Map document. Using the Face Map layer as a reference, use Transform mode to rotate and scale the face image to match the UVs of the map as closely as you can.

STEP 6: TWEAK THE FACE TEXTURE

Cut the eyebrow away from its original placement and move it higher up above her eye to match the geometry. Also, the mouth is too low; select the lips and then Ctrl/⌘ + X to cut away the mouth and a Ctrl/⌘ + V to paste it back. Use the Move(V) tool to reposition her lips a few pixels above its original position.

Skin fill

The mouth from the source image is too small for the geometry of the model. Just do a Ctrl/⌘ + T to transform the scale of the mouth. Then use the Burn and Dodge Tools to add the dark area between her lips and the highlights of her lipstick. With the Clone(S) tool, add some subtle creases to her lips to lessen the slick look of them. You could even add a tiny bit of noise for more texture.

STEP 7: SOFTEN EDGES

Two other problems with the source image are that the edges need to be softened and the skin tone needs to match the Skin Fill layer that serves as the background.

To soften the edges of the Face, choose the Eraser(E) tool with a small, soft brush set with a Roundness of 45, and quickly remove the hard edges and the darker areas that could never be made to match the background. The next step is to get the skin tone to match up. Do an Image➔Adjust➔Variations➔Darker and click OK. Then, adjust the Hue/Saturation of the Master with a -19 Saturation.

STEP 8: ADD VARIATION TO SKIN TONE

Now let's add a little variation to the surface of the background skin tone. Go back to the Face Source image and, with the Rectangular Marquee(M) tool, draw a selection on her left cheek. Hit V on the keyboard and click and drag the selection in to the master document. Then do a Ctrl/⌘ + T to increase the scale of the swatch to cover the entire image, add some more noise, and hit Enter. Do an Image➔Adjust➔Variations and click OK (the tool will be set to how it was used last). To complete the color correction, do an Image➔Adjust➔Hue Saturation and lower the saturation of the Master by 19. Name this layer "Skin Variations" and set its Opacity to 75%. Place it over the Skin Fill layer in the layer stack.

STEP 9: TEST THE TEXTURE

Do a Ctrl/⌘ + S to save over the first JPEG test and reapply the texture to the model to check the mouth's position. It may take a couple tries to get the position of the lips in the right spot over the geometry of the mouth.

Time for some fine-tuning. One thing that needs doing is to change the color of the model's pupil. Simply use the Elliptical Marquee(M) tool to select the pupil, then do a Ctrl/⌘ + J to create a new layer with a new pupil. Adjust the Hue/Saturation to change the eye to a darker brown, and then place it over the original with the Move(V) tool.

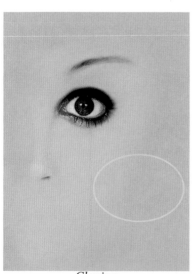

Cloning

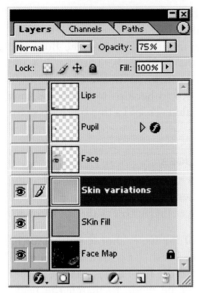

Layer stack for the skin tutorial

STEP 10: FADE SKIN EDGES

Next, use the Clone Stamp(S) with Use All Layers checked to fade out the edge of her face. First, clone with a 75% Opacity, then, as you paint outward, reduce the Opacity to first 50% and then, finally, 25% in order to create a seamless transition between the skin of her face and the skin tone of the background. This technique is fine to use, because the texture itself is meant to be soft. Clone in more of a cheek and add a lighter skin underneath her lips and to her chin, using the original source image as a guide. The goal here is to reconstruct the curves and planes of the woman's face with a subtle and gentle use of the Clone(S) tool, painting over the digital imperfections and pixelations of the source image. To finish up, use the Dodge(O) tool with a low exposure to bring out highlights on the end of her nose and her lips.

Human skin can be as simple or as complex as you would like it to be. With this map, you could also add jewelry or tattoos - whatever strikes your fancy.

The skin

Altered eye

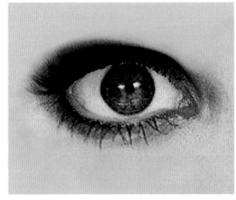

Original eye

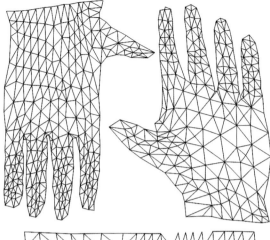

UV map for the hands

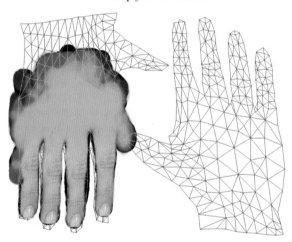

Fingers

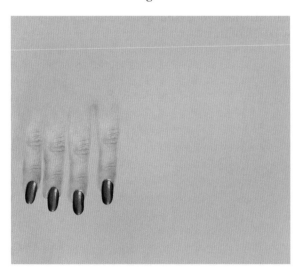

The hands

EXERCISE — HANDS

Open the HandsMap.tif and HandsDone.psd files.

Since the Hands need to match the Face, the first step to take is to add the Skin Variations layer and the Skin Fill layer to the HandsMap. Using the Move(V) tool, click and drag while depressing the Shift key to place the layers in the Hands Map document. You can make them invisible or reduce their Opacity later. (Refer to the HandsDone.psd to check progress.)

Once again, I downloaded images of a hand and fingernails that roughly match the texture map. After a little color correcting, clone one finger to create the four represented here and then you can use Transform mode to scale them down, or up, to the appropriate size corresponding to the UV map of the hands. Next, erase the hard edges of the hand. Once that's done, use the cloning and healing tools to blend the edges of the hand in with the background skin tone.

Now add the fingernails over the nail area of the original hand. Again, use Ctrl/⌘ + T to scale and rotate the fingernails to match the scale and shape of the hand.

Some things to add: since only certain portions of the hands are visible in the final composition that this character is for, the thumbs and palm of the map aren't added to beyond the background skin tone. It could be a cool idea to add palms to this model and maybe a bump map to emphasize the wrinkles and creases of her hands. Rings could be added to the map, as well as more defined knuckles, veins, and pores.

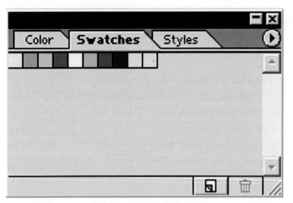

Hair strands palette

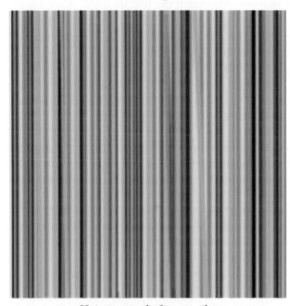

Hair texture before overlay

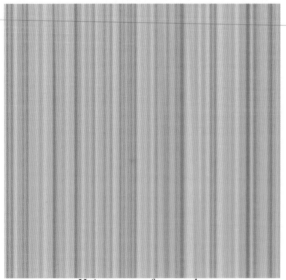

Hair texture after overlay

EXERCISE - LONG HAIR

Open the HairDone.psd.

Do a Ctrl/⌘ + N to create a new document. Set the Width and Height at 128x128 with a transparent background. Go to the Swatches palette and, while holding down Ctrl/⌘, click to cut out all of the swatches currently loaded into the palette. You are going to choose a selection of hues to serve as a Hair palette.

Depending on what hair color you want this model to have, you may need to customize parts of this step. I've chosen blonde for this character's hair. With the empty palette, access the Color Picker by clicking on the Foreground color swatch. Use the slider to move into the yellow area of the spectrum. Next, begin to choose a variety of hues that well represent different shades of blonde, from dark brown to light, pale yellow. Add each to the palette as a new swatch. After you have chosen your hues, pick a middle-of-the-road yellow and use it to fill Layer 1. Name the layer "Hair Fill".

Now hit U and select the Line(U) tool. Make sure it is set to Create a New Fill on the Options bar and set the weight to 3. 3 will be the largest strand of hair. Select a darker color from the palette. Do a Shift + Ctrl/⌘ + N to create a new layer and name it "Brown Strands". Using the Line(L) tool, Click and drag while holding Shift to draw a series of brown strands on the layer. Don't worry about placing them evenly - they will look more natural unevenly set along the layer.

Draw 9 or 10 strands and then create another new layer. Name this one according to the next swatch you choose to draw with. I used a light brown. Set the weight of the Line(L) tool to 2 and draw your strands again. Draw 20-25 of them.

Layer stack for the hair tutorial

Create another new layer and repeat the process with a new hue from your Hair Swatches palette. Continue this process until you have a lovely texture of fine strands. As you draw, alter the weight of the Line(L) tool to suit your tastes. In this case, we want a nice, fine texture for the blond hair, which requires many thin lines on separate layers.

Finally, when all the strands are in place, create a new layer on the top of the stack and fill it with the blond hue you like the most from the Hair palette you have created. Reduce the Opacity to 55%. Try the texture out on your model and tweak until you have the results you like the most.

JEANS: AT A GLANCE

TOPICS COVERED

Learn how to create a seamless jeans texture map for the babe character in this tutorial.

YOU'LL LEARN HOW TO:

Make Denim with Four Sections tiling
Color Correct the source photos
Fix the seams of the characters pants

MATERIALS REQUIRED

thebabe.mb or thebabe.dxf
JeansMap.tif
Denim.psd
DenimButt.psd
DenimHips.psd

TUTORIAL: JEANS

The UV Snapshot map of the pants geometry has five main areas: hips, butt, and front, back, and sides of the legs. In the case of the different sides of the legs, the UVs have been doubled up to save space and to maximize the texture space. All of the leg geometry that is represented by UVs in this document will be transformed into a pair of jeans. That means the denim pattern, details of the jeans, thick seams, and whatever else you feel like.

STEP 1: SORT OUT THE UVS

The first thing to do is figure out which UVs represent what. Flip between your 3D app and Photoshop to determine what is what, if the UV snapshot texture map is a little hard to sort out. The UV snapshots for the clothing and skin of this character were set at 512 x 512. This is large enough to get great detail, and can be scaled. (Use the JeansMap.tif for this tutorial).

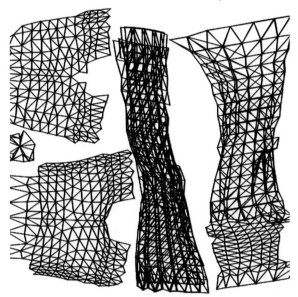

UV map for the jeans

Tiled denim swatch

STEP 2: FOUR SECTIONS TILING

Do a Ctrl/⌘ + O to open the Denim.psd you have downloaded. Click and drag to load the Denim layer into the JeansMap document. We will make use of the Four Sections Tiling tutorial from earlier in the book. Using Ctrl/⌘ + T, scale down the denim swatch until it is believably the size of actual denim. Then, rotate it 90 degrees counterclockwise so that the swatch is oriented horizontally. Place the swatch in the bottom-right corner of the Pants document. Now hit V for the Move (V) tool and, while depressing the Alt Key, click and drag to create a new swatch. Do a Ctrl/⌘ + T to surround the new swatch with a Transform bounding box and then right-click→Flip Horizontal. Do a Ctrl/⌘ + E to merge the 2 swatches. Use the Move(V) tool duplication trick again to duplicate the merged denim swatch. Drag this layer above the first layer of denim, do a Ctrl/⌘ + T, then right-click and choose Flip Vertical. Hit Enter to finalize. Do a Ctrl/⌘ + E to merge and duplicate this layer until the entire area of the texture map is covered. Either Merge Down as you work, or merge them all at the end. The goal is one layer. Right-click, choose Layer properties, and name it Denim Photo.

STEP 3: CREATE A FILL LAYER

Do a Shift + Ctrl/⌘ + N to create a new layer and call it Denim Fill. Mouse over to the Swatches palette and choose a fitting hue to represent the blue of the denim jeans; dark cyan will do nicely. Hit G and click to fill.

STEP 4: ADJUST THE FILL HUE

Lower the Brightness a bit. Next, choose Filters→Noise→Add Noise and set the Noise to 2.0, Gaussian, and Monochromatic. After running this Filter, apply the Crosshatch Filter located under Filter→Brush Strokes→Crosshatch. Set the Stroke length to 9, the Sharpness to 6, and the Strength to 1. Hit OK to finalize.

Do a Ctrl/⌘ + S to save

STEP 5: TEST THE TEXTURE

Time to do a texture check. Save the image as a JPEG and apply it to the model in your 3D application. Let's say that after examining the model, you decide that the pants are just too blue. So, back in Photoshop, click on the Create New Fill or Adjustment Layer button located on the bottom of the Layers palette and select Hue/Saturation. Set the Master Saturation to -35 and the Lightness to -1. Do a Ctrl/⌘ + E to merge the Denim Fill, Denim Photo, and Hue Saturation Adjustment layer. Name the layer Denim.

STEP 6: START SEWING THE PIECES TOGETHER

Now to start sewing it all together. Start with the butt. Go on over to the DenimButt.psd and, with the selection tool of your choice, select an area that will become half of the character's rear end. Be sure to select pixels inside of the dark outlines around these jeans. Otherwise there will be dark lines in the texture that won't look so hot. With the Move(V) tool selected, click and drag from the DenimButt to the main texture document. Now do a Ctrl/⌘ + T to rotate the half of her rear counterclockwise 90 degrees. Duplicate with an Alt + V + click and drag the second half down. Do a Ctrl/⌘ + T and then a Flip Vertical. Ctrl/⌘ + E to merge, then Ctrl/⌘ + T to resume transforming your newly created Butt. Use the UV Map as a reference or use the already created details layer of the master file downloadable for this book as a guide. Right-click on the layer and name it "Butt".

Jeans source image 1

Jeans source image 2

Now we will follow essentially the same process for the front of her hips. Zoom in on the hips area of the DenimHip.psd. Select the area of detail that includes the pockets, fly, and creases, then drag the selection in to the main Jeans file. Do another Ctrl/⌘ + T to rotate the hips 90 degrees counterclockwise, then scale them to fit the area of the map.

Repeat the same process to add detail to the sides of her legs as well. Employ what you know about how jeans look and what happens to them after they're worn for awhile.

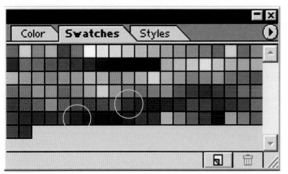

Cyan swatches

Denim Swatches

STEP 7: TEST YOUR STITCHING

Do a Ctrl/⌘ + S to save the Photoshop document, then do a Ctrl/⌘ + Shift + S to save the file as a JPEG. Now test out what you've created so far on your model. You'll notice that there are several very noticeable seams messing the texture up and the hues of each do not match.

STEP 8: COLOR CORRECTING TEXTURE SECTIONS

The denim hips and butt sections in for this tutorial are corrected with a combination of the Color Balance (Ctrl/⌘ + B), Hue/Saturation (Ctrl/⌘ + U), Variations, and Brightness/Contrast Tools. For each pair of jeans, the Magenta Levels and the Yellow levels were significantly reduced, the Cyan was added once with Variations. Hue/Saturation was used to reduce the Cyan's saturation and lightness. The last step was tweaking the Brightness/Contrast slider to get the denim sections perfect.

STEP 9: ADD IN DETAILS

Now go on back to Photoshop. Hit E for the Eraser(E) tool and with a medium-sized, soft brush, erase around the hard edges of the hips and butt Denim. Create a new layer and name it "Details". Now, with clever use of the Clone(S) tool and the Healing(J) tool, use the creases of the hips as the source points and paint on some creases along the area of the texture map that represents the sides of the model's legs. You will also need to add half of a pocket, coupled with the jeans details, to the side of her legs to match the texture on her rear end. Keep referring back to the model, trying on her pants every time you make a major edit to make sure you're on the right track. The edges of the character's texture sections need to be soft and need to match the hue and saturation of the background texture layers. When you are satisfied with your Hips, Butt, and details, duplicate the original document, and merge them all onto one layer. Name the layer "Details".

The jeans

Once you have done your time getting the Jeans to where they need to be, you can add whatever else you like. In this case, the Dodge(O) tool is used to create lighter, more washed out areas on the jeans on top of the thigh area. I also added a little heart-shaped logo, and a belt with a buckle.

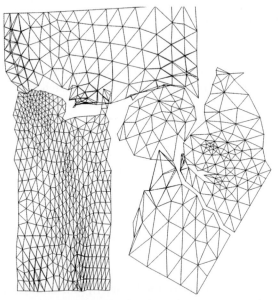

UV map for the sweater

Sweater texture

EXERCISE — SWEATER

Open the SweaterMap.tif. Look carefully at the UV snapshot layer. This texture map is even more difficult to sort out than the jeans UV Snapshot. Once again, you will need to refer to the character model, select some UVs here and there, and determine what's an arm, what's a shoulder, etc. Once you have that information you can begin.

Create a new layer with a Shift + Ctrl/⌘ + N and name it "Noise". Hit X on the keyboard, and then G to fill the layer with Black. Next, run a Noise filter on the black fill, setting the noise to 22 or so, Gaussian, and monochromatic. Drag the cloth layer to the Create a New Layer icon at the bottom of the Layers palette. Right-click and call it "Angled Strokes". Do a Filter→Brush Strokes→Angled Strokes and set the filter to Direction Balance 62, Stroke length 15, and Sharpness 4. Hit Enter to finalize.

Now do a Ctrl/⌘ + T to Transform. Zoom out to view the entire bounding box and, holding down Shift to constrain, rotate 45 degrees or until the angled strokes are oriented vertically. Hit Enter to finalize.

Now duplicate the Angled Strokes layer. Right-click and name it "Stripes". Turn off the Noise and Angled Strokes layer for now so you can work on the layers below with an unobstructed view. Hit E for the Eraser(E) tool and choose the Spatter 25 pixels brush. With the Eraser, erase horizontal streaks from the layer all down the canvas, winding up with a striped pattern. Now do a Filter→Liquefy. Choose one of the Twirl brushes and set the size to 64, Brush Pressure to 50. Now repeatedly click along the black stripes of the Stripes layer, creating a slightly warped and irregular pattern. Repeat along every stripe. Hit Enter when done, then turn all of the layers back on. Set the Stripes layer to Overlay with an Opacity of 52%.

Now it's time to pay attention to how to orient the sweater pattern correctly along the UVs of the mapped model. The fast way is to select the Stripes layer and then Ctrl/⌘ + E twice to merge all three. Duplicate the layer and reduce the Opacity of the Noise copy layer to 65%. Then turn off the Noise layer. With the Noise copy layer selected, do a Ctrl/⌘ + T, zoom out to view the entire bounding box, then rotate the layer 45 degrees clockwise. Use the Lasso(L) tool to create a selection around the shoulder and arm section of the map, do a Ctrl/⌘ + Shift + I to Invert the selection. Do a Ctrl/⌘ + X to cut away the unnecessary portions of the layer. Return the Noise copy layer to 100% Opacity and turn the Noise layer back on.

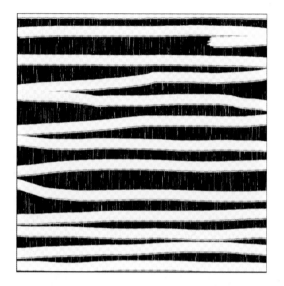

To complete the texture for the Sweater Map, run the Add Noise Filter again on each layer with the same settings.   10% was added to mine.   Do an Image→Adjust→Brightness/Contrast,   +8   for Brightness and a +10 for Contrast. If you wish, you can finish up this texture with an Unsharp mask.

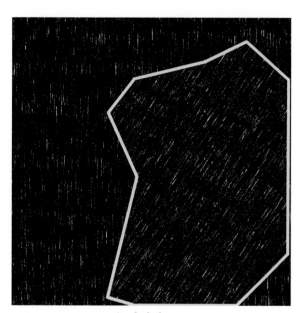

Angled sleeves

The sweater

EXERCISE — HAT

The last step to complete the Babe is to add a material to her hat. A basic black suede is perfect.

Do a Ctrl/⌘ + N to create a new document. Set the dimensions to 128x128. Hit D on the keyboard to reset the Foreground/Background swatches to default, and then select the Fill(G) tool. Click inside the image to fill with black. Double-click on Layer 1, choose Layer Properties, and name it "Black Suede".

Next, choose Filter→Noise→Add Noise from the top menu bar and specify a low percentage of noise: 25%. Check Uniform. Leave Monochromatic unchecked. Hit Enter to finalize.

Next go to the Edit menu and select Fade Add Noise. Reduce the noise by 50% or so, so that the range of color is there, but subtle. Save this as a JPEG, and then apply it to an object within your 3D application. This simple texture can also be inverted and used as a bump map to further emphasize the tactility of the hat.

ORC HEAD TEXTURE: AT A GLANCE

The Orc

TOPICS COVERED

Time for more advanced character texturing techniques with the Orc tutorial. Learn how to an evil Orc head.

YOU LL LEARN HOW TO:

Paint a scaly hide with Layer Styles
Reuse and Recycle for Arms and Legs

MATERIALS REQUIRED

LizardSource.psd
OrcMap.tif
Orc.mb or Orc.dxf

TUTORIAL: ORC HEAD

Once you have compiled your source file, do a Window→Tile and examine it closely. Use Z to zoom in and out, paying attention to what is repetitive about the texture, and what is not. Will most of the texture be created with Photoshop's features? Or will the source images be relied upon? Will you concoct a mixture of both? For the Orc Head tutorial, a combination of both the source image and the tools of Photoshop will be used.

STEP 1: OPEN THE SOURCE ART AND MAKE A PALETTE

Create a palette. Open the LizardSource.psd image and select the Eyedropper(I) tool. Use it to move around the image collecting swatches for your texture's palette. Once a sample is taken, click in the Swatches palette. Enter a reference name, and hit Enter. Select new swatches in order: choose a range of yellows, move to browns, then grays, and finally select the darkest values of the image. In this way, when you glance at your palette, you will be able to see exactly what range of hues and values you have to work with, and it will be a simple matter to pare them down if you are working within a limited palette.

STEP 2: CREATE THE FOUNDATION FOR THE TEXTURE

A basic texture can be used to fill the background and serve as a blending pattern along the seams of the UVs. Open OrcMap.tif, and do a Shift + Ctrl/⌘ + N to create a new layer. Name it "Snakeskin". Click on the Styles palette and then the Options arrow. Choose Replace Styles, and select Image Effects from the list of styles. Scroll down the Image Effects list and click on Snakeskin. Now jump to the Layers palette and double-click on the Bevel and Emboss effect. Click on Texture.

Also add a Bevel and Emboss.

Set the Blending Mode of the Snakeskin layer to Hue.

STEP 3: CREATE A BROWN FILL LAYER

Create another new layer and name it "Brown Fill". Drag it into position below the Snakeskin layer in the stack. Fill the entire layer with a brown hue like R 101, G 81, B 66. Do a Filter→Noise→Add Noise and set the filter 15-20% with Gaussian and Monochromatic checked. Add a Pattern Overlay with the settings to the right.

STEP 4: CREATE A GREEN FILL LAYER

Now create yet another layer. Name it "Green Fill". Do a Ctrl/⌘ + A to select the entire image and click on the Foreground swatch to specify the Fill color. Choose a lighter grayish-green such as R 236, G 236, B 190. Use the Paint Bucket(G) tool to fill the selection. Now double-click on the layer to access the Blending Options and add an Inner Bevel using Bevel and Emboss.

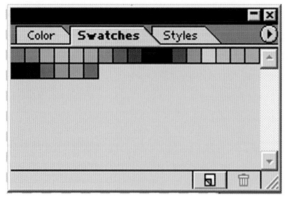

Orc palette

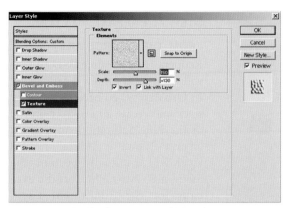

Snakeskin pattern dialog box

STEP 5: MAKE A LAYER OUT OF THE GREEN FILL

Now right-click on the Green Fill Layers Effects Icon and select Create Layers. This command will change your Layer Style into separate layers. Notice that there are now separate layers for the Bevel and Emboss, Highlights, and Shadows. Click on the eyeball of each to see the effect they add to this texture. Next, click back on the Green Fill layer. Set the Blending Mode to Color and the Opacity to 100%. Click on the Green Fill's Highlight layer and set this layer to Overlay, 67%. Finally, click on the Shadow layer and set it to Multiply, 75%.

STEP 6: MAKE A NEW LAYER SET

Since the Basic Snakeskin texture is optional, I'm going to create a Layer Set folder in the layer stack to contain all of the relevant layers. To accomplish this, do a Layer→New→Layer Set. Type in "Basic Texture" and hit Enter. A Folder will appear in the layers stack. Now, being careful to keep the layers in order, click on each of them in turn and drag them onto the folder. Everything is now neatly contained and easy to turn on an off as needed.

Create a new Hue/Saturation Adjustment Layer above the Basic Texture Layer Set and set it to Master Hue –12, Saturation –23, and Lightness +30. This will even out the hue values a bit and blend all those layers more cohesively together.

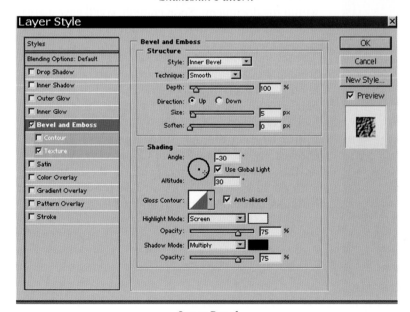

Snakeskin Pattern

Inner Bevel

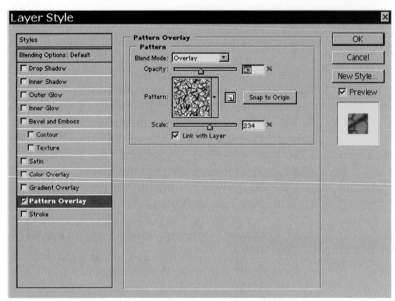

Metal Landscape Pattern

Brown pattern

Green fill

Hue/saturation adjustment layer

STEP 7: PREPARE TO CLONE FROM THE SOURCE ART

Reopen LizardSource.PSD. This will be used to clone details from. In OrcMap.tif, go back to the layer stack and create a new layer on top of the Hue/Saturation Adjustment layer. Name it "Hide". This layer will eventually become the main one. Next, click off the eyeballs for the Adjustment Layer and the Basic Texture in order to see the UV snapshot at the bottom of the stack. This is the layer needed in order to see where the hide details need to go.

STEP 8: CLONE FROM THE SOURCE ART

On this map, it's easy to see what is what, for the most part. Remember to check the UV placement on the main model in your 3D app if there's any confusion about which UVs represent what section of geometry.

Decide on a starting point. Find patches of scales on the lizard that work well and clone a few onto the Hide layer of the UV map. Next, do Ctrl/⌘ + T to scale up the scales a little because they are a little small. (Not too much, though, or the scales would be blurred.) Then clone that small group of scales over and over within the document. Soon enough, you'll have a great scaly hide with nice relief and depth to it.

The second thing to do is choose a larger detail to work around. Look at the source lizard and find the great big knobby thing that will look good placed in the cheekbone area of the head. (Don't forget - this UV map looks like only a half, but the UVs are mirrored.) So, with a large brush and Aligned and Use All Layers checked on the Clone(S) tool Options bar, Alt + Click on the source image, then paint on the bump thing onto the hide layer. With a smaller brush of medium hardness, add more detail around the large lump.

Lizard source art

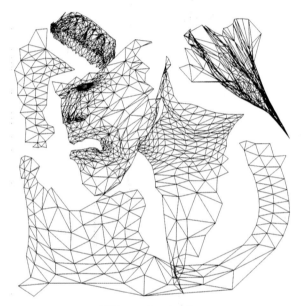

UV map for the Orc

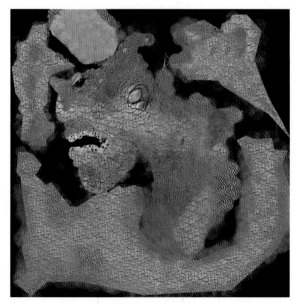

The Orc's head

Another technique I use for adding detail is to simply click on the "Spots" Layer of the Lizard source image and drag it right into my Main Texture. With the Ctrl/⌘ + Alt + V (for the Move tool) command, I can quickly replicate this pattern and transform it to fit into the UV Map. It's always a good idea to keep everything on separate layers until the end. Keep your freedom intact for as long as possible.

Continue to clone in the details you like from the source lizard. For each new pattern that you introduce, create a new layer and invent a name for the pattern. Once the whole map is covered, do a Ctrl/⌘ + S to save your work, convert the image into a JPEG or a GIF or a TIF, and try it out on your model. After looking carefully at the model, you will clearly see where the edges of the textures meet. Downplay those seams as much as possible: figure out where the mismatched areas of the textured model are in relation to the Photoshop document you are creating. This may take time; the goal is to make the orc's hide meet together in a believable, if not absolutely perfect, fashion.

STEP 9: COLOR CORRECT TO MATCH

The final step is color correcting . I wound up with a foundation hide and two layers of further detail and variation culled from the Lizard source image. To get all three to match, click on each layer in succession and use the Image➔Adjust➔Hue/Saturation command to match the patterns' hues. Use the basic texture as a guide for the Hue, Saturation, and Lightness levels of each layer, but don't make them match exactly: some variation is good.

Do a Ctrl/⌘ + S to save your orc face texture. Try it out on the model. Rework and revise. Save, and try it on again

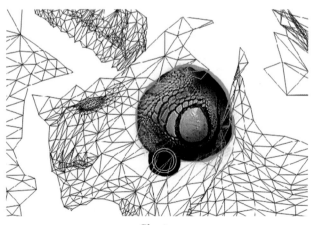

Cloning

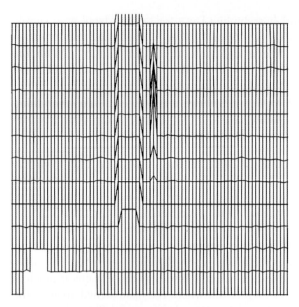

UV map for the fur skirt

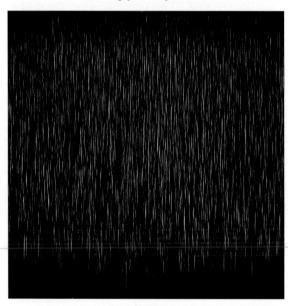

The Fur

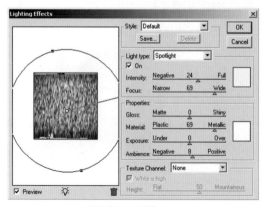

Lighting Effects

EXERCISE — FUR

Open the OrcFurSkirtMap.psd document for the furry, nappy hide kilt the Orc wears. Do a Shift + Ctrl/⌘ + N to create a new layer. Right-click and call it "fur".

Go to the Swatches palette and select a dark brown. Hit G on the keyboard and fill the Fur layer with the dark brown. Next, access the Filter menu and do a Noise➔Add Noise. Set the Noise to 22-25, checking Gaussian and Monochromatic. Hit Enter.

Go back to the Filter menu and do a Blur➔Motion Blur. Set the Angle to 90 degrees and the Distance at 25. Hit Enter.

Do File➔Save As... (Ctrl/⌘ + Alt + S) to save the PSD. Name the file "FurSkirt.psd".

Go back to the Fur layer and do a Filter➔Texture➔Texturizer. Click on the Texture drop-down arrow and select Load Texture. Go to the directory where the FurSkirt.psd has just been saved and select it as the file to be loaded. Make sure the scaling is at 100% (or else there will be unsightly seams) and bump up the Relief. I used a value of 22. Set the Light Direction to Right, and hit Enter to finalize.

Time to test out the fur skirt on the orc character. Do a Ctrl/⌘ + Alt + S to save as a JPEG and load the file into the texture editor of your 3D application. Do a quick render, just to be sure.

However, to increase the depth of the fur texture, a little burning is a good idea. Hit O for the Burn(O) tool. Create a very skinny brush that matches the approximate width of the fur strands. I chose a brush with a Roundness of 0, a Hardness of 50%, and an Angle of 90 degrees. Use the Burn(O) tool to burn in some darker shadows amongst the hairs. Paint in some chunks here and there, concentrating on darkening up the bottom portion of the skirt.

Once satisfied with the burning job you've done, it's time to perform the last operation for this character: tone down the bright whites.

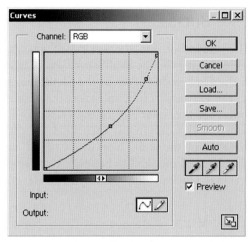

Curves

Make sure the Fur layer is selected and choose Filter→Render→Lighting Effects. Click on the top white box, the hue of the light. Set the light to R 254, B 237, B 219. Click and drag on the point opposite the source point in the Preview box. Manipulate the points until you have an even circle around the texture and the light coming from the right. Set the Intensity to 24 and the Focus to 69. Hit Enter to finalize.

The overall image is still a bit light. Go to the bottom of the Layers palette and click on the Create New Fill or Adjustment Layer icon. Select Curves from the drop-down list. Refer to the illustrations and place two points onto the graph. Click and drag on these points until they reflect the illustration, or until the values of the images are set to your own preferences. Hit Enter to finalize.

Do a Ctrl/⌘ + S to save again and try the texture out on the Orc.

Note here that in order to achieve a jagged edge to the bottom of the fur skirt, an Alpha channel must be created and mapped to the fur skirt texture.

For this Alpha channel, draw a jagged edge along the bottom of the skirt shape. You want the orc's clothing to look dirty, old, and ragged. Now select the new shape the jagged edge and do a Select→Save selection. You now have an Alpha in the skirt file that will take away everything not included in the jagged skirt shape.

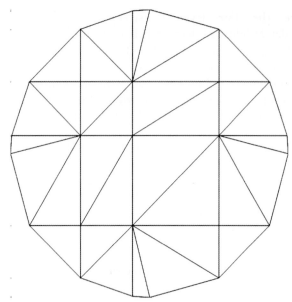

UV map for the belt buckle

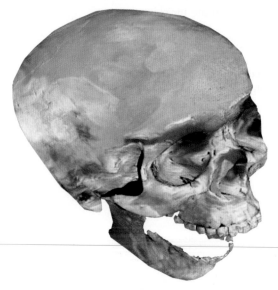

Skull source image

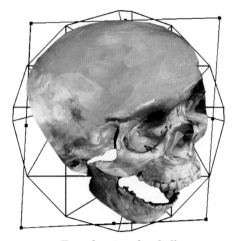

Transforming the skull

EXERCISE — BUCKLE

Open the UV snapshot for the orc's belt buckle (OrcBeltBuckleMap.tif) and the SkullSource.psd. Click and drag on the Background layer of the Skull image and drag into the UV map. Hit E and select the Magic Eraser(E) tool. Set the Tolerance of the eraser to 5, check Anti-Alias and Contiguous, then click in the black area surrounding the skull. Now do a Ctrl + T to Transform the shape of the skull to better fit the shape of the belt buckle. Click off the visibility of the layer, for now.

Do a Shift + Ctrl/⌘ + N to create a new layer. Name it "Buckle". Bust out the Polygonal Lasso(L) tool and use it to create a selection around the edge of the buckle's shape. Do a Select→Save Selection. Now head to the Swatches palette created especially for the Orc and choose a medium gray. Use the Paint Bucket(G) tool to fill in the buckle shape. Choose Filters→Noise→Add Noise, and set the Noise filter to 2 with Gaussian and Monochromatic checked. Next, run the Plastic Wrap filter located under Filter→Artistic→Plastic Wrap. Set the Plastic Wrap filter to Highlight strength 15, Detail 9, and Smoothness at 7. Hit Enter to finalize.

Now go to the bottom of the Layers palette and click on the Create a New Fill or Adjustment Layer icon, and choose Curves. Place points along the top of the curve to bring down the highlights of the overall image.

Now right-click on the Buckle layer and choose Blending Options, add add a Bevel and Emboss.

Return to the Skull layer and make it visible. Hit L for the Lasso and, while depressing Alt to alternate between the polygonal lasso and the freehand lasso, remove the dark areas from the eye sockets, nose, and open jaw of the skull. Use Ctrl/⌘ + X to cut. A rough edge in this case is actually desirable because it fits well with the buckle concept.

Next, double-click on the skull layer to access the Blending Option. Reduce the Fill Opacity (located under Advanced Blending) to 33%. Put a check in the Blend Interior Effects as Group Box.

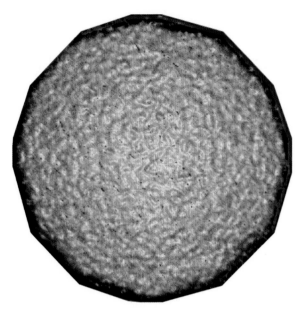

Basic belt texture

This texture has some interesting things happening, but it needs just one more detail to finish up. Time to add some very small, but bright red, blood spatters to the skull area. You want detail that would complement and contrast with the rest of the palette, and Red and Green are complementary colors.

Create a new layer and name it "Spatter". Hit B for the Brush(B) tool and select a small brush with a 50-65% hardness. Use the brush to paint on some tiny drops, maybe a smear here, and a drip there.

Now you can test out this image on your model, and save your work.

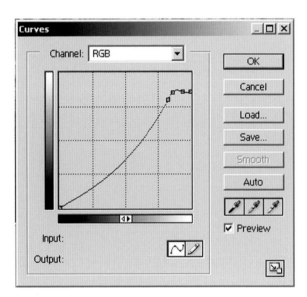

Curves

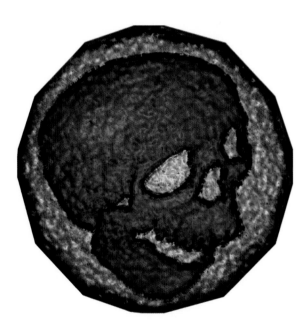

The Belt Buckle

EXERCISE - LEATHER

Start with a new document 512 x 512. Use G to fill it with a brown hue that matches the palette of the rest of the image. Add some subtle noise for detail. Access the Blending Modes or Filters Menu and use your knowledge of Photoshop to pick effects that will work as a leather texture. Refer to the original file for help or idea.

Add a new layer and name it Rivets. Copy the Rivets layer style to this image from the Styles Palette. Select a gray to use with a round brush, and place rivets along the edges of the belt UV map. Use the Line(U) tool with a Bevel and Emboss effect to create the leather seams that travel horizontally along the image. Use the Eraser(E) tool to remove some chunks along the edges of these seams to break them up a bit.

ORC ARMOR: AT A GLANCE

The Orc

TOPICS COVERED

Time for more advanced character texturing techniques with the Orc armor tutorial. Learn how to make metal.

You'll learn how to:

Make armor metal with Filters

MATERIALS REQUIRED

Orc.mb or Orc.dxf
OrcArmorMap.tif
OrcArmorDone.psd
Celticgraphic.psd

TUTORIAL: ORC ARMOR

STEP 1: OPEN THE FILES

Open the OrcArmorMap.tif map to begin this tutorial.

STEP 2: CREATE THE GREY FILL

Do a Shift + Ctrl/⌘ + N to create a new layer and name it "Grey Fill". Use the Rectangular Marquee(M) tool to select the rectangular shape of the breastplate map.

To continue creating the gray fill, select a medium gray, select the Paint Bucket(G) tool, and click inside the marquee to fill it with gray. Now right-click on the fill layer and choose Blending Options, and add a Bevel and Emboss

STEP 3: SET LAYER BLENDING MODE

Set the Grey Fill layer to Blending mode Normal, Opacity 100%. Complete this layer by running a Noise filter. Do a Filters→Noise→Add Noise. Set the percentage to 15-20%. Hit Enter to finalize.

Add Noise

STEP 4: MAKE THE BLACK FILL

Create a new layer and name it "Black Fill". Reselect the same area filled by the gray value. Hit D to restore the default swatch settings on the Tool bar and hit G, then click to fill the selection marquee with black.

STEP 5: ADD A NOISE FILTER

Repeat the noise filter with a percentage of 10-15%. With this color overlay in place, the overall value of the armor can be changed very easily by using the Opacity slider. Configure to your taste.

STEP 6: MAKE THE METAL TEXTURE

Next, make the metal texture. Begin by creating another new layer, and naming it "Metal". This texture will be created with a series of Filters. Listed below is the combination of filters used to create a metal texture for armor.

Do a Select All (Ctrl/⌘ + A) and apply the Filter→Render→Clouds, with default foreground and background color swatches.

Filter→Sketch→Chrome, Detail space to 10, Smoothness 0

The metal texture

The graphic

Filter➔Noise➔Add Noise, set to 20 %, Gaussian, Monochromatic

Filter➔Distort➔Shear, with Wrap Around Checked and an "S" Shaped pattern of points

Filter➔Artistic➔Palette Knife, with the Stroke size space to 25 and Stroke Detail set to 3. Softness set to 0

Filter➔Brush Strokes➔Spatter, with a Spray Radius of 5 and a Smoothness of 5

Filter➔Texture➔Grain, with an Intensity of 20, a Contrast of 50, and Grain Type set to regular

Filter➔texture➔Craquelere, with Crack Spacing set to 100, Crack Depth set to 10, and Crack Brightness set to 10

Filter➔Noise➔Dust and Scratches, with a radius of 40 pixels and a Threshold of 60 levels

Layer style applied to graphic

Lastly, do an Image➔Adjust➔Brightness Contrast, with a Brightness of -20, and a Contrast set to -40.

STEP 7: ADD ADJUSTMENT LAYERS

To adjust the layers below, add a couple of Adjustment layers at the top of the stack that has been created so far. Remember that Adjustment layers are an absolutely excellent way of manipulating the contents of your layers without ever having to alter the actual contents of the layer.

First, a Hue Saturation Adjustment layer was added and set to the following:

Master Hue: -12
Saturation: -51
Lightness: +18

Then, add a Curves Adjustment Layer to brighten up the whites of the metal texture. See the illustration or load the Metal Texture Curve into the Curves Dialog.

STEP 8: IMPORT A GRAPHIC

Open the CelticGraphic file. Click and drag the black and white graphic into the Breastplate.psd. Since this graphic is too small, do a Ctrl/⌘ + T to scale the graphic up until it covers at least two-thirds of the total area of the plate. Remember that this graphic will be mirrored on the geometry of the model when the UV map is applied to a material shader in a 3D application.

Do a Ctrl/⌘ + S to save your work.

The Breastplate

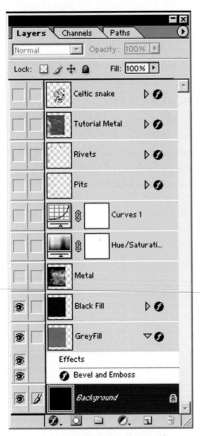

Layer stack for the Breastplate tutorial

STEP 9: SET THE BLENDING OPTIONS

Once the graphic has been scaled, right-click on the layer and name it "Celtic Graphic", and access the its Blending Options. The goal is to come up with a Layer Style that will closely match the rest of the armor texture that's been built so far. The right hues and the correct surface are important. I added a Drop Shadow, Bevel, Texture, and Stroke.

Once the blending modes are set, click on the New Style button to preserve the settings as a preset for later use. Type in something you'll remember for the name of the preset, like "Armor Graphic".

Test the breastplate on the model and test the placement of the graphic based on what you think looks best. Once you're satisfied, save your work.

EXERCISE - RIVETS

Create a new layer and name it "Rivets". Next, access the Blending Options by right-clicking or double-clicking on the Rivets layer. In this case, the Layer Style will be set first, and content added to the layer second. That way, when the rivets are painted on, they will be immediately transformed into what looks like a metal head. Add Drop Shadow, Inner Shadow, Bevel, Color and Pattern Overlays, and Stroke.

Now bust out the Brush(B) tool. Open up the Options and set the brush to a diameter of 20 and a hardness of 100%. If you want, you can type in a name for the brush (like Rivets) and click on the preset icon to the right to preserve the brush in the Photoshop presets for all time. Hit D on the keyboard for the default swatches and begin placing dots along the perimeter of the texture. I chose to add my rivets about a half-inch in from the edge of the texture.

The last phase of detail for the armor breastplate pits and dents are added to a new layer, so create a new layer and name it "Pits". Hit B for the Brush(B) tool and choose a brush with a rougher edge, such as one of the splatter brushes. Now paint a few marks with black paint here and there on the surface of the breastplate. Bear in mind that anything too large and obvious is not going to work because it will be a lot easier to tell that the pattern has been mirrored.

Once you're happy with the variety of marks, double-click on the Pits layer to access the Blending Options, and once again add Drop Shadow, Inner Shadow, Bevel and Emboss, Color Overlay, and Stroke.

Rivets

Pits

Notice that the Layer Style settings throughout have been very similar. The fast way to create blending modes that match together well is to first come up with a good combination of Blending Options for the main detail – in this case the CelticGraphic – and then use the settings for the lesser details to retain some consistency. Then you can just go back in there and change the established settings however they need to be customized. To copy a Layer Style for another layer, right-click on the layer with the style and select Copy Layer Style. To paste, make sure the destination layer is selected, right-click, and select Paste Layer Style. Another option is to load the style you created (Armor Graphic) right into the layer by simply selecting the layer and then clicking on the Armor Graphic Style swatch in the Swatches palette to automatically apply the Layer Style.

Now save your work and, as usual, test the texture out on the model.

CONCLUSION

Characters are complicated. They are challenging to model, animate, and texture, so it takes a lot of patience. Characters are also great fun and are satisfying to make. People put a lot of stock into the characters they meet as they travel through the lands of entertainment and the more detail, personality, and sheer coolness you can add, the better.

QUIZ

1) WHAT IS THE FIRST THING TO DO WHEN EVALUATING A CHARACTER MODEL?

    a) Decide what the costume and details of the character will be

    b) Figure out which UVs correspond with what areas of the UV map

    c) Locate where the seams will be

2) WHAT IS THE SECOND STEP TO TAKE WHEN WORKING WITH A CHARACTER MODEL?

    a) Figure out which UVs correspond with what areas of the UV map

    b) Decide what the costume and details of the character will be

    c) None of the above

3) WHAT IS AN EXCELLENT RESOURCE FOR SOURCE ART FOR REALISTIC CLOTHING TEXTURES?

    a) Looking at games for examples

    b) Your own wardrobe

    c) Both A and B

4) WHAT IS IMPORTANT TO REMEMBER WHEN TEXTURING A MAP THAT HAS UVS POINTING IN DIFFERENT DIRECTIONS?

    a) That the texture will disregard the direction of the UVs

    b) That the texture must be rotated to follow the direction of the UVs as they are positioned on the map, corresponding to the model

    c) That the UVs must be rotated to match the direction of the texture

5) WHAT IS THE TRADITIONAL WAY OF MAKING SKIN LOOK "ALIVE"?

    a) Scanning photos

    b) Building up thin "glazes" of paint

    c) Scanning the side of your face

6) HOW CAN YOU SAVE ALL OF THE SKIN TONE HUES YOU ACQUIRE FROM YOUR RESEARCH?

    a) Create a new palette, name it "Skins", and save it

    b) Create a new document, paint on little blobs of skin color, then save it

    c) Keep your source art in a safe place

7) WHY IS IT NECESSARY TO HAVE A FILL COLOR FOR CHARACTER TEXTURES THAT MATCHES THE OVERALL HUE OF THE TEXTURE?

    a) Because it looks nice

    b) Because such a fill hides the seams of the characters mapping

    c) Neither

8) WHAT IS THE PURPOSE OF USING MANY HUES TO CREATE A HAIR TEXTURE?

    a) To create the illusion of depth and dimension

    b) To add creativity

    c) To imitate Shakira

9) WHAT MUST YOU ALWAYS KEEP IN MIND WHEN WORKING WITH THE HUMAN FORM?

    a) Hair color

    b) Scale

    c) The depiction of form through light

10) LOTS OF BLENDING MODES STACKED TOGETHER CREATES GREAT DETAIL QUICKLY.

    a) True

    b) False

    c) What's a Blending Mode?

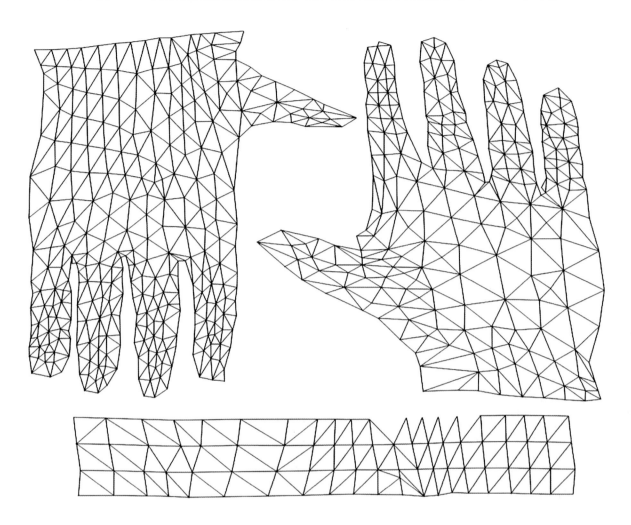

IN THIS CHAPTER YOU WILL LEARN ABOUT:

- Maya Texture Mapping Terminology
- UV Coordinates
- The UV Texture Editor
- How to take a UV Snapshot
- How to use the four mapping types of Maya
- How to create an image plane

INTRODUCTION

Texture mapping is the process of applying textures you create with Photoshop to the surface of 3D models.   The process begins by identifying how the model must be "unwrapped" in order to achieve the best results when projecting a square 2D image onto the surface of a (probably not square at all) 3D model.   Most projects will also have texture and geometry budgets (limits), set by the parameters of the technology in use, such as the game engine.

Texture unwraps of 3D geometry can be done in a myriad of ways. This chapter explores some of my favorite methods for getting that texture on the model.

This chapter assumes you have a basic working knowledge of Maya.

TEXTURE MAPPING TOOLS AND TERMINOLOGY

There are some basic definitions and tools you should know about. The terminology in this chapter is specific to Maya, but the concepts themselves are found in other 3D applications, as well. For instance, the concept of UV Coordinates is also used in both 3ds max and XSI. The tools (such as the UV Texture Editor) aren't called the same thing in other software, but the concepts are the same.

UV COORDINATES

Before you can assign a texture to a model, Maya needs to know how areas of a texture map correspond to areas of a 3D model. How a texture is placed upon a model is a concept called UV Coordinates.

Low-poly dragon model by Rick McCann

UVs are points that match the vertex points of a model, but are used for moving around the texture, instead of moving around geometry. Each UV is used as a texture reference point that you can select, move, rotate, and scale to get a texture to match a model.

Texture map for dragon model by Rick McCann

You can then export the UV coordinates as an image file, and use that image as the foundation for creating your texture. In the case of a polygon model, they will look like the wireframe of the model, peeled apart and flattened out. Paint a face onto the part of the image that was where the UV coordinates of the model's face were laid out, save the image, and in Maya load that image as the texture map for the model, and it's got a face!

UV TEXTURE EDITOR

The UV Texture Editor is the Maya tool you use to do the actual laying out of a model's UVs. This Editor can be found in Maya by doing a Modeling➔Window➔UV Texture Editor. This is where all the UV manipulations you make for texturing models take place. Once a model is final, it's time to examine it closely and decide the best way to map and unwrap it.

I think of the "unwrapping" process in sewing terms. If you have ever seen a sewing pattern that has cut out sections making up a whole piece of clothing, you'll get the idea fast. An unwrap is two things: how you slice up the "skin" of a model, and how you lay the skin out to be painted.

The UV Texture Editor is where the model skin is arranged. The Editor displays a gray grid framed by a black box, that is intersected with X (red) and Y (green) coordinates. These are two-dimensional coordinates. There are four squares in the Editor, each measuring 1 x 1. In order to export the unwrap so that it can be painted, the UVs are arranged in the top-right square of the grid.

There are two main rules to follow when unwrapping. The first is to keep all of the UVs within the top-right 1 x 1 square of the UV Texture Editor. You want to do this because it's the only square in the Editor from which you can export the image of the UV arrangement for painting. The other half of the rule is you want to keep the UVs confined within the 1 x 1 space in order to avoid texture overlapping as the texture applied to the model appears tiled over and over in the Editor. Any UVs sticking out of a 1 x 1 square will show parts of the repeating texture.

The second main rule is to use as much of the space in the top-right 1 x 1 space in the Editor as possible. Think of this area as prime real estate in Tokyo: every millimeter is precious. It's precious because the more space your UV unwrap takes up, the better the resolution and detail of the texture on the model. Make the most of the limited space.

A couple of ways to make the most productive use of this area are to use the More Space for Detailed Areas technique, and the technique of "doubling-up" UV shells.

To decide what parts of a model are the most detailed, take look at the source art. The areas that have the most detail will be the areas that need the most space in the UV Texture Editor. The UV coordinates for these areas will need to be scaled up, and low detail UVs scaled down. This way, what's most important will be represented best.

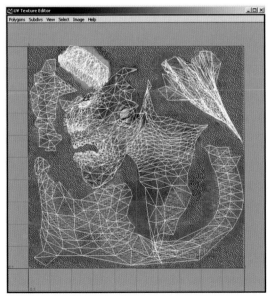

The UV Texture Editor of Maya 4.5

Doubling-up UVs is another clever way to maximize your valuable texture mapping real estate, and is a technique taken into account by Art Directors as they design assets. The idea is to look at the model and determine which areas can use the same section of texture. For example, say you have a character that's got a basic pair of pants on. There aren't any separate details on either leg. This means you can get two legs for the price of one, by placing the UV shell for one leg right over the top of the other leg in the UV Texture Editor. Now, you only have to paint one leg and you're saving a leg's worth of space!

UV SNAPSHOT

The UV Snapshot command takes a picture of the UV coordinate layout in the UV Texture Editor, creating an image file to work from in Photoshop.

Once you've got a model's UVs mapped, unwrapped, and arranged in the UV Texture Editor, hit F8 on the keyboard and make sure you're in object mode. (You can tell because the whole model will be selected and the geo borders will be green.) Now go to the UV Texture Editor and do a Polygons→UV Snapshot…. (The UV Snapshot feature will not work if you are in component mode.) A dialog box will pop up prompting for a title and the dimensions of the resulting image. Here is where you also specify the file type of the exported image. I always use Targa because they're compatible with the Unreal Engine and Photoshop.

Hit OK when the settings are complete. Now go over to Photoshop, open the newly-exported UV snapshot, and you are ready to paint!

DIFFERENT MAPPING TYPES

UVs are "projected" from a model onto the flat texture space in the UV Texture Editor using four different mapping methods. You have a choice between Planar Mapping, Cylindrical Mapping, Spherical Mapping, and Automatic Mapping. The decision of what mapping tool to employ is based on what sort of geometry is about to be mapped. A Planar Map is designed for flat projections at any (and multiple, if needed) angles. A Spherical Map is designed to enclose something that is round. Cylindrical Mapping works best on shapes that are roughly cylindrical, and Automatic Mapping does a fair job of automatically unwrapping shapes of simple to medium complexity.

You can combine all the different mapping types for a particular model, because they can all be used on just one part of a model. For instance, for a human character, you might select the polygons on an arm and unwrap its UVs using a Cylindrical Map, then select the head polygons and use a Spherical Map, then select a hand and use Automatic Mapping, etc., until all of the model has been mapped in one way or another. Next, you open the UV Texture Editor and make additional tweaks and changes, and rearrange the UV coordinates to fit in the top-right 1 x 1 square.

PLANAR MAPPING

A Planar Map takes a straight-on shot of the geometry from one angle (at a time) and plants it in the UV Texture Editor. For example, if you were adding a texture to a car, you could use a Planar Map to take UV snapshots from above for the top of the car, from below for the bottom of the car, and another from the side. The UVs would then be visible in the UV Texture Editor for further manipulation (if necessary), and to save out to an image file to start painting the texture with Photoshop. Once the texture is painted according to the UV snapshot wireframe, just load the texture in Maya again and the car is mapped!

SPHERICAL MAPPING

Spherical Mapping attempts to project a texture (or unwrap the UVs, depending on how you look at it) correctly on a surface that is roughly round. Things like heads, planets, rocks… you get the idea.

I use this method of mapping only when I have a smaller sphere that doesn't need a lot of detail, as it has a tendency to distort the poles of spheres. I recommend you choose an alternative method for mapping spherical objects with Maya.

CYLINDRICAL MAPPING

Cylindrical mapping unwraps UVs well on shapes that are roughly cylindrical, like an arm, or a tree trunk.

This mapping method is handy and I use it regularly.

AUTOMATIC MAPPING

Automatic mapping uses Maya's mind to decide how the UVs get laid out in the UV Texture Editor. It looks at a model, evaluates how many faces there are, and lays them out to make the most of the texture space by assigning an equal amount of space to every face it's told to map.

Automatic Mapping is a good option for simple to medium complexity models because it produces UV shells that can be selected, moved, scaled, and rotated fairly rapidly.

I mostly use it for simpler things, such as basic architecture or box-shaped game assets.

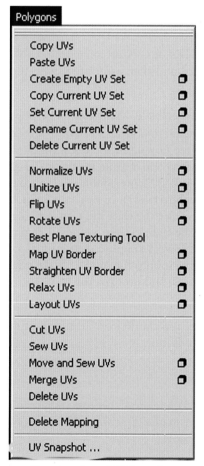

How to take a UV Snapshot

UV MANIPULATION IN THE UV TEXTURE EDITOR

Fortunately, the UV Texture Editor provides some handy features to make things easier. Commands found in the drop-down menus of the UV Texture Editor that I use frequently are Select Shell, Convert Selections, Cut, Sew, and Display Image.

I use Select→Select Shell to make sure that every UV of a shell is selected. Sometimes it's impossible to find and select all the UVs of an unwrapped section in order to manipulate them. With this command, you only need to select one, and Maya will do the rest. It saves a lot of time and untold amounts of frustration. Another quick way to see what's going on with a model and make UV selections is to use the Convert Selections commands in the Select menu of the Editor. You can select a group of UVs and then convert them to selected faces, now visible on the model, and vice versa. I use this command to determine how UVs are assigned to their corresponding faces. This comes in especially handy with models that are more complex and harder to unwrap.

Cut and Sew follow the sewing idea of unwrapping UV patterns. As you work, you'll find that some UVs need to be sliced apart in order to make the most of the texture space. Or, perhaps your first decision on how to chop apart the skin isn't working out. Use the Cut UVs command to separate parts of a UV shell. To do this, right-click and hold, and choose Edge mode. Once in Edge mode, go to the model and select the correct edge to cut. Then do a Polygons→Cut UVs. Now the UVs are separated. Sew UVs performs the opposite function: instead of cutting skins apart, it pieces them back together. Follow the same set of commands as Cut UVs, except choose Sew UVs under the Polygons menu of the UV Texture Editor.

Finally, the Display Image command is simple, yet crucial to laying out UVs. This command lets you turn on or turn off the texture image you're working with in the UV Texture Editor. Having the image on is usually the way to go because you can then see how each UV lines up with the texture you're working on. Since you'll be making a lot of changes and re-importing the texture over and over trying to get it perfect, this visual reference is key. My advice is to always keep Display Image checked when working with a texture.

Texture mapping and unwrapping is a tricky business and it's important to know it takes a lot of practice to get really good at it. I enjoy it because I think of it as a game: me against the machine. Even after a long time, it's still a fun challenge.

ADJUSTING UV DISPLAY SETTINGS

The following settings make it easy to see exactly where the borders of a UV map begin and end. To set it up before you start unwrapping a model's UV coordinates, go to the top menu bar and select Display→Custom Polygon Display→Option Box. Reset the tool to default with an Edit→Reset Tool, then set the border size to 5, and check UV Topology. The UV Coordinates will now show up on polygon models, with any cut borders showing up thicker.

ASSIGNING TEXTURES TO YOUR MODEL

You know what to do to get a model unwrapped and laid out. Now you need to know how to assign the texture you produce to a material and then associate it with the model.

Do a Modeling→Window→Rendering Editors→Hypershade. A new window pops up with all of the tools you need to create materials. Now do a Create→Materials→Lambert. You'll see a gray sphere pop up in the top window of the Hypershade. Hold down Ctrl, double-click, and type in a name for the material node. (I usually go with what it is, such as "brick wall".) Now double-click on the new Lambert. This calls up the Attribute Editor for the Material you've made. Click the checkerboard to the right of the Color option, click File, click the manila folder icon to the right of Image file, browse to the file in the right directory, and hit Enter. You'll see the texture appear on the new Lambert. Now it's simply a matter of clicking on the material with texture assigned and dragging it onto the model. Make sure you hit 6 on the keyboard (this mode displays textures) and presto! You've now got a texture on the model.

When you make changes to the texture and resave, use the Reload Texture button located beneath the Image File field in the Attribute Editor.

EXERCISE — PLANAR MAPPING

My favorite way to map models is using the Planar Mapping tool, because it's fast and easy. It works great as a way to map faces that all face in one direction, and is the tool I use to fix distortion caused by the other mapping tools.

(Make a note that if you can help it, don't triangulate a model before you map it. If you do that, you'll have at least twice as many faces to select, the process will take twice as long, and will be twice as complicated.)

In this exercise you'll take a house model and learn how to use Planar Mapping to quickly lay out the UVs for its texture. Open the planar_mapping_house.ma file to begin.

The first order of business is to inspect the house like you're buying it. Circle around it, check out the roof, inspect how the walls are built; in other words, get familiar with your property. The goal is to get a good idea of what areas can share the same texture and how much space the UV shells will need to best represent the texture.

It's important to note that UV unwraps can be done in as many ways as there are people. Everyone develops a system that works for them. For now, however, you're using my system.

Start with the front and back walls of the main house. Hit 4 on the keyboard to enter wireframe mode, and find the four faces making up the front and back of the larger part of the house. Once they're selected, hit 5 to enter grayscale mode. Now do a Polygons→Texture→Planar Mapping→Options Box. You will see the Polygon Planar Projections Dialog pop up. Put a check in the Smart Fit box and click in the Fit to Bounding Box circle. This enables the four Mapping Direction options just below. Since the selected faces point in the Z direction, click the Z-axis Mapping direction and hit Apply. Hit 6 so you can see the texture. Go to the UV Texture Editor and scale down the map of those faces using R. Note here that even though it looks like only one wall of the house has been mapped, actually what you're seeing is both mapped walls, automatically doubled-up by Maya so you don't have to do it. Isn't that convenient? You bet it is!

Use your judgment on how far down you need to scale. Click in the empty area to deactivate the mapping projection, and finalize it.

Now go back to the house and select the faces that comprise the sides of the main house. In the Polygon Planar Projections Dialog, click the X-axis mapping direction and hit Apply. Just like you did above, scale those walls down. You want to make sure the checkerboard pattern matches the front and back walls, and each square is perfectly square. Basically, each UV shell needs to be approximately the same shape as the face it was taken from. This shape can be smaller or larger, but it needs to be the same shape as the geometry – or close.

The main house is mapped, and it's time to do the roof. Select the top faces of the roof – the one on the main house and the top of the smaller roof. Go back to the Polygon Planar Projections Dialog and click in the Y-axis Mapping direction. This time, you get two shapes in the UV Editor. The smaller square represents the texture information for the little roof, and the large rectangle is the roof of the main house. Decide whether or not these shapes will share the same texture, scale them down to fit the 1 x 1 space, and move the UVs into position. Be sure to keep them from overlapping the UV shells for the walls. If they do, you'll get wall where there should be roof.

Now use this method of mapping to complete sectioning off and mapping the house model. Your goal is to lay all the UV shells out in a way that gives the most space to the walls, the second most space to the roof, and the least amount of space to the chimney and porch details. If you need some help, refer to the planar_mapping_house_after.ma file to see how I laid out the map.

Once your ready to take a snapshot, hit F8, make sure the model is selected in object mode, and do a UV Texture Editor→Polygons→UV Snapshot... Fill in the dialog box using the dimensions of 256 x 256, hit Enter, and you have a UV image to paint on. A 256 x 256 texture will give you just enough resolution to paint some decent detail onto this house. You have just mapped a great game asset! Now, head on over to Photoshop and get working!

EXERCISE — CYLINDRICAL MAPPING

Cylindrical mapping is designed especially for texturing cylindrical shapes. I use it for all things tubular, such as trees. Trees are an example of a game asset that is used often and this exercise shows you when and how to apply Cylindrical Mapping.

The best time to map an object is before you begin to refine the faces, edges, and vertices of the geometry. This is because it's much harder for Maya to understand the UV information of vertices that have already been transformed. The two trees in this exercise represent the right time to map and the wrong time to map. Open the cylindrical_mapping_tree.ma file. You will see two trees. One tree has straight limbs and the other has bent limbs.

Make sure the UV Texture Editor is open. Hit 5 on the keyboard, and then select the straight tree. Right-click, choose Faces, and click on all the faces of the main trunk to select them. Now do a Edit Polygons→Texture→Cylindrical Mapping. Go into the UV Texture Editor and use the scaling tool to move the UVs into a shape that roughly corresponds with the shape of the tree (about a third of the space in the Editor). Your goal is to make the checkerboard pattern assigned to the tree look like it's made of perfect squares.

Once you have that, go over to the bent tree and follow the exact same steps. You'll notice that you don't have as nice a texture for this tree. There's warping and distortion – very bad. You could try and fix it, but that would take a long time, and might not work. The reason that you have a bad mapping for the second tree is because Maya is having a hard time understanding which UV is supposed to go where. Check out the cylindrical_mapping_tree_after.ma if you need help.

Follow the Cylindrical Mapping steps to map the rest of the branches of the straight tree. You will need to use Maya's manipulation tools to rotate the Cylindrical Mapping wireframe in the correct direction for each branch. To make the Cylindircal projection transformable, click once on the small red handle. Once you click this handle, you'll see move, scale, and rotational points to click and drag.

Use the select, move, scale, and rotate tools to manipulate the UVs just as you would while modeling in Maya. Look at the checkerboard to make sure the texture isn't warping and that the pattern looks like it's supposed to: nice and straight, and square. Once you have all the shells arranged in the UV Texture Editor, hit F8, make sure the model is selected, and do a UV Texture Editor→Polygons→UV Snapshot... Fill in the dialog box, hit Enter, and you have a UV image to paint on. Head on over to Photoshop and get working!

I always make a point to remember to map my object before it gets too refined. Sometimes I write "MAP" on my fingers so I can see the reminder while I work. It's easy to get involved in what you're modeling and forget all about the mapping.

EXERCISE — SPHERICAL MAPPING

For this exercise, you'll apply a spherical mapping to a simple, low-poly sphere. The purpose of this exercise will be twofold: you'll see how this mapping type works, and you'll see why it's not used very often.

Open the spherical_mapping_sphere.ma file. You're looking at a sphere that has a checkerboard Lambert on it, but isn't mapped yet. Make a note to check out how the texture warps at the north and south poles of this object. It's always a problem area.

The first thing to do is get it mapped. Click on the model to select it, and in Modeling mode, do an Edit Polygons→Texture→Spherical Mapping. Now open the UV Texture Editor using Window→UV Texture Editor. Be sure that Display Image is checked on. Now you can see how the spherical mapping projection is affecting the texture's placement.

Again, the top and bottom of the sphere texture are distorted. This happens because the UVs combine at each end point of the primitive, forming triangles instead of squares. These two shapes represent the texture differently, so you don't get a match.

To fix this warping at the points on this sphere, select the faces that have the messed up texture and do a Planar mapping from the top down (Y-axis). You'll see a new circle of UVs appear in the UV Texture Editor. Select this shell and use the Move tool to slide it over to a neighboring 1 x 1 space. Hit R for the Scale tool and use that tool to scale down the UVs so that the size of the squares in the checkerboard match those in the main body of the sphere. The goal is to get the textures from both mappings to match up. It takes a steady hand, and patience, but the result is worth it.

Make a note here that if you need to start over, you can delete a map. Go into faces mode, select the mapped faces, and do a UV Texture Editor→Polygons→Delete UVs. This will nuke that bad map and let you start over.

To see the difference between just a Spherical map and a Spherical map with Planar Mapping, open the spherical_mapping_sphere_after .ma file. Pay especial attention to the difference between how the texture appears at the top versus the bottom. See what I mean?

EXERCISE — AUTOMATIC MAPPING

Automatic Mapping is similar to Planar Mapping, except you can get projections from all axes combined into one. This is helpful, because it can be a very quick and easy way to map a model.

This next exercise will show you how to take a simple 3D prop and turn it into a texturable asset with lightning speed efficiency. Open automatic_mapping_pyramid.ma to get started.

You've got a basic, four-sided triangle shape sitting in the interface waiting to be textured. Make sure you're in grayscale mode (hit 5) and select the model. Do a Polygons→Texture→Automatic Mapping→Options Box to call up the Automatic Mapping Options dialog box.

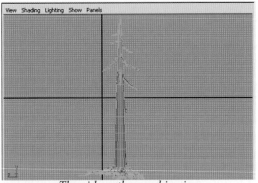

The side orthographic view

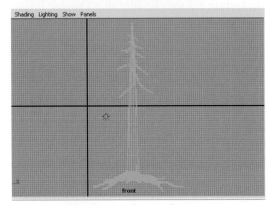

The front orthographic view

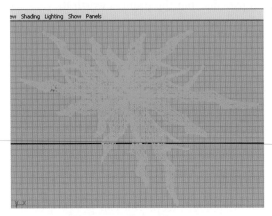

The top orthographic view

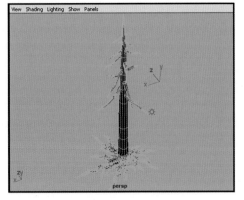

The perspective view

At the top, you'll see a drop-down arrow next to the word "Planes". This is where you set how many UV shells you want the tool to slice up for you. I always set this to 6 because 6 always gives me shapes that are closest to the faces of the geometry and therefore less distorted. (Don't worry about any of the other settings.) Now click Apply to project the mapping, and then close the dialog. As before, look over in the UV Texture Editor.

In the Editor you have four perfect triangles, one for each side of the model, mapped from the X- and Y-axes. You could leave the map just like this, but that would break the first rule: make the most of prime texture space. It doesn't take any time to double up these four shells and scale them up. Doing this will give you better texture resolution on all four sides and you'll only need to paint one side of the pyramid instead of four sides. You can see the potential here!

To go about this, hit Q to get the Select tool and click and drag around the top UV of the top-right triangle. Right-click and do a Select→Select Shell to make sure the entire shape is selected. Hit V for the Move tool and drag the selected triangle shape into the center of the 1 x 1 space. Select the top-left triangle and do the same, placing this second shell directly over the first triangle in the center. Go to the bottom right triangle, select the shell and hit E for the rotate tool. Turn the triangle to match the other two in the center of the space and add this third shell over top of them via the Move tool. Repeat the process for the fourth triangle shell. You should wind up with the four sides of the pyramid piled up on each other in the middle of the texture space.

The next step is to grab all four shells and scale them up to fit into the space. Using the Q (select) tool, click and drag around the top points of the triangle. Right-click and do a Select→Select Shell to make sure every UV is selected, and then hit R for the Scale tool. Pull the top (green) handle of the scale tool straight up. The UV shells will grow with the mouse movement. Scale them up until they are just barely inside the 1 x 1 space. Now repeat for the sides. Scale until the bottom points of the pyramid reach the bottom corners of the space.

Now you'll notice that these triangles aren't exactly the same size, so here's an important tip to get them that way. Click and drag to select all four points of the top of the pyramid. Now hit R for the Scale tool. Drag first the X handle, and then the Y handle, to the center square (light blue) of the tool. You can see how the points of the triangle all pull together to look like one point instead of four. This is perfect! Repeat for the other two points of the shape. You'll wind up with a UV set that looks like one clean and beautiful triangle.

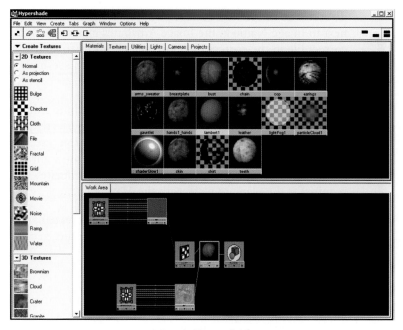

Maya's Hypershade

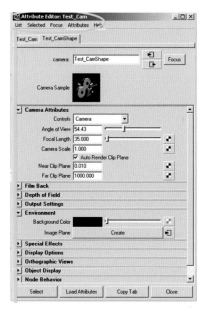

The Camera Attribute Editor Dialog

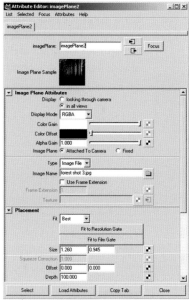

The Image Plane Editor

Hit F8 and do a UV Texture Editor➔Polygons➔UV Snapshot… to take a picture of this layout. You're ready to begin painting this pyramid and the whole mapping process took only a few minutes!

To see the finished product, you can open the automatic_mapping_pyramid_after.ma file and assign the pyramid.tga to the pyramid1 Lambert saved in the Hypershade.

IMAGE PLANES

Sometimes you need a background in a 3D scene, from a stormy sky full of clouds to a forest backdrop. An Image Plane is like a backdrop curtain in a theatre: a quick and dirty way to add a background image in the 3D scene itself. Image Planes are attached to the camera, and follow it.

SETTING UP AN IMAGE PLANE

Do a Display➔Show➔Cameras, go to an Orthographic view (Top, Side, or Front), and look for the Perspective camera. Once the camera is selected, look to the top-right in the Channels menu to see if the name of the camera matches the one you want to add the image plane to (only an issue if the scene has multiple cameras).

Do a Ctrl/⌘ + A to call up the Attribute Editor for the Perspective camera. Roll down to the Environment drop-down menu and click the arrow to access the controls. Now click on the large Create button to the immediate right of Image Plane. You are now in the Attribute Editor for the Image plane.

Go up to the top far-right of the interface to the Channels menu and rename the image plane to something easy to find later.

Doubling up UVs over a specific area of texture

To attach an image to the image plane, click on the folder icon next to Image Name in the Image Attributes menu. Find the correct file in the correct directory and click OK to attach it. Do a quick render from the Perspective view to see how it looks.

In the Placement menu of the Image Plane Attribute Editor, click on Fit to Resolution Gate to fit the image perfectly into the camera's field of view. In addition, you can use the Placement attributes to specify how near or far you want the plane from the camera, as well as the exact coordinates you require for the plane to work with the Maya scene.

Open a new Maya scene (or one you've already created), and create an Image Plane using the image_plane.ma file.

CONCLUSION

Often, it's a challenge to determine the best way to map out a model in order to represent all of that model's facets with consistent, quality textures. You'll need to think about which of the four mapping tools is best to use, and then how the UVs of the model will be arranged within the UV Texture Editor. It's a good idea to look over the model carefully, in order to understand the geometry and save yourself time. However, if a map isn't working after all, don't be afraid to start over. It's always better the second time, anyway.

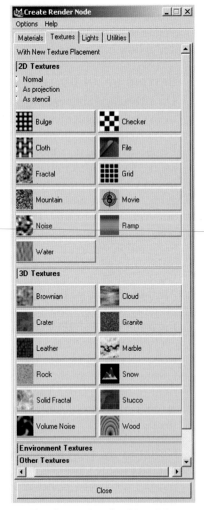

The Create Render Note Menu

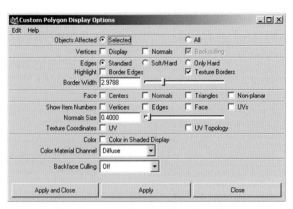

The Custom Polygons Display Menu

QUIZ

1) WHAT ARE THE FOUR TYPES OF MAPPING IN MAYA?

    a) Spherical, Rectangular, Triangular, and Planar
    b) Planar, Cylindrical, Spherical, Automatic
    c) Automatic, Cylindrical, Rectangular, and Spherical

2) UVs CAN BE MANIPULATED IN THE UV TEXTURE EDITOR WITH THE

    a) Scale, Select, Rotate, and Move tools
    b) Cut, Sew, and Select Shell tools
    c) Both A and B

3) WHICH MAPPING METHOD USES THE "DOUBLING-UP" TECHNIQUE AUTOMATICALLY?

    a) Automatic Mapping
    b) Planar Mapping
    c) Cylindrical Mapping

4) WHICH METHOD OF MAPPING IS GREAT FOR TREE TRUNKS?

    a) Spherical mapping
    b) Automatic Mapping
    c) Cylindrical mapping

5) WHICH MAPPING METHOD IS USED TO MAP FROM THE X-, Y-, AND Z-AXES AT THE SAME TIME?

    a) Planar Mapping
    b) Automatic mapping
    c) Cylindrical mapping

6) WHICH METHOD OF MAPPING WOULD BE PERFECT FOR A PLANET?

    a) Automatic mapping
    b) Spherical mapping with Planar Mapping
    c) Cylindrical mapping

7) A UV SNAPSHOT IS TAKEN TO:

    a) Map a simple object
    b) Assign a material to a model
    c) Export a texture layout on which to paint

8) TO APPLY A TEXTURE TO A MODEL, A _____ IS CREATED AND ASSIGNED TO IT.

    a) A 3D model
    b) A UV shell
    c) A Lambert material

9) WHAT IS THE PURPOSE OF THE UV TEXTURE EDITOR?

    a) To view the UVs that define the texture placement on a model
    b) To manipulate the UVs that define the texture placement on a model
    c) Both A and B

10) HOW IS THE IMAGE PLANE ATTRIBUTES DIALOG ACCESSED?

    a) By selecting the camera the Image Plane is attached to
    b) By doing a Ctrl + A
    c) By selecting the image plane

ERIC KOHLER

ART DIRECTOR

MONOLITH PRODUCTIONS

What is your job?

I'm the Art Director for the Tron 2.0 team at Monolith Productions in Kirkland, WA. I do the character and weapon concepts for the game, as well as modeling, texturing, and directing animations. I draw guns and robots for a living… what more could you ask for?

How did you get started in the game industry?

Blind luck – and not even my luck. Me and my friend Matt moved out here from Michigan after getting art degrees, and set up shop digitally coloring comic books. Then one day, Matt was outside his place smoking his last cigarette and started talking to his neighbor, who happened to be the head of the 3D department (and founder) at Monolith Productions. After that, Matt kind of disappeared, and it turned out he'd gone to work for Monolith. So, through him, I eventually got an interview with them as well. At that time, they were making their first game, Shogo: Mobile Armor Division and in order to get hired, I had to learn the Japanese anime style. So, I went out and bought some Masamune Shirow graphic novels, made a "Leave Behind" poster specifically for the interview, and they hired me.

How did you learn the tools you use?

I mostly learned by trial and error. With Photoshop, I had to figure it quick so I could pull my weight in the comic book coloring company I joined right out of college. With 3D, first Softimage and then Maya, one day somebody showed me a model, I didn't like it, so I sat down and set about fixing it, and just went from there.

How do you use Photoshop?

We use Photoshop to make skins for our characters and textures the fastest way possible. Everyone approaches it from a "whatever works for you" point of view. One our favorite Photoshop tools is Actions. Actions help us automate the more menial tasks involved in producing in-game content, this in turn helps us keep from going insane. Some of the guys here have these incredible action sets that create complex effects with a single keystroke. We are also starting to use Actions in conjunction with custom Maya scripts; once again this makes life a heck of a lot easier.

Photoshop is my favorite program in the world. It's very intuitive and supports many different ways of doing things.

How long have you worked in the industry?

I've worked for Monolith for 5 Years. Games is the industry to be in. Electronic entertainment is surpassing the film industry. The line between games and film is beginning to blur. Games are costing more and more to make; eventually the budget for a game will be the same as the budget for a Hollywood film. That's gonna require legions and legions of production artists. There's a lot of opportunity.

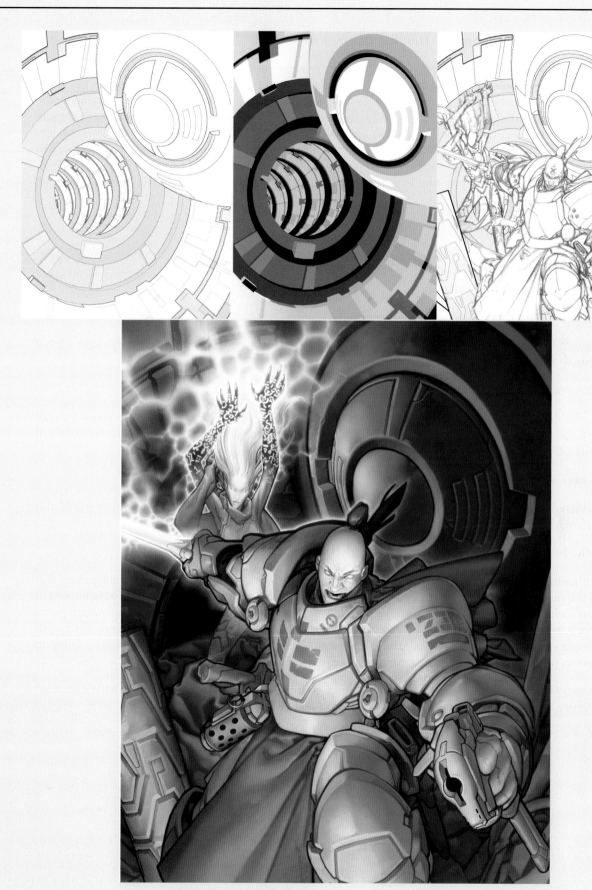

From the book ARSENAL, Copyright Perpetrated Press 2002

How early do you have to get up? How late do you have to stay?

As an Art Director, I'm pretty busy. I am responsible for the overall look and visual quality of the game... combine this with the in-game asset production I'm scheduled to do and I don't have much free time. If you want, you can work in the games industry and keep a 9-5 schedule, you just need to be focused and producing the entire time you're in the office. Most of us prefer to take it easier at the office, but that means we stay more than 8 hours a day. We expect a lot, but you can keep your own hours, just as long as everyone is around during the core hours of 11-4. That way, communication can take place and everyone knows what's going on. We try to take good care of our people, cause that's how you produce top-quality products. You can't make games without talented, dedicated people. Our long-term goal is to eradicate the crunch time stress and burnout that the games industry is famous for.

What are your interests outside the job?

I collect guns and make knives. I like to collect old battle rifles and restore them... after that sometimes I keep them to shoot, but most of the time I just sell them off and buy another one that needs work. The fun is in restoring the tool to its past beauty.

What games do you play?

My favorite video game is still Blood, Monolith's first FPS (first-person shooter). I actually don't have a lot of time to play games any more... I'm too busy making them.

Where do you find inspiration for your work?

I am inspired by the work of other artists... I constantly search comics, the web, books, and movies for cool ideas, styles and techniques. Also, historical reference and imagery from other cultures are a treasure trove of great ideas...especially for those interested in character design.

Do you have an ultimate goal for your career?

I've considered it. I want to be the best. I want to be the best artist in games. Period. I think it would also be cool to maybe get into movies some day, and do more book covers.

What's the best advice you could give to new artists entering the industry?

Monolith looks for people who have done work in the genre we work with. If you don't have anything that matches the genre in your portfolio, it's a good idea to come up with a sample anyway. We're always impressed with people who go the extra mile that way. We also like to see people who have basic art skills and can paint. We'd take a painter over a Maya whiz because we can always teach the painter how to use Maya. Monolith wants people who do low-poly work and painted textures. It also helps to be interested in games. Being in games now is probably the best and most exciting place to be. Enthusiasm is really important.

In getting a job in general, research the company. Never go into an interview "dry". Find out what they want to see – genre, poly count, texture examples... whatever) - and give it to them.

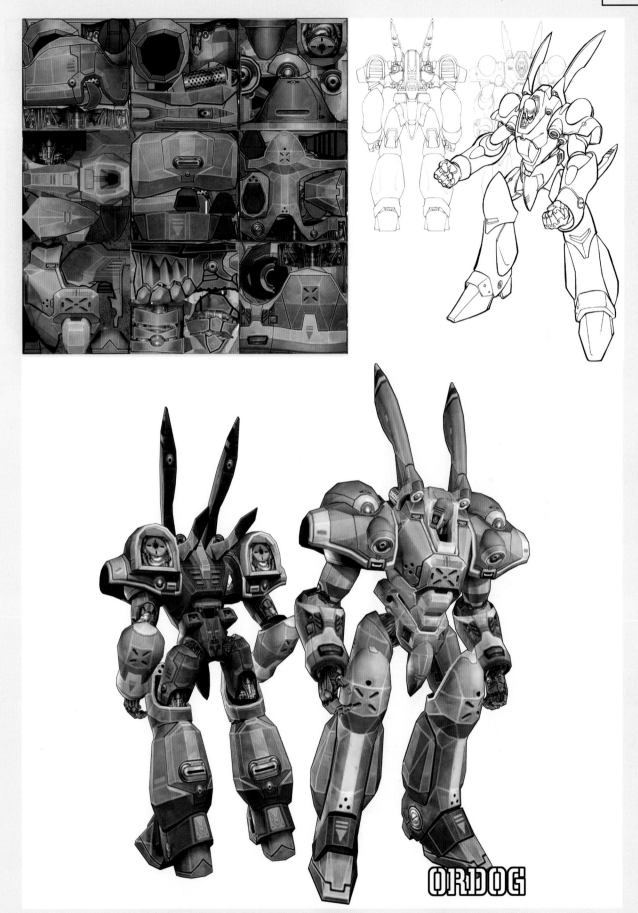

ORDOG

Concept Design and Texture by Eric Kohler, Model by David Longo. Copyright Monolith Productions 2002

Concept Design and Texture by Eric Kohler, Model by David Longo. Copyright Monolith Productions 2002

IN THIS CHAPTER YOU WILL LEARN ABOUT:

- Sources and Clips
- Importing images to XSI
- Clip Effects
- Using PSD files in XSI's compositor
- Using the UV Editor

INTRODUCTION

Softimage XSI is an integrated 3D animation and special effects package. While it does have a compositor, it doesn't yet (as of version 3.01) have an integrated paint system. Since you will often want to use outside art and content in any 3D program, Photoshop is an important part of working in 3D.

SOURCES AND CLIPS EXPLAINED

All images that you use within XSI must first be brought into the program and associated with your scene. Each image (or image sequence) from Photoshop needs to be located on your hard disk or network, and a reference stored to that location in your XSI scene. This reference has two parts, called the Source and the Clip.

The Image Source is the object that stores the name of the image file or sequence, where it is on disk, how fast you want the sequence to play, how long the sequence is, and a few options related to rendering.

The Image Clip refers to an Image Source, and adds new properties, like the image size, crop, color balance, and more. We'll examine these Clip properties later in this chapter.

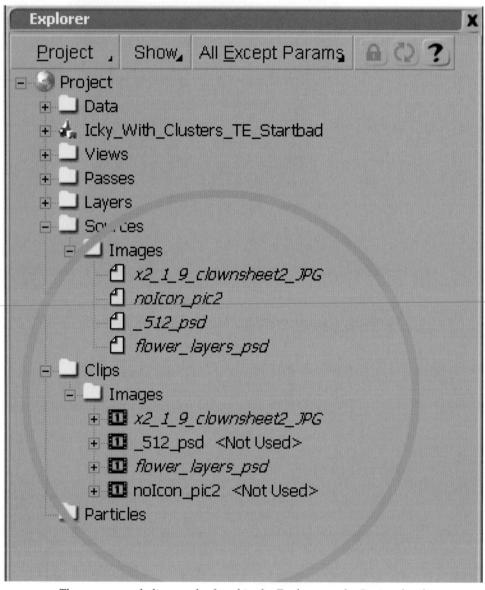

The sources and clips can be found in the Explorer, at the Project level.

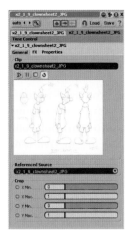

The Clip properties include cropping and clip FX.

Both Image Sources and Clips can be viewed in the Explorer, at the Project scope (level). There must be at least one Source for each Clip, although there may be many Clips referencing each Source. Because the Source is really just the file location of the image on disk somewhere, the images are not really stored inside the scene file. That means you can modify them on disk and see the results in XSI.

So while we might say we are "bringing images into XSI" or "importing images", we are really just making references to them on disk.

IMPORTING IMAGES WITH THE IMAGE CLIP VIEWER

It's a good idea to bring all your imagery into your XSI scene all at one time, to optimize your productivity and workflow. You do this with the Clip Viewer, and optionally with the Browser window.

If you open the Clip Viewer into one of your four View windows, you can create Sources and Clips by either using the File→Import Clip menu or by opening your Browser into another View window, and dragging images from the Browser into the Clip Editor.

If you have a single image to import, you can locate the image in the Browser, drag it to the middle of the Clip Editor, and let go to create a Source and a Clip. The image will then appear in the Clip Editor. When you drag and drop another image into the Clip Editor, it is added and shows up in the Window. You can use the Clips drop-menu to switch back and forth between the images.

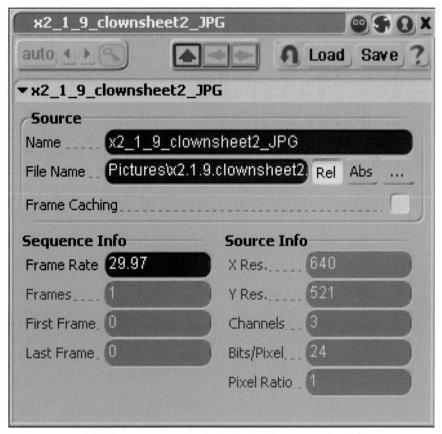

The Source properties include the filename and path.

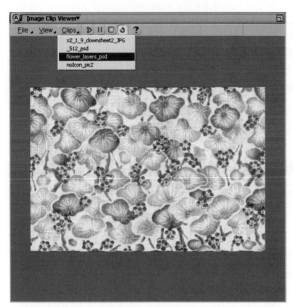

The Clip Viewer shows you all the clips imported into your scene.

The Browser is just a file dialog with image icons.

If you have a sequence of images that you want to use, for instance as an animated texture map, they need to be named like this: name.number.extension (powerup.1.tif for instance).

When you look at the images in the Browser, XSI combines all the numbers together and shows you only one Icon; when you drag and drop it into XSI, only one source and one clip will be created, no matter how many individual images there were in the sequence.

If it happens that you only really want one of the images, you can double-click on the icon in the Browser to drill down into the sequence and drag just one into the Clip Editor.

You can import almost any file type that Photoshop will write. XSI will happily read TIFF, Targa, JPEG, and even the native Photoshop file format, PSD. However, if you choose to use PSD files in the RenderTree portion of XSI, only the first layer will be accessible. (The compositor can extract layers, though.)

I mentioned above that the images are merely referenced in the XSI scene. That might lead to problems if you took the scene somewhere else and tried to open it. The images would not be there, because they did not travel with the scene.

You can solve this problem. When you save your XSI scene, if you check the box marked "Copy External Files Under Project" then during the save XSI will locate, gather, and move all the referenced images from where you found them into the Pictures directory in the current XSI Project. Then you transport the entire project, now containing both scenes and images, to the new location, and it all works properly. This collection feature is extremely convenient.

UPDATING REFERENCES

If you open the Explorer and switch to the Project scope, then open the Sources folder and inspect one of the clips you have created, you'll see the path to the file.

If at some point it's necessary to swap this image with another, you could manually change the file path here, and the same source would reference a different image. The clip you use in the scene would therefore also point to the new image.

DYNAMIC UPDATE FROM PHOTOSHOP

You can also use Photoshop to edit a file used by XSI, and see the results immediately after you save the file from Photoshop, even if both applications are running. The user preference named "Reload Externally Modified Image Clips on Focus" in File→User Prefs→Interaction Tab controls this behavior.

REMOVING UNUSED CLIPS AND SOURCES

Since Clips and Sources can also come in with Model imports, after working with a scene for a long time, sometimes there are lots of Sources and Clips that you no longer wish to use.

Since Clips depend on Sources, you can remove the clips without removing the sources, but not the other way around. While you can delete Sources in the Explorer with the Delete key, it's usually easier to use the Clips→Delete Unused Sources and Clips command from the right-hand menu stack in the Render module.

USING THE CLIP EFFECTS

Frequently, after you have prepped an image in Photoshop for use as a texture of some kind, then imported it and used it, you discover that it is not quite right, and some adjustment must be made. If you are the one that made the file, and have both Photoshop and XSI running on the same computer, that is easy enough. But alas, that is frequently not the case. XSI has a solution for the most frequent minor image editing problems, called the Clip Effects. Clip Effects are filters and changes to the image that occur non-destructively, after the image has been read from the file on disk. That means that you can crop or blur or flip an image in XSI without damaging the original file, and without going back to Photoshop to complete the edit. The Clip Effects are also animatable, which is a neat feature.

The Clip Effects are located on the Clip itself, so you can see them all by locating the clip in the Explorer and inspecting its properties. However, it is usually faster and easier to use the Clip Editor to examine the Clip Effects.

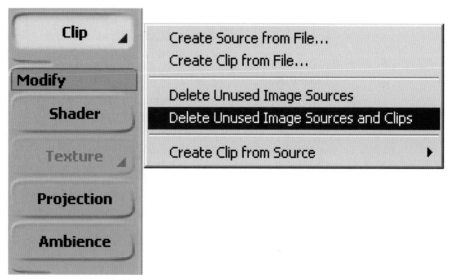

Use the Clip Menu to eliminate old, misdirected and unused clips.

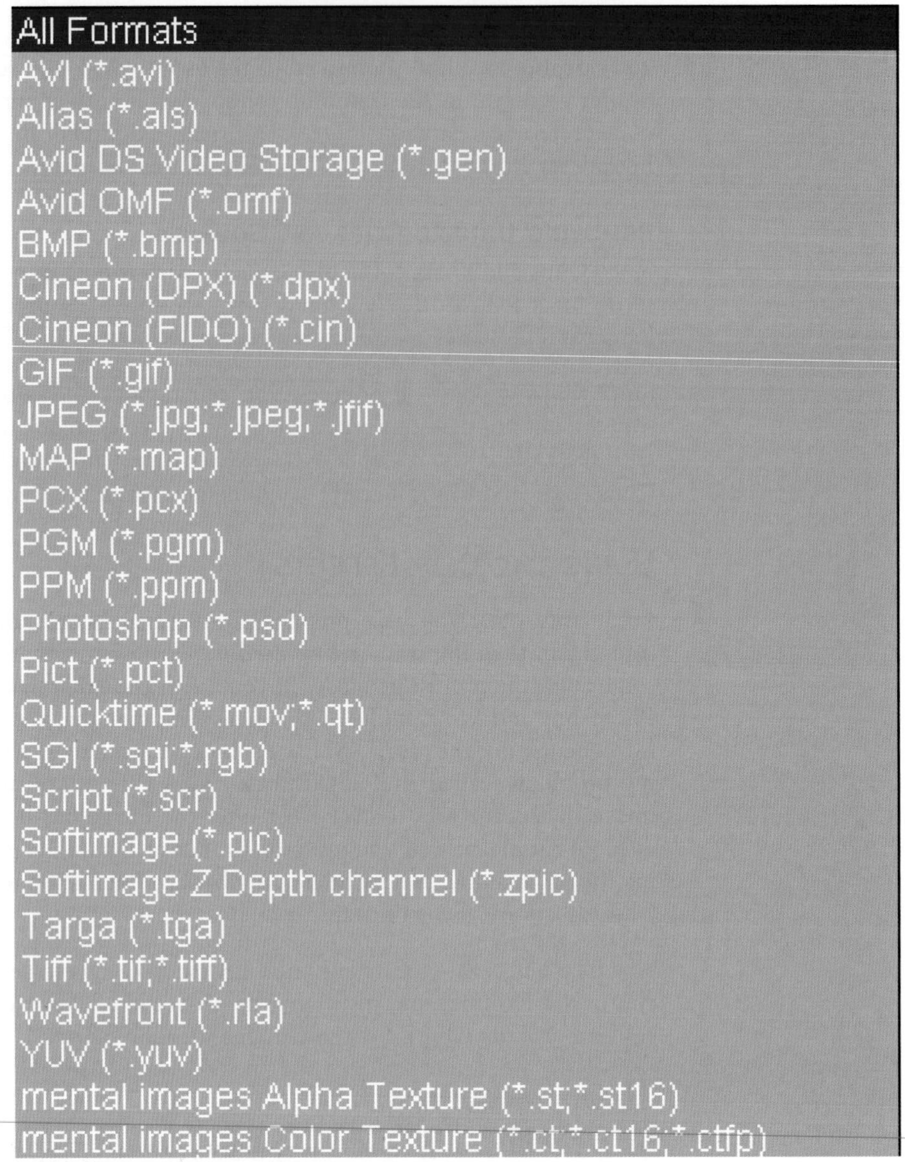

All Formats
AVI (*.avi)
Alias (*.als)
Avid DS Video Storage (*.gen)
Avid OMF (*.omf)
BMP (*.bmp)
Cineon (DPX) (*.dpx)
Cineon (FIDO) (*.cin)
GIF (*.gif)
JPEG (*.jpg;*.jpeg;*.jfif)
MAP (*.map)
PCX (*.pcx)
PGM (*.pgm)
PPM (*.ppm)
Photoshop (*.psd)
Pict (*.pct)
Quicktime (*.mov;*.qt)
SGI (*.sgi;*.rgb)
Script (*.scr)
Softimage (*.pic)
Softimage Z Depth channel (*.zpic)
Targa (*.tga)
Tiff (*.tif;*.tiff)
Wavefront (*.rla)
YUV (*.yuv)
mental images Alpha Texture (*.st;*.st16)
mental images Color Texture (*.ct;*.ct16;*.ctfp)

XSI can import all these files from Photoshop.

CROPPING

You will often find that the image you plan to use is too big, includes more than you want, or has too much space around the edges. In these cases, the solution is to crop the image. This can be done non-destructively in XSI. Simply show the image in the Clip Editor, then pop up the context-sensitive menu over the image with Alt-right-click (or just right-click if you have Nil mode on) and choose Clip Properties. Then again right-click (or Alt-right-click) in the middle of the image in the Clip PPG, and choose the Crop Tool. Thin yellow lines will be drawn on the image, and you can adjust them to crop the image on the top, bottom, left, and right sides.

If you want a more precise or numeric crop, use the crop sliders in the Clip PPG, just below the image.

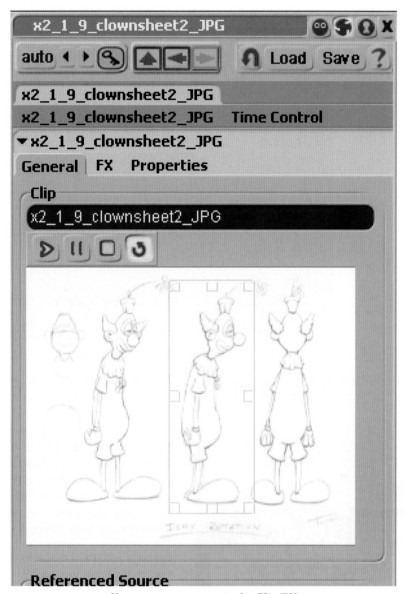

You can crop images in the Clip FX.

FLIPPING

When mapping a texture to a NURBS patch, the initial orientation of the image on the patch is determined by the U and V direction of the surface. Sometimes the image is upside-down, or perhaps mirrored (backwards). While you could go adjust the Texture Projection to solve these problems, it is often easier to just flip the image horizontally or vertically with the Clip Effects. You can use the Clip Effect PPG for this, by popping the context-sensitive menu from the Clip Viewer

The one thing you cannot do with flipping is rotate the image 90 degrees. If the image is laying on its side and you need it up and down, you will have to Swap UV in the Texture Projection.

You can flip but not rotate!

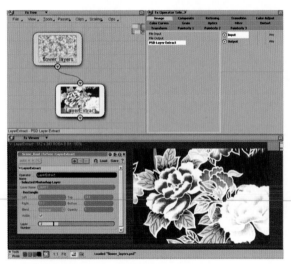

You can pull layers out of PSD files in the Compositor!

MONOCHROME, INVERT, AND BLUR

If you are using Photoshop reference material to bump or displace a surface, you frequently need to adjust the image once you see the rendered result. The Clip Effects are again useful here. Since Bump and Displacement are calculated using the luminance of the image (all the Red, Blue, and Green info added together, and clipped to a maximum value of 1.0), it helps to be seeing the image in that way as well. The Monochrome Clip Effect does this.

Perhaps now the Displacement is the opposite of what you want, dipping in where you want it pushed out. You can use the Invert Clip Effect here.

If the results of your Bump or Displacement are too chunky and crunchy, perhaps you need a finer displacement Tesselation, or a different Bump filter. Or, you could in some cases get away with applying a Gaussian Blur filter to the original image. The Blur Clip effect helps here.

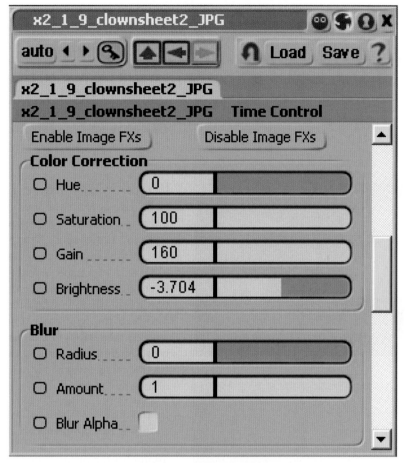

Color correction and blur.

NON-DESTRUCTIVE COLOR CORRECTION ON PSD

Since the Clip Effects are animatable, you can use one Photoshop file as texture input, and then animate changes in the Hue, Saturation, Gain, and Gamma to change the effect it produces over time. You can't animate over time on a single frame in Photoshop, and rember that using the Clip Effects won't harm the saved image on disk.

USING PSD FILES IN THE COMPOSITOR

The XSI Compositor is a bit like a collection of Photoshop effects that can be chained together, by plugging one into the other, as far as you want to go to achieve a given effect. That tree of connected effects (called Operators in the XSI compositor) is evaluated at each and every frame, and the results presented to you. In this way, it too is dynamic and non-destructive.

Let's say you take a picture of a cherry tree with pink blossoms against a blue sky, and you select the sky and blur it, then apply a Mosaic filter to the whole image. Now you think you might want to go back and make the sky more blue. In the XSI compositor, each filter is run only when you need it, and the original images are never changed. So you could go back to extract the blue sky from the image, color correct it, and add it back to the original, even after a Mosaic filter was also added.

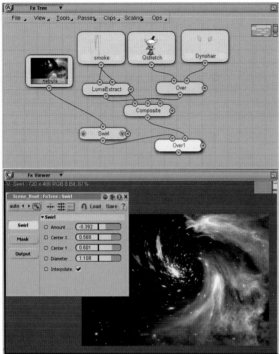

Now the Swirl operator is stuffed under the clown.

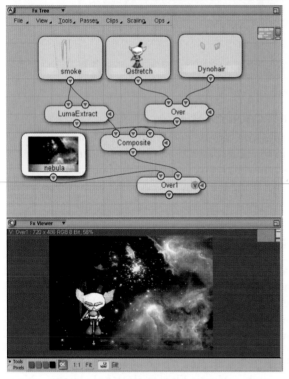

The completed (simple) composite.

You can also use the compositor to extract specific layers from a PSD file, using the PSD Layer Extract image operator.

LAYERING ANIMATION OVER A BACKGROUND

Open the FXTree in one XSI view window (perhaps the top-left) and then open the FX Viewer in the lower-left view. The FX Tree is where you chain operators (filters) together, and the Viewer is where you see the results.

In order to plug together like Legos, each operator must have at least one input, and one output. In fact, most operators have at least two inputs: one color input and one Mask input. The Mask determines in what part of the image that operator will have an effect, just like a selection mask in Photoshop. However, the difference is that you can use another image as that selection mask, which is why there is another input for the Mask. If the operator is one that mixes or combines images, there would be one color input for each image it can operate on. For instance, an Over operator layers one image over the other, using the matte to determine which parts of the foreground are transparent.

In this case we want to layer foreground animation from XSI over an image created in Photoshop.

To import the images into the FX Tree, first make clips of them. Use the File→Import Images menu item in the FX Tree to create the Clip and the Source, and to load the image into the FX Tree interface.

In this case there are two images: the clown foreground and the stars background.

To combine them we'll need an Over operator. Open the Operator Selector in a floating window with the View→Operator Selector menu command in the FX Tree view.

In the Composite tab, select the Over effect and examine the inputs. The fast way to use the Over is to middle-click first on the background image, then on the foreground, then middle-click in the FX Tree where you want the node placed. But in this case, let's do it the long way to reinforce the concepts.

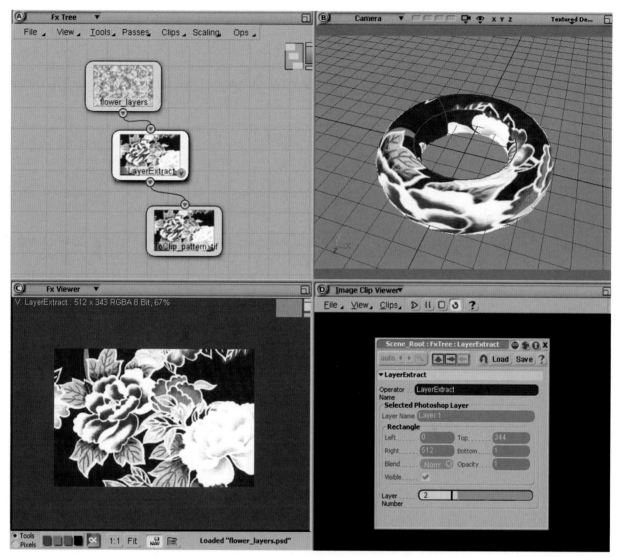

You can extract Photoshop layers with the Compositor.

With the Over selected in the Operator Selector, middle-click in the FX Tree window to place the node. It needs to have both the background (nebula) and the foreground (Qstretch clown) connected to it. Click on the small triangle dropping from the bottom of the stars image (the output) and drag it to the left top input triangle on the Over operator. This plugs the output of the stars image into the background input of the operator. Now repeat for the foreground, plugging the Clown output into the foreground input on the Over. That's it – you are done.

You can test your work by hovering the mouse over each node and clicking the right-bottom V button, which will display the results in the FX Viewer. See how the final Over node combines each original image!

Now let's put a filter on the Stars. From the Distort tab of the Operator Selector, choose the Swirl operator, and middle-click to drop it in the FX Tree. It needs to be connected after the Nebula, and before the final Over.

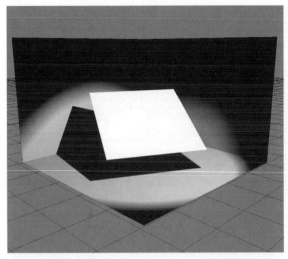

The starting scene, no textures applied.

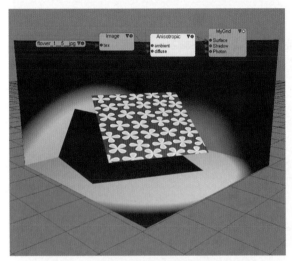

The image is applied to the diffuse and ambient channels.

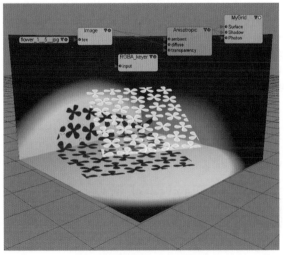

Now the flowers are cut out.

Unplug the Nebula from the Over by right-clicking on the part of the line that enters the Over from the stars. Now plug the output of the stars to the input of the Swirl, and the output of the Swirl to the background input of the Over. Load the result into the FX Viewer with the V button to see the result.

You can always adjust the properties of an operator. Hover your mouse over the Swirl and click the E (Edit) button to see the property page. Adjust the sliders to your liking. For extra credit, try applying the Lens Flare operator to the whole stack, and the Glowing Edges operator to just the Clown.

EXTRACTING PSD LAYERS WITH THE COMPOSITOR

Extracting layers from a PSD file for use in XSI also uses the compositor, but it requires a bit of trickery. Basically, we're going to rewire from the compositor back to the Clip, then use the Clip in the rest of the program normally.

We need two clips: one has the layered Photoshop file, and the other is a dummy, which can be blank. When both are imported into the FX Tree, you'll note that Clips have two parts: a node called the "FromClip" which points to the source file on disk, and the actual Clip node.

If you add a LayerExtract node to the Photoshop layer clip (here called flower_Layers) you may pull out any layer that you wish. Then if you plug the output of the LayerExtract node to the input of the dummy clip (here called Clip_Pattern), then you would be replacing the input that was coming from disk, and instead using the layer extractor from the Compositor. Then, you could use that clip in the Render Tree, and in fact the image would be coming from the compositor, not from the disk. In addition to making it possible to read Photoshop layers, an infinite number of other possibilities present themselves using the compositor to modify Photoshop files, then pumping them into the renderer.

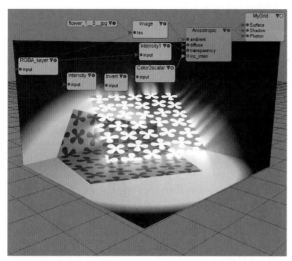

The flower pattern is extracted, and glows.

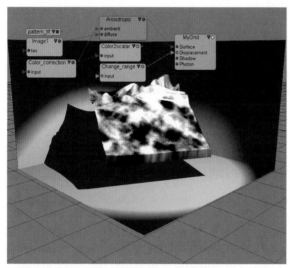

Now the roughness pattern actually creates a new surface

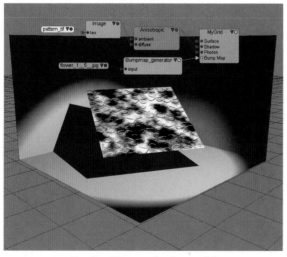

Do the Flowers look rough?

RENDERING TEXTURES FROM PHOTOSHOP

What can you do with Photoshop files in XSI? The short answer is that you can do almost anything. Generally speaking, Photoshop images are wrapped onto a scene object using a texture projection, which precisely controls which part of the image falls where on the object.

Then, that image can be used in the Render Tree as inputs to any number of shaders. As the image varies over the surface of the object, the input to the shader varies, and the rendering engine creates a different result. Since the image can be used in almost any input on almost any shader, and because the shaders can be plugged together like operators in the compositor, the results are infinitely variable.

However, there are some standard uses. In this section each use is briefly described, the original Photoshop image is shown, and the rendered result is shown with the Render Tree connections used to make it happen composited over it.

COLOR MAP

The simplest use of a Photoshop texture is as a color map, changing the diffuse, ambient, and specular colors across the surface of an object.

TRANSPERANCY

Rather than model a complex shape or pattern, an image can be used as a transparency mask, to cut out the parts of the object that you want to be invisible.

LUMINOSITY

In this example, the luminosity of the pattern has been extracted, and applied to transparency to cut out the flowers, then to the incandescence channel to create luminance, and to the diffuse channels with a color correction. Finally, a glow was added.

BUMP

Bump is an optical illusion creating the impression that the surface is rough.

DISPLACEMENT

When an image displaces a surface, the surface actually changes shape during the render. That means it will cast shadows correctly, and look more complex.

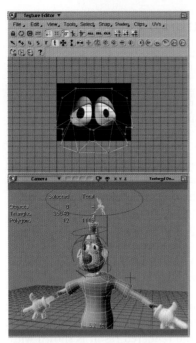

The UV Editor, and Icky's eyes

Icky needs some vision.

Now the UVs for Icky's head are stamped into the image.

USING THE UV EDITOR

People using XSI for game development frequently make use of Photoshop for creating textures. The Photoshop textures need to be connected precisely with the models built in XSI, so the results can be exported to a game engine.

The Texture Editor is the XSI interface that a texture artist uses to connect each specific polygon on the model with each specific part of the texture file.

In this case, the model is a Sub-Division Surface, which is derived from a simple polygon cage. We have images of Icky's eyes and mouth, which need to be mapped correctly onto his head.

The eyes and mouth have been created and processed using Photoshop. (In real life they are actually sequences of animation, so Icky can look around, blink, smile, etc.)

A texture projection is created, and the polygons of Icky's face are unwrapped using the Texture Editor.

The Eye image is imported as a Source and Clip, and positioned correctly onto the unwrapped UVs in the Texture Editor.

The Eye image is now mapped onto the area of Icky's face in the Render Tree, and the results may be rendered out.

USING XSI TO STAMP FILES FOR PHOTOSHOP

Sometimes you will have a model file, but not a texture file. You might want to paint on the model, adding makeup or other details, using Photoshop. But in order to paint on the object in Photoshop effectively, you need to know what part of the model you would be painting on, were you actually painting in 3D. The solution is to stamp the polygon edges from the model directly into an empty texture file from Photoshop, then re-import the file into Photoshop and, in a new layer, paint what you want on top of the stamped file, using the lines of the model as a guide.

To do this, first unwrap the model using the Texture Editor (this takes a good deal of manual labor). Then, use the Stamp UV Mesh function from the Edit menu of the Texture Editor. This adds the lines, and saves the file back where it came from. Now you can simply open the UV Mesh image in Photoshop and paint away. When the file is saved from Photoshop with the same name, the results will immediately become visible back in XSI.

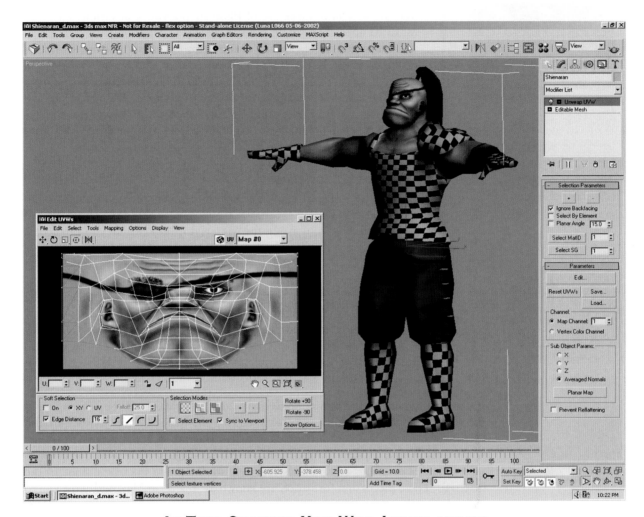

IN THIS CHAPTER YOU WILL LEARN ABOUT:

- How to use the Material Editor
- How to assign texture maps to a material
- The application of materials to objects
- The uses of UVW Maps and Unwrap UVW
- How to export UV information as a template for painting

INTRODUCTION

Photoshop is a tool that almost every 3d Studio Max artist has in their graphics arsenal. The 2d tools that Photoshop provides you with are a tremendous aid for creating texture maps, and compliment Max's 3d capabilities quite well. Discreet, the developer of 3d Studio Max, is very much aware of this fact, and has striven to make workflow between the two programs as fast and seamless as possible.

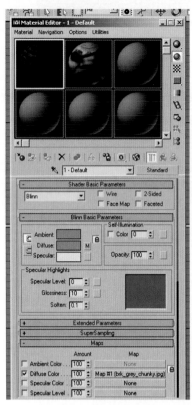

Using the Material Editor

DEALING WITH TEXTURES IN THE MATERIAL EDITOR

Max allows you to make use of Photoshop artwork in various ways. In Max, the appearance of an object's surface is determined by a material, which may consist of various texture maps. Each of these maps within a material may influence the overall appearance of the object's surface in different ways. This may mean the color, the bumpiness, the shininess, etc. There are various attributes available within a material, and you can use Photoshop-created textures in each of them. What we use to control, prepare, and alter these materials is known as the Material Editor, which is a powerful and sophisticated tool for this type of task.

MATERIALS AND MAPS

In Max, the color, texture, and overall appearance of an object's surface is determined by the material that you apply to it. Materials can be created in Max by using the Material Editor, which you can access from the Main Toolbar, by hitting the hotkey M on the keyboard, or by accessing it from the Rendering Menu. You can think of the Material Editor as a painter's palette, where you can prepare your paint before applying it to your canvas, which is an object in the scene. Once the Material Editor is open, you will have various sample slots available to you in the upper part of the dialog, which allow you to preview the materials that you are preparing. If you want to access more slots, move your mouse to the border between the slots, and click and drag. More slots will become visible.

If you click on one of the sample spheres in a material slot, it will become active in the material editor, allowing you to begin editing the material. The border around the slot will turn white, letting you know that this is the material that you are currently working on. Within these materials are some shading controls and basic parameters, and also various components that help to determine the overall look of the material. These pieces of information are known as "maps" in Max, and allow you to control the color, shine, bump, and other aspects of the material's overall appearance.

USING BITMAPS

To access the maps for a material, click on the Maps rollout for the material whose slot is currently active in the Material Editor. The various maps will become available, each marked with a None on their button, letting you know that no maps are currently assigned. If you are having trouble seeing all of the maps, move your mouse over a blank area of the dialog, where there are no buttons. The mouse pointer will change its appearance, resembling a hand. Click and drag down to scroll vertically in the dialog, allowing you to see the other maps. To add a texture map to one of the components, click on the button next to the attribute that is marked None. The Material/Map Browser will appear, allowing you to choose a variety of different map types. To utilize an image created or edited in Photoshop, you will want to choose a new Bitmap as the map type. At this point, another dialog will appear, allowing you to select an image from your hard drive or network. If you are curious to see what file types are supported by Max, click on the drop-down arrow next to the Files of Type field. A wide variety of file types are supported, but since you are working in Photoshop, it is usually best to choose a PSD file.

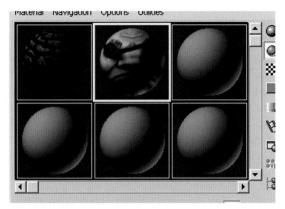

Material slots

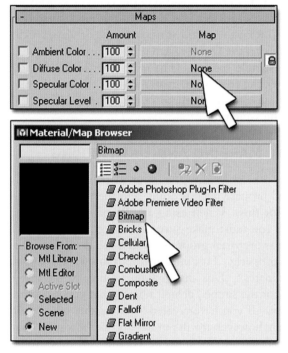

Click on the None button next to the map, then choose Bitmap.

When you choose a PSD file, you will be asked whether you would like to use Collapsed Layers, or individual layers. If you choose Individual Layers, you will get a preview of each of the layers before you hit OK, but in reality it does not always matter which option you choose here. Once you hit OK, the PSD is assigned to the map component, and should be visible on the sample sphere in the material slot.

You will now be at the Map level of the material editor. At this level, you have various controls including the rotation and tiling for the map. When you want to get back to the root of the material, click on the Go to Parent Icon, which is located just below the sample spheres, toward the right of that row of controls. An alternative is to click on the Material/Map Navigator button, located at the bottom of the column of options to the right of the sample spheres. This will bring up a floater dialog with a hierarchical display of the material and its maps. Just click on the level in the hierarchy that you want to be, and you will move up or down in the hierarchy, as you wish. Once you are back at the root of the material, you can then add more maps to other attributes, such as Bump, Shininess, etc.

BITMAP AND PSD FEATURES

Once a texture map is assigned to a specific attribute, you can choose to go back into Photoshop and make any changes to the file that you wish. As soon as you resave that image file, the map will automatically be updated in Max, reflecting the changes that you have made. This can be a tremendous time saver, since you do not have to reload the map in Max to see any of the tweaks or adjustments that you have made in Photoshop. This is done automatically as soon as you re-save in Photoshop.

Max handles information from PSDs quite well, making this format a favorite for Photoshop artists. Max will be able to understand complex layered files without any trouble, allowing you to work as you wish in Photoshop, with little restriction. Whether it is just a relatively simple piece with several layers in Normal color mode, or one with dozens of layers in various blending modes and numerous effects, Max shouldn't have any trouble interpreting the information.

ASSIGNING MATERIALS TO OBJECTS AND UVW MAPPING

In this section we will be covering exactly how you should go about assigning materials to objects in your scene, so that they are displayed properly. In addition to this, we will also look into UVW mapping, which dictates exactly how a bitmap will be applied to a more complex piece of geometry.

ASSIGNING MATERIALS TO OBJECTS

Once you have a material prepared in the Material Editor, you will need to assign it to an object in your scene. An easy way to do this is to click and drag the material's sample sphere from its slot in the Material Editor to an object in your scene. If you have a scene with numerous objects, this can be a little challenging to do correctly, so there is an alternative method of assigning a material. You can first select the object(s) that you want the material assigned to, and then in the Material Editor, click on the Assign Material to Selection button, which is located below the sample sphere slots. After assigning the material, the material slot will be flagged with white triangles in its corners, indicating that this material is assigned to an object in the scene.

When you assign a material to an object in Max, you will see the object change colors, letting you know that it has been successfully assigned. However, by default, you will not see the maps that make up the material displayed in the viewports. Max will just show the default shaded color of that material, in order to put less demands on your graphics card. Usually, you will want to override this, so that your maps are displayed on the object. To do this, click on the Display Map in Viewport button, which is located centrally, just below the sample spheres. The icon looks like a checkerboard box. You can do this at either the root of the material or at the map level. I usually do this at the root level, because it allows me to view the main diffuse color and the results of opacity maps at the same time.

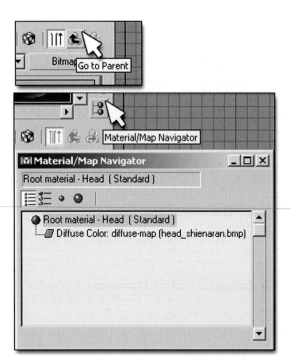

When you are at the map level, use Go To Parent, or the Material/Map Navigator to get back to the root of the material.

UVW MAPPING AND UNWRAPPING

There is a possibility that your maps will not be displayed properly at this point, and there is an explanation for this. When using any Bitmap images in textures, you must make sure that the geometry in your scene is prepared properly, so that the textures will lay on it properly. This information is known as mapping coordinates. This information is already present in many of the simple, default objects that you can create in Max. If you have created some unique object from scratch, however, it will not have proper mapping coordinates, and so they must be assigned. If they are not assigned, you will get an error when you try to render, as Max gets confused about how the bitmaps should be displayed on the objects.

To assign mapping coordinates, you will need to apply either a UVW Map modifier, or the Unwrap UVW modifier. The UVW Map modifier gives you straightforward controls that dictate how the map will be applied to the object. These include planar mapping, spherical mapping, cylindrical, and more, which allow you to choose a map shape (or "projection") that most approximates your model.

Click and drag the material onto the object, or select the object, and click on Assign Material to Selected.

Show Map in Viewport

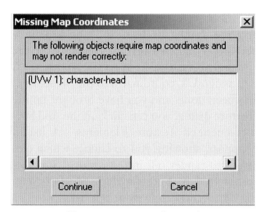

No mapping coordinates!

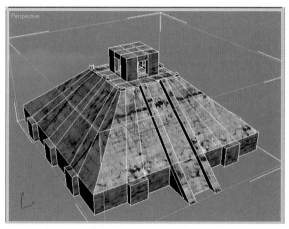

An object with a UVW Map applied to it in the viewport.

The Unwrap UVW modifier allows you to edit the mapping assignments more specifically, dictating exactly how the UV coordinates affect different areas of the mesh, and can also be used to assign planar mapping to different portions of the object. By using this modifier, you can edit the alignment of the vertices to their texture map by clicking on the Edit button, and can assure that everything is lined up properly. This is done in an Edit UV dialog, which shows you a wireframe of the mesh, flattened out and overlaying the texture that is assigned to it. From here, you can select portions of the mesh, and position them over the correct area of the bitmap, ensuring that you get the UV information lined up just how you want it.

SAVING UV INFORMATION FOR REFERENCE

Many experienced Max/Photoshop artists who are working with custom models will usually prepare their UV mapping coordinates before ever touching Photoshop. This UV information will always be necessary so that the bitmaps will be displayed on the object properly, and this information can also be useful to you when working in Photoshop.

TEXPORTER PLUGIN

There are several methods that you may use for preparing a UV mesh. One of the tried and true tools for doing this is to use the Texporter plugin, which may be downloaded for free on the Internet. This plugin will work for Max 5 and 4, and there are earlier versions of the add-on software available for even earlier versions of Max. After installing it, this plugin allows you to save an image of your UV information to a 2d bitmap file, which you can use as a template for painting over in Photoshop.

To use this plugin, you must first assign UV coordinates to your object. Once this is done, you can access the Texporter plugin by going to the Utilities Panel, and clicking on the More button. A dialog will appear with a list of utilities. Select Texporter from the list, and various options will appear in the Utilities Panel. Scroll down a bit, and determine the size for the bitmap that will be created. After this, determine exactly what you want to be displayed in this image. You can choose wireframe, shaded, and many more options. Once you have designated how the UV mesh is to be rendered, just activate the Pick Object button, and then click on the object. Texporter will calculate for a moment, then you will see a flattened version of your UV coordinates, which you can save in several formats by clicking on the save dialog in the upper-right corner of the window.

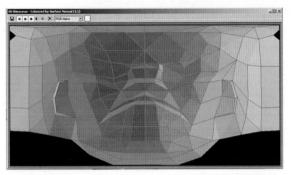

A texported UV template, ready to be painted in Photoshop.

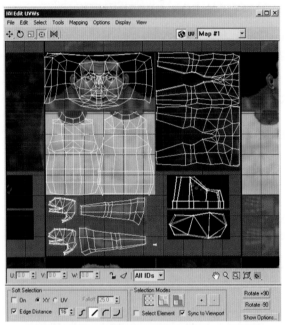

Editing UV coordinates using Unwrap UVW.

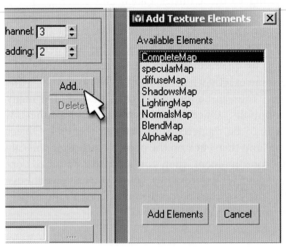

Click on Add, and choose which texture elements you want to generate.

Once this image is saved, you can open it in Photoshop, and use it as reference for painting over. Generally, you will create a new layer on top of the UV reference, and begin your painting. Doing this allows you to preserve the reference in case you make mistakes. As you continue to make progress with your PSD, you can then load this new painted version into the material editor, and assign it to your object. The detailing on the PSD should line up quite well with the geometry in the scene, and you can continue to work on the image until you are satisfied.

RENDER TO TEXTURE

There are several alternatives to the Texporter plugin for extracting UV information as a bitmap image file. Some MaxScripts are available that perform many of the same functions as this plugin. Even more promising, however, is the Render to Texture function that is built into Max. This option is new to Max 5, and can be found under the Rendering Menu.

Once opened, the Render to Texture dialog will allow you to generate UV-mapped texture elements for the object that is currently selected. As with Texporter, it is a good idea to assign UV coordinates to the object first. Once this has been done, and you have brought up the Render to Texture dialog, you can click on the Add button next to Generated Texture Elements. A list of options will appear, allowing you to choose which elements you want to render out into a texture. Options such as CompleteMap, SpecularMap, ShadowsMap, and LightingMap are available from this list.

Some of these elements take into account any lighting and other information in your scene that you have prepared, and "bake" this shading into the rendered image. This can provide you with an excellent head start when it comes to using Photoshop, as you will not need to spend as much time trying to paint subtleties in lighting and so forth, particularly if you are preparing textures for a real time application. Once you have determined which elements are to be included, you must select an image size for the file to be output to, and must designate a name for the image, and a folder to be saved to. After this, just click on the Render button from the dialog, and a 2d map will be created, taking into account any element that you have included. This map can then serve as a template to further Photoshop work, and can be reloaded as a texture map in a material when it is ready.

Choosing Render to Texture

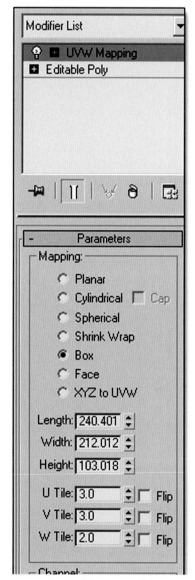

UVW Map controls

CONCLUSION

Photoshop is an outstanding image editing and paint package that really complements the 3d capabilities of 3d Studio Max. Max allows you to work hand-in-hand with Photoshop, throughout the production pipeline. You can save the UV information out of Max as a template for painting in Photoshop, do what you need to do in Adobe's fine product, then can easily load this freshly painted PSD as a texture map into Max's Material Editor. Of course, if you should need to do some touchups on your 2d texture artwork, Max will automatically update as soon as you save in Photoshop. These capabilities, along with others make Max and Photoshop an excellent combination of tools for any 2d/3d artist.

COMBUSTION AND PHOTOSHOP

IN THIS CHAPTER YOU WILL LEARN ABOUT:

- Using Photoshop Plug-ins with combustion
- Photoshop Filter Emulation
- Bitmap versus Vector Graphics
- Importing and Using PSD Files
- Effective Methods of Working with PSD Files
- Digital Matte Painting: A Case Study

INTRODUCTION

combustion and Photoshop are two of the most powerful image editing programs available for the desktop computer, and fortunately for digital artists, they work together extraordinarily well. In this chapter, you'll learn about some of the features and settings that apply to Photoshop and combustion integration, what kinds of things combustion can do with PSD files, and see a working example of the two programs' interoperability.

USING PHOTOSHOP PLUG-INS WITH COMBUSTION

Most third-party Photoshop plug-ins work with combustion. Professionally produced plug-ins created by software companies to meet Adobe's API standard, such as Corel's Kai's Power Tools or Alien Skin's Eye Candy, are most likely to function correctly. A complete list of fully supported third-party plug-ins is available on the Discreet web site (http://www.discreet.com/support/combustion/), in the FAQs list. Unlisted or "homemade" plug-ins might work, but you'll have to test it yourself.

Using Photoshop plug-ins in combustion

INSTALLATION

To install a Photoshop plug-in in combustion, put a re-named copy of the plug-in folder in combustion's Plugins folder, and copy any associated DLL files to the main combustion directory. Or, if the plug-in uses an executable (EXE) installer, just run the installer and point it at combustion's Plugins folder instead of Photoshop's. That's it!

USING PHOTOSHOP PLUG-INS

Installed Photoshop plug-ins will appear in the Operators drop-down menu, sorted according to category, and sometimes in their own new category. Simply apply the third-party filter just like you'd apply one of the combustion operators.

PHOTOSHOP FILTER EMULATION

Photoshop Filter Emulation is a preference set in File→Preferences→General. When it's checked, any Photoshop filter plug-ins will be organized and function like they would in Photoshop. Palettes and controls for the filters will appear as sliders in combustion, some of which can even be animated. The translation to combustion sliders doesn't always work, though, in which case you'll probably be presented with the plug-in's custom dialog box when you apply it to a Layer.

Why apply Photoshop filters to an image in combustion instead of Photoshop? Animation. All of combustion's operators can be animated over time, and combustion can generate animation curves for the controls of many Photoshop plug-ins.

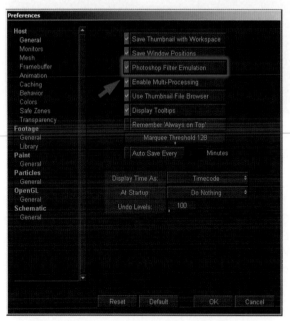

The Photoshop Filter Emulation preference

Vector graphics scale and animate well.

PAINTING: BITMAP VS. VECTOR

There are two major types of image editing: bitmap and vector. Both Photoshop and combustion have at least some capability to create with both, and if you're using them together, you should understand the difference so you can manage your workflow appropriately.

BITMAP

Bitmap graphics are composed of pixels. The file itself is a "map" of how many pixels there are and what color each pixel is. Almost every major image file type stores image information as a bitmap, though they use different methods of organizing and compressing the pixel color data. Bitmaps are excellent for fine detail and a more traditional painting approach to image editing. Use Photoshop for creating the bitmap elements of your work.

VECTOR

Vector graphics are composed of points and curves between those points. These curves are frequently closed to form shapes — such as a circle, or the letter M - that are in turn filled with color information, like a solid color, a gradient, or even a bitmap image. Because they are defined by curves and not a particular pattern of pixels, vector graphics can be scaled and morphed while retaining smooth edges and without losing detail. Vector graphics are excellent for animating and a graphic-design approach to image editing. Use combustion for creating the vector graphics elements of your work.

COMBINING THE TWO

One of the biggest advantages of combustion is being able to animate over time. However, Photoshop's image editing tools are more effective for creating certain types of images. You can simply create those images in Photoshop, then import them to combustion for animation and addition of vector elements.

COMBUSTION OUTPUT TO PSD: RENDERING

One of the file types combustion can render is a Photoshop Sequence (PSD). However, the PSD images that combustion renders don't have any layer or blending information, and are effectively a flattened RGBA image. You'd be better off rendering a different file type with lossless compression, such as TIF or PNG. They are the same quality, but in a much smaller file size.

PSD INPUT TO COMBUSTION: IMPORTING

You can import PSD files into a combustion workspace the same way you import any footage: File→Import Footage, browse to the appropriate directory, and select the file. If the PSD you select has multiple layers, you are presented with an Import Options dialog, with three import mode options: Merged Image, Grouped, and Nested. If you select Merged Image, a Layer will be created with the flattened PSD as the footage. If you choose Grouped, combustion creates a separate footage source and Layer for each PSD layer, and a Null object (named the same as the PSD file) that all the Layers are parented to, so they respond to transformations applied to the Null as if it were the master object in a group. Nested does the same thing as Group, but includes the Layers and Null object in a master Layer as if you had selected them all and chosen Object→Nesting... Selected Layers.

The Import Options dialog

Grouped or Nested should be selected in almost every case. If you only need a flattened image, the file should be saved as a type other than PSD, because the file size is smaller and will be faster to work with. An exception is if you only want to use one layer from a multi-layer PSD, you can import the PSD as Merged, then uncheck Merge Layers in the Source tab of its Footage Controls and select the layer you want to isolate from the drop-down menu above the Merge Layers box.

Note that if you create a workspace by using the Open command and selecting a PSD, you aren't given a choice of import type: it's always Merged. Create the Composite workspace first, then Import Footage.

WHAT COMBUSTION CAN SEE IN A PSD

The most important aspect of a PSD that combustion recognizes is the color and alpha information, or what the image looks like. You can isolate pieces of this information, such as telling combustion to show you only one layer, but you can access any layer or color information with the Footage Controls and Layer Properties at any time.

However, combustion can tell a lot more about a PSD than just what it looks like. When a multi-layer PSD is first imported, combustion examines its setup and translates that information into equivalent combustion Layer settings. When you import a PSD as Nested Layers, the Layers are named the same as they were in Photoshop. The stack order (which layer was on top, which was below that, etc.) in combustion is the same as it was in Photoshop. If one of the layers was turned off (eyeball icon unchecked) in Photoshop when the file was saved, that Layer will also be turned off (yellow icon grayed out) when combustion opens it. Blending Modes and Opacity are also translated: if a layer in Photoshop is set to Multiply and 75% Opacity, the Layer that combustion creates for the footage will have its Transfer Mode set to Multiply and its Opacity set to 75%.

The beach.psd file in Photoshop, and imported into combustion. Note the layer order, naming, and Transfer Mode.

WHAT COMBUSTION CAN T SEE IN A PSD

Although combustion can translate vector graphics from some applications, like Adobe Illustrator, it doesn't recognize vector information in PSDs. If you want to use text, paths, or shapes from Photoshop in combustion, you'll have to Layer→Rasterize them into bitmaps first. However, you'd be better off using combustion to create the vector-based elements of a piece anyway.

Another PSD element that combustion doesn't recognize is Layer Style. For instance, if one of your Photoshop layers has a Bevel and Emboss layer effect applied to it, the bevel effect will only be visible in combustion under certain circumstances. The data that describes what the layer looks like with the bevel is present in the PSD, but ignored by combustion unless the image is merged (either imported as a Merged Image, or with the Merged box checked in the Source Layer section of the Footage Controls). Since the main advantage of using PSDs instead of other image types in combustion is multiple layers, only being able to see Layer Styles on merged PSDs isn't very useful.

A good workaround is to merge the Layer Style with the layer it's applied to, in Photoshop, though that isn't as straightforward as it sounds. Right-click on the Layer Style and choose Create Layer from the list that pops up, which turns your Layer Style into its own, normal layer. Select the new layer, and choose Merge Down from the Layer menu, cooking together your original layer and the Layer Style that was on it. Although it's not totally flattening an image, you should probably save a copy, for the same reasons it's a bad idea to flatten an original multi-layer PSD.

EDITING THE SOURCE LAYER

Even though the information in a PSD can be translated and arranged in different ways on import, the image information in the file itself is all still there no matter what. In the Source tab of the Footage Controls for PSD footage, there is a section on the far-right called Source Layer. There you can toggle the footage between Merged and un-Merged using the Merge Layers checkbox, and if the box is unchecked, select which layer is displayed using the drop-down menu above the check box. Note that when you import a PSD as Nested or a Group, the footage created for each Layer references the same PSD file, but each footage reference has a different Source Layer selected.

The Source Layer settings

MAXIMIZING PSDS IN COMBUSTION

If you're using Photoshop imagery to augment a combustion scene, or using combustion to animate a Photoshop image, you will almost always want to import Photoshop creations to combustion, not the other way around.

If you're creating an animation or video clip, your final output will be from combustion, not Photoshop, and combustion can read more information from a PSD than it can render into one.

DYNAMIC REFERENCING

The exception to the "save Photoshop file, import into combustion" flow is making changes to a Photoshop document that you've already imported into combustion. Using the two software packages together in this fashion can be extremely dynamic.

When you import image sequences into combustion, a Layer is created with the image sequence as its footage. The footage isn't actually saved inside the combustion workspace (CWS) file; its location on disk is referenced. If you make changes to a referenced image sequence without changing its name or duration, then reload the CWS, the changes show up without any additional messing around.

This is very useful, because if you want to make a change to an image, you don't have to re-import it. If you have any animation or operators applied to a Layer, the footage changes beneath it without removing or changing any aspect of the transformations or operators applied to it.

3D COMPOSITING

In most image editing and compositing software, all the layers are stacked directly on top of one another and all the work is done in two dimensions. If an element needs to appear three-dimensional – for example, text tilted away from the camera and foreshortened – the third dimension has to be faked using skew, scale, and other distortions. If there is any animation – for example, that text needs to twirl like a revolving door and fly towards the viewer – faking the dimensionality and maintaining its believability becomes extraordinarily difficult.

This isn't true in combustion, because instead of faking changes in the third dimension, you can actually move, rotate, and scale Layers in all three axes. The Layers themselves are always two-dimensional, but they can flip and twirl, fly towards the camera, cast shadows on each other, and more. There are many possibilities for cool effects using 3D compositing, and actually moving objects in 3D is not only easier than faking it, it looks better.

This composite uses bitmap and vector graphics elements animated in 3D.

CASE STUDY: DIGITAL MATTE PAINTING

To demonstrate some of the features and possibilities of using Photoshop and combustion together, and to give a sample workflow, I am going to walk through the creation and implementation of a background plate. You can follow along using the beach.psd file located in the file package that accompanies this book (which you can download from www.mesmer.com's File Bank, if you haven't already).

EXAMINE THE PSD FILE

This scene is mostly hand-painted in Photoshop, though some of the elements (like the sand and the water) started with a photograph and were cleaned up and augmented using the Clone tool and color correction. There are six layers: beach, hills, mountains, clouds, sky, and the locked Background, which is turned off (invisible). All the layers are set to 100% Opacity and Normal Blending Mode, except the clouds, which are set to 90% Opacity and Hard Light Blending Mode. Although this plate is intended for use in an NTSC resolution (720x486) video, it is much larger than that (1024x768) in case I want to pan or zoom. Having more resolution than you need is always better than having less, though your computer speed and available disk space may limit your ability to work with large files.

beach.psd opened in Photoshop

beach.psd imported into combustion

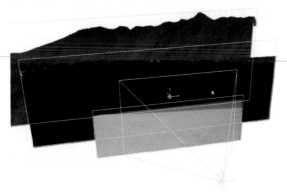

Move the background Layers backwards in Z and adjust their Scale and Y Position so they are framed correctly.

Back in combustion, open the beachStart.cws workspace and import beach.psd, selecting Grouped for import method. I recommend working in Draft quality mode for a while, the 1024x768 PSD is slow to work with.

Examine the file in the Workspace tab. One combustion Layer was created for each Photoshop layer, named as they were in Photoshop, and all six layers were each imported as a separate Footage reference. The Background layer is turned off just like it was in Photoshop, and the clouds Layer has its Opacity set to 90% and its Transfer Mode set to Hard Light, in the Surface tab of its Composite Controls.

Because the beach.psd image is so much larger than the resolution of the workspace, only a small part of it is visible. Frame the shot by selecting the camera in the Workspace tab and dragging on the Position Z slider in the camera's Transform tab, zooming out. As you can see, combustion correctly interpreted and retained all the layer information from Photoshop, so the beach image looks the same in combustion as it did in Photoshop.

ADD DEPTH IN THE Z-AXIS

Switch to dual-view mode using the monitor-shaped drop-menu at the left of the center playback bar, and switch one of the view modes to Perspective.

The Dolly and Orbit tools are now available in the Toolbar tab; use them to zoom out and skew the camera at a bit of an angle. Hide (turn off) the sky and clouds layers for a moment, and move the hills and mountain Layers backwards in Z, with the mountains about twice as far back as the hills; about 250 and 500 worked for me. Adjust the Scale (with Proportional checked) and Position Y for the hills so they are framed in the shot approximately the same way they were before the move in Z, and do the same for the mountains.

TEST YOUR WORK

The scene looks the same as it did before, except that if the camera is panned across it, the foreground (beach) will move across the screen faster than the background (hills) and distant background (mountains), just as they would in real footage of a three-dimensional landscape. Try it out by animating the camera: go to the first frame using the Home key, select the camera and move it forward and to the left so that it can only see the left portion of the beach Layer. Turn on Animate by hitting the A key, go to the last frame by using the End key, and move the camera to the right edge of the beach. Preview your animation by hitting Play (Space bar).

DEFINE THE BACKGROUND

Turn the sky and clouds back on. The hills and mountains are no longer visible in the Camera view, because they're behind the sky. The most obvious fix would be to change the sky's Position in Z, putting it behind the mountains. However, to keep up the depth illusion, the sky would have to be moved extremely far behind the rest of the scene and scaled to an enormous size. There is a more efficient solution.

When there are multiple layers in a composite, combustion has to decide which layer to show on top, which to put behind that, and so on. The two obvious methods combustion uses to decide which order to show the Layers are their order in the layer stack in the Workspace tab, and their physical location on the Z-axis. If two Layers are in exactly the same place (which is usually the case), whichever one is on top in the layer stack is shown in front. Location on the Z-axis (distance from the camera) overrides the layer stack, so if Layer A is closer to the camera than Layer B, it will be shown in front, even if A is below B in the layer stack.

However, there is a third method that overrides both of these, called Depth Order, located in the Layer tab of a Layer's Composite Controls. If you set the sky and cloud Layers' Depth Order to Background, they will always show up behind every other Layer, regardless of where they are in Z or where they are in the layer stack. The clouds will still show up in front of the sky: since they are both set to Background, combustion falls back to their Z position and layer stack order to determine which to put in front.

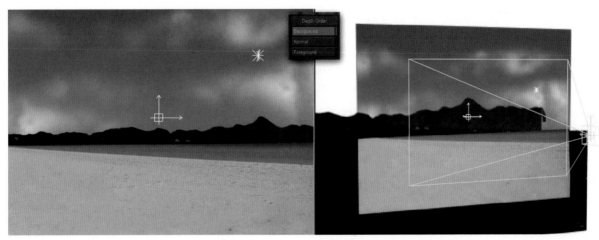

The sky and clouds Layers set to Background Depth Order

ATTACH THE SKY TO THE CAMERA

There's one more problem with the sky that needs to be fixed. To maintain the depth illusion when panning, the sky needs to move even slower than the mountains, if at all. Simply select the sky Layer, go to the Composite Controls, and using the Parent drop-down on the far right, set its parent to the camera, and do the same for the clouds Layer. Now they will inherit the transformations of the camera, and no matter where the camera points, the sky will move with it, creating the illusion it's not moving at all.

The beach scene has fake Depth of Field added using Gaussian Blur.

FAKE DEPTH OF FIELD

Real cameras (and eyes, for that matter) can only keep a certain range of distance in focus. The area that's in focus can be near or far, but anything closer or farther than that area gets increasingly out-of-focus. This effect is called Depth of Field. The virtual cameras in combustion (and 3D applications) can keep everything in perfect focus no matter how great the distance range in the shot, but it looks unnatural to a human viewer. For an effective composite, Depth of Field should be added in.

For a quick fake Depth of Field, add a Gaussian Blur operator to the layers that are out of the hypothetical focal range. In this case, the foreground should be in focus, so put a 1-pixel blur on the hills, and a 2-pixel blur on the mountains and clouds.

ANIMATE THE CLOUDS

Even if there is very little wind blowing the clouds, and the water is a placid bay, there would still be some slight movement. The fact that they are absolutely, perfectly still ruins the believability of the plate. A viewer might not be able to articulate exactly what's wrong with the shot, but they'd notice something about it looks fake. Some subtle movement will counteract this.

First, add an Operators→Distort→Crumple to the clouds Layer. Leave the Amplitude at 0 for the first frame. Turn on Animate with the A key, go to the last frame with the End key, and change the Amplitude to 2. The clouds will animate changing shape just a tiny bit, but even this barely perceptible movement breaks the bad effect of the clouds being totally static.

Next, add some drift (X Position animation) to the clouds. First, turn off Animate, and Scale the clouds up a little (110% works) so you can move them without seeing the edges of the layer. Then, turn on Animate and animate the clouds drifting over the course of the clip. This too should be just a tiny bit of movement (too much movement would give the impression of a very windy day; that would be distracting, and the rest of the scene doesn't appear to be shot during a windy day anyway).

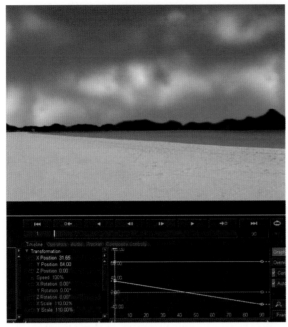

The changes to the PSD file show up in combustion without having to re-import the PSD file, leaving the Layer animation intact.

ANIMATE THE WATER

Finally, add some similar animation to the water. Turn Animate off and go to the first frame. Select the beach Layer, and choose Operators→Selections→Draw Selection, and draw a selection around the water area to confine the Crumple operator to just the water and not the sand. This time, leave the Amplitude low (1%) over the duration of the clip, raise the Octaves as high as it will go (10.0) to make the ripples more fine, and animate the Time Slice changing from 0.0 to 0.1 over the course of the clip. Some sparkly white particles to imitate the sun glaring on the water would be an appropriate addition, but don't overdo it.

DYNAMICALLY ADJUST LAYER ELEMENTS

Looking at the whole thing together, I think this scene would look better with some more clouds. Starting all over would be a drag, but fortunately that isn't necessary. Open beach.psd in Photoshop, and paint some more clouds on the clouds layer. Save the PSD, then go back to combustion and choose File→Save Workspace, then File→Revert Workspace to reload the workspace without closing it or exiting combustion. The clouds footage is updated to include the alterations to the PSD layer, and all the animation and operators on the clouds Layer are intact. The background plate is finished, ready to nest together and for the foreground elements to be added. Open up beach.mov (QuickTime 6 movie, MPEG-4 codec) to check it out.

CONCLUSION

In this chapter, you've read all about features and functions that integrate combustion and Photoshop, like plug-in support, importing PSD footage, and manipulating PSD files with combustion's unique features. You've also learned about the difference between bitmap and vector graphics, and should know which is appropriate in a given situation. You've also seen an example of a PSD in combustion in action, and learned effective techniques and methods of working with PSD files. Photoshop and combustion are powerful tools that can be combined into a workflow greater than the sum of its parts.

MIKE NICHOLS

ART DIRECTOR AND CO-FOUNDER

SURREAL SOFTWARE

What is your job?

Art Director and co-founder of Surreal Software. As the Art Director, I take a look at all the creative work that we do, and I like to work on modeling and texturing. I try and keep the art team honest and push them to do the best they can.

How did you get started in the game industry?

I got started in the game industry back in high school. One of my best friend's parents, Ivan and Carol Manley, were game producers and they asked me to help them out with some artwork. It was cool and I thought it could help pay for college. In school I was getting frustrated with my art classes because I was learning more from the job working with games which caused me to have something of an epiphany: I liked the games industry (though back in 1988 it wasn't even an industry yet). I left school early to join Sierra as an Art Director and Designer, worked for a few other game companies in the Seattle area, and eventually helped to found Surreal in 1995.

Which 3D packages do you work with?

Maya.

How did you learn the tools you use?

I've used 3D studio max forever, since it was a beta. Same with Photoshop. I think I started off with version one. I've just gone with growing and evolving with the software.

How do you use Photoshop?

We use it for our texturing work. I mainly use the airbrush tool and many layers to build up my textures. Alpha channels are also a very helpful concept to have included in the program for the kind of work we do.

How early do you have to get up? How late do you have to stay?

We work a lot at Surreal. One guy slept here just last night. In the past during crunch time, we've had six months of 24 hours a day, with people sleeping here all the time. One of our goals, with 52 people on board, is to try and even that out a bit. We've worked hard on our production management to create a series of checks and balances to help reduce our crunch periods. People here like their jobs, though. Surreal is a great place to work.

What are your interests outside the job?

My three-year-old daughter Madison. I like to spend my free time with her, doing things kids like to do. Next year I'm going to teach her to ski.

What games do you play?

I play games that don't take up too much of my time, like car racing. I also like an occasional role-playing game, if I know it's really good. I try to stay away from PC games altogether, because they have the potential to take me away from my family for too long – and they don't like that!

Where do you find inspiration for your work?

Form really follows function. When we work on a project, we research the details so we know exactly what it is we need to be looking at, and then we find that information from whatever sources we can. I look for inspiration from really anything. I like the work of Francis Bacon. I like things that have good lighting, and I also used to be into photography quite a bit.

Do you have an ultimate goal for your career?

Over the years, my career and goals have changed. I really like where I am right now and my main goal is to make Surreal a successful company where everyone can be proud of the work they do. I want people to be happy. We try very hard to create an open and creative culture here, and I want to maintain and improve that. It's reflected in the quality of work we do.

What's the best advice you could give to new artists entering the industry?

Listen. Observe. Appreciate both the good and the bad sides of things. Keep an open mind. Have a good work ethic and take pride in your craft. Take your work very seriously. All of these will help enormously while working in the game industry.

JERUSHA HARDMAN

LEAD ARTIST

SURREAL SOFTWARE

What is your job?

I'm a Lead Artist here at Surreal Software. My job is part management and part creative work. I make sure that all the work that gets done on my team is great, down to the nitty-gritty details, manage the employees on my team, and work on the art and modeling for the game project. I go to a lot of meetings, and really like the job.

How did you get started in the game industry?

I went to the Art Institute to study computer art, wanting to work in the film or games industry. It was a good program, and took a lot of self-motivation. At the portfolio review that they have, I met a guy from a game company, and he gave me a couple of numbers to call for a job. One of the numbers was Surreal's. I called up, they interviewed me, and I got the job, starting as an entry-level artist. My first project here was working on a small game called Everest. Then I worked on Drakan: The Ancients' Gates. Now I'm the Art Lead for a new project.

Which 3D packages do you work with?

Maya and our proprietary software.

How did you learn the tools you use?

I learned Photoshop and 3D studio max while at the Art Institute. But I really got comfortable with using these tools my first six months here at Surreal. I also learned Maya on the job.

How do you use Photoshop?

We use it for texturing and doing concept work mostly. For texturing we work between Photoshop and Maya, like a lot of 3D artists do.

How long have your worked in the industry?

Three years.

How early do you have to get up? How late do you have to stay?

I work a lot. Average day is 8-10 hours, crunch time hours run 12-16. The latest you can get here is 10am, and the earliest you can leave is 5pm, but you can work your hours around those core times. You have to be really obsessive to be in this industry and really like what you're doing. If not, with such long hours, you'll be miserable.

What are your interests outside the job?

I like movies, games, and reading. My place is filled with tons and tons of books. I read a wide variety of books. I'm also really into art and like to paint, draw, and sculpt when I have time. We have a plastic covered room in our apartment to use as a studio. Really, I have a too many interests to list.

Bump map texture used for wall texture

Cement texture made for use on the final wall texture

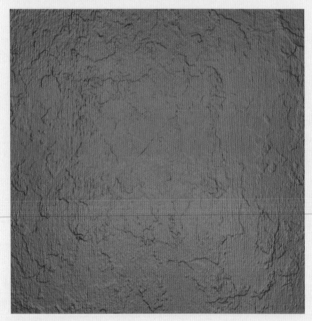

Green half of wall texture from the bump map texture.

White half of wall texture made from the same bump map used to make the Green wall.

What games do you play?

The last game I finished was Drakan: The Ancients' Gates. I played it through to see how it was, and it was a blast. Mostly I like action-adventure games the best. At home we have a PlayStation 2, an Xbox, a Dreamcast, and a Nintendo 64. I think the only one we're missing in the GameCube. I also play racing and fighting games. My current favorites are Halo, Metal Gear Solid 2, and Grand Theft Auto 3.

By combinding all these textures we can make these two textures.
All images © Surreal Software

Where do you find inspiration for your work?

Everywhere: books, movies, nature, TV. Just recently, I got the new "Art of The Lord of the Rings" book full of all these incredible images. I look at things and take little elements from everything and put it together. That's how it's done. Another thing I do is take pictures of things I see that are interesting. One time I was in Boston with my in-laws, and everyone was wondering why we had to stop so I could take a close-up shot of an old brick wall. Not the entire brick wall, just a small spot of the brick wall. It was a cool texture. Inspiration can be found anywhere.

Do you have an ultimate goal for your career?

I like where I am right now, and what I'm doing. Someday, I might be interested in starting my own company, but not any time soon. Right now I'm happy at Surreal doing what I'm doing.

What's the best advice you could give to new artists entering the industry?

Learn how to put a portfolio together, and how to apply for a job. Take a class on it if you have to. If your portfolio is online, I want to be able to see an example of work in three clicks. Be critical of your work, judge whether something belongs in your portfolio based off its merit, not based off of how much time you spent on it or how dear to your heart it is. A portfolio is there to show your best stuff, not justify the time you spent working on something. Make a demo reel geared towards the offered job. Read between the lines of the job description: if it's a modeling job, don't show animation. Learn to use good judgement. Don't include inappropriate references in your reel (and by this I don't mean you can't show nudity, just use some common sense). Don't make it too over the top – it's important to take your work seriously and be confident about it. You can be funny and entertaining but don't make that the center of your demo reel.

And of course, you must get some training. I don't care how many times your friends and family tell you you're a good artist; you still need some schooling and training. Most of all it's important to be an artist. You need to know how to look at the world through an artist's eye, and be aware of what art is.

This is a great industry to be in. I'd like to see more artists look at it as a possible career path. Especially some more women, I think the industry turns off a lot of women since video games are stereotyped as a guy thing. But they shouldn't, this is a fun, and wonderful art form. I highly recommend it for any aspiring artist.